BULL THRESHERS
AND BINDLESTIFFS

BULL THRESHERS AND BINDLESTIFFS

Harvesting and Threshing on the North American Plains

Thomas D. Isern

University Press of Kansas

© 1990 by the University Press of Kansas
All rights reserved

Published by the University Press of Kansas
(Lawrence, Kansas 66045), which was organized
by the Kansas Board of Regents and is operated
and funded by Emporia State University, Fort
Hays State University, Kansas State University,
Pittsburg State University, the University of
Kansas, and Wichita State University

Printed in the United States of America
10 9 8 7 6 5 4 3 2 1

The paper used in this publication meets the
minimum requirements of the American
National Standard for Permanence of Paper for
Printed Library Materials Z39.48-1984.

Library of Congress Cataloging-in-Publication
Data

Isern, Thomas D. (Thomas Dean), 1952–
    Bull threshers and bindlestiffs : harvesting and
threshing on the North American plains /
Thomas D. Isern.
       p.   cm.
    Includes bibliographical references.
    ISBN 0-7006-0468-5 (alk. paper)
    1. Grain—Great Plains—Harvesting—
Technological innovations—
History.   2. Threshing—Great Plains—
Technological innovations—History.   3. Grain—
Great Plains—Harvesting—Machinery—
History.   4. Threshing machines—Great
Plains—History.   5. Farm life—Great
Plains.   I. Title.
SB189.73.I74   1990
633.1'045'0978—dc20   90-11967
                                              CIP
British Library Cataloguing in Publication Data is
available.

Make this one for Stan, since he stayed on the farm. It'll surprise him.

CONTENTS

TABLES AND FIGURES

PREFACE

Years ago, as I was researching my dissertation, which became the book *Custom Combining on the Great Plains,* I realized that my study was the sequel to a book that had not yet been written. *Custom Combining* portrayed itinerant custom wheat harvesters, thousands of whom have practiced their profession up and down the plains since World War II as an elite, as plainsmen nonpareil. They represented to me the ultimate in mobility and flexibility in employment of resources as an adaptation to life on the plains. But they have never numbered more than a few thousand. As I probed the earlier history of harvesting and threshing, although I was concerned with it at first mainly as background, I uncovered a different saga. This one involved not just thousands, but hundreds of thousands, even millions of plains people in the United States and Canada. It was the story of harvesting and threshing on the North American plains before the advent of the combine. It is the story I tell in this book.

My intent here is primarily descriptive: to tell what harvesting and threshing were like before the combine. This sort of description inevitably turns expository and analytical, because the mass of detail is so great and because the relationships among the parts are as complex as the prairie. The historian in me strives to make sense of it all through categories and causations.

Moreover, I cannot quell the thought that this description touches the heart of the culture of the plains, and the Great Plains of North America are my abiding interest and my home. As I uncover the head and shoulders of harvesting and threshing, I feel like some nineteenth-century Yalie come to Kansas who has unearthed a great lizard, the report of which must substantially augment the sum of paleontological knowledge. I want to describe the animal I have found and in so doing make possible a sounder, more comprehensive historical interpretation of life on the North American plains. I claim the continental plains of the United States and Canada as the scope of the work, but I cannot claim to do equal justice to all parts. The plains are broad, and intensive research everywhere is an endless agenda. I do not think I have done falsely by any section, even where I may have done slightly. (I should also note that monetary amounts in this book are in either Canadian or U.S. dollars, depending on which country I am discussing.)

I owe thanks to people from Texas to Alberta. Many of them are archivists, librarians, and curators, of course, who were just doing their jobs, and I do not think I taxed any of them too heavily for this project—except maybe Steve Hanschu, interlibrary loan librarian at Emporia State University. So as I mention him, he stands for all you other good foresters.

Besides those people who loaned photographs to me, several individuals graciously opened private manuscript collections, and to them I tender thanks beyond words. Moses H. Voth, Hartford A. Lewis, Spike Jensen, and Mr. and Mrs. Lowell Ayers—you will find your names in the notes.

So will you—Milo Mathews, Alexander Boan, Richard Goering, Floyd Bever, Hartford A. Lewis (again), and Ernest Claassen. The detailed, extended recorded interviews you gave me are much of the flesh of this work. Of comparable account are the contributions of Michael Ewanchuk, Alexander Boan (again), George Hitz, William J. Lies, Ted Worrall, J. A. Boan, A. O. Krueger, Ned McKinney, and Guy Bretz. Although the notes say you sent me only questionnaires, we exchanged much more. The questionnaires were simply introductions, after which I was amazed again and again at how you replied conscientiously to the thick yellow sheets of individual questions I mailed to you.

Two fellow scholars, John Herd Thompson of McGill University and R. Bruce Shepard of the Fort Calgary Museum, allowed me to steal data from tables in their publications, and I thank them. Thanks likewise to the editors of three fine scholarly journals who allowed me to cannibalize parts of my articles that appeared in their columns and use them in this book. The articles were "Adoption of the Combine on the Northern Plains," *South Dakota History* 10 (Spring 1980): 101–18; "Folklife of the Threshing Outfit," *South Dakota History* 16 (Spring 1986): 18–34; "The Header Stack-Barge: Folk Technology on the North American Plains," *Social Science Journal* 24 (Autumn 1987): 361–73; and "The Adoption of the Combine on the Canadian Plains," *American Review of Canadian Studies* 16 (Winter 1986): 455–64. The last article was coauthored with R. Bruce Shepard, who deserves credit for its contributions to this work.

The Faculty Research and Creativity Committee of Emporia State University made a grant for the purchase of many of the photographs included in this book. In preparing the manuscript I was doubly blessed to have the help of two excellent computer hands—Jacqueline Fehr of the Division of Social Sciences and Nancy Gulick of the College of Liberal Arts and Sciences. My wife, Lotte, put in many hours of proofreading and other assistance.

Having mentioned photographs, I feel compelled to defend their integrity as documents by explaining the origins of their captions. The photos came from myriad sources, public and private. Some were unidentified, some were identified orally by informants, and for those identified in writing (usually on the backs of the photos), the scrawls themselves were of uncertain provenance. Having no clear or consistent provenance to preserve, I composed the captions, which are intended to link with my text. Cover up the captions, and the photos become pure documents again.

Finally, let me explain the title of the book. I am not one to shy away from an alliterative phrase, but there is more to the title than that. The bull thresher represents capital, particularly machine capital; the bindlestiff represents human labor. These two elements came together in wonderful and peculiar ways in harvesting and threshing on the North American plains.

CHAPTER ONE.
ANTIQUITIES

Out from the albums, the trunks, the shoeboxes, and the closet shelves spill the fine old albumen prints, card-mounted in the style of the late nineteenth and early twentieth centuries. Some of the images are obscure; others release stored recollections. Here stands a favorite team hitched to a binder. Here pose faintly familiar ancestors and neighbors and forgotten hired men with a long-ago-scrapped steam engine and a steel separator that now rusts back in the hedgerow. Here loom perfect grain stacks that grand-dad constructed with care and forbade the children to slide upon.

Historians debate whether there was a golden age of American agriculture, a time before wartime boom and post-war recession disrupted the developing agricultural economy, when farmers prospered and waxed content. The golden hue of the old photographs, however, is not entirely the product of the photographer's toning, for there is evident in them a golden age of rural

culture and agricultural endeavor on the Great Plains of North America. Admittedly, the photographs are questionable evidence. They owe perhaps more to a golden age of itinerant professional photography, before every family snapped its own mediocre photographs with Polaroids, than to the agricultural situation. The people, machinery, and circumstances portrayed also are the product of selection by the subjects and by the photographers. The nostalgic reminiscences they stimulate may also be products of selective memory.

Return, though, to the images. Surely their omnipresence, their vainglory, their evocation, demand consideration of the possibility that they captured men and women engaged in a proud enterprise and that this enterprise, the harvesting and threshing of small grains, was the focus of a great web of rural culture and institutions. That web, comprising the means and methods by which people on the plains

Alfred Isern (back center), Alvin Isern (far right), and forgotten hired men of the header harvest in Barton County, Kans., ca. 1915. (Courtesy of Bernice Isern)

harvested and threshed prior to the advent of the combined harvester, or combine, is the subject of this book.

The technology and practices of harvesting and threshing that people carried onto the plains were the products of millennia of adaptation and refinement. This evolution was relevant to the history of the plains both because it established the level of technology first available for use there and because it illustrated principles that also governed developments on the plains.

Although after the advent of the combine, terms such as "harvesting" and "threshing" came to be used indiscriminately, descriptions of earlier operations with small grains required more exact usage. Harvesting and threshing were distinct. Harvesting was merely the gathering of unthreshed grain from the field, including both reaping or gleaning (cutting of the heads) and attendant movement of the grain (gathering, making sheaves or bundles, shocking, and so on). Threshing was the breaking loose of the kernels of grain from the straw and chaff. A third operation, winnowing, was the separation of the kernels from the chaff.

The ancient peoples who first employed tools for reaping left scant remnants for archaeologists to examine. More than three thousand years before Christ, inhabitants of the Middle East reaped grain with straight flint knives, imparting to their tools an unmistakable sheen. Contemporaries in Babylonia and Egypt crafted hard-baked clay into sickles with serrated blades angled forward from the handle for easier wrist action.[1]

Egyptians some two thousand years later left a richer record—paintings and artifacts—of harvesting in the Nile Valley. Itinerant harvest laborers enjoying exemption from military service moved down the valley with the progression of the harvest. Methods varied, but usually male laborers grasped the heads of grain in their left hands and clipped them off with angular sickles held in their right hands. Women followed to gather up the gleanings.[2]

If the Egyptians recognized labor as a crucial element in the harvest, the evolution of reaping tools focused on the sickle as of primary importance. The Egyptians, evidently somewhat later than the Babylonians, had converted from clay to bronze in toolmaking. With the advent of the Iron Age (about 1200 B.C.) the material, although not the basic design, changed again. A needed change in design came early in the Iron Age and was proliferated through Roman conquest and administration: The blade was balanced by curving it back from the line of the handle and around past the handle again. With such a balanced blade, the motion of reaping was no longer a backward pull but rather a circular sweep, easier and longer. With this improvement the sickle reached perfection in basic design, although it was always subject to debate as to optimum angles and curves.[3]

Roman chroniclers documented both the widespread use of the balanced sickle and its succession by the scythe. Marcus Varro wrote in the first century before Christ of various styles of reaping with a sickle—cutting near the ground, cutting near the heads, or cutting midway up the stalk. Roman art of the preceding Bronze Age, however, had also depicted use of the scythe, a blade similar to a sickle but attached to a handle that extended down from the arm and hand of the harvester. In the Iron Age the scythe blade became shorter and straighter. When after the Middle Ages European agriculture began to emerge from stagnation, both the sickle and the scythe were common implements. During this time the scythe undoubtedly gained on the sickle, given that the scythe was a superior implement for making hay. By the twelfth century the handle of the European scythe was curved and hand posts had been added to facilitate use.[4]

If the scythe was to be superior to any other tool in gleaning grain, and not just in cutting hay, some method had to be developed by which the cut grain could be laid aside in orderly piles to be gathered or tied into sheaves. The answer was to attach wooden fingers behind the blade in an arrangement known as a cradle, depicted in a psalter as early as the thirteenth century. The cradle caught the falling grain, which could then be laid aside on the stubble.[5]

The advent of the cradle made the cradle and scythe the premier implement for reaping in western Europe and established the technologies and customs that would be transplanted to the European colonies of North America. Still, its use was not universal, or even predominant where common, because of human and environmental circumstances. Cradling required a strong body; many women, old men, and children could not do it, but they could wield a sickle. Simple tradition opposed the cradle in some areas, and in parts of Britain, law backed tradition to protect sicklers' jobs. Environment also could be an ally against the innovation, for cradling required ground that was free of stones or other obstructions.[6]

The first documentation of the use of animal motive power in reaping occurred in the first century. Roman writer Pliny the Elder described how on great estates in Gaul the Romans employed a stripper for harvesting. Later historians generally termed this invention "Pliny's reaper," although he had mentioned it only in passing. Pliny's reaper was a two-wheeled cart pushed through the field by oxen. On the front of the cart were mounted teeth in a comb arrangement that embraced the stalks and stripped the grain from them. A man walked behind the oxen and pushed up and down on a bar that regulated the height of the comb. Another walked alongside the cart and raked out grain that stuck in the teeth. After Pliny's time the Gallic reaper was depicted in

stone and, with better detail, in the writings of Palladius about 400.[7]

Despite these classical precedents, it was apparently mere coincidence that when in 1780 the London Society of Arts discussed offering a premium to the inventor of a reaping machine, a few inventors made proposals or models of strippers. William Pitt of Pendleford, England, constructed a stripper that refined the Gallic principles by replacing the fixed teeth with a revolving tooth-studded cylinder that was powered by a ground wheel. These tinkerings were important mainly as an expression of awakening interest in the mechanization of harvesting.[8]

The musings of inventors mean nothing unless conditions are conducive to their efforts. In the late eighteenth and early nineteenth centuries the Napoleonic wars gave impetus to the mechanization of harvesting by absorbing the supply of harvest labor. English landowners mourned the necessity of hiring Irish laborers who, they said, fought and drank and, according to one source, did such a poor job that "a sheep could be lost in the stubble." Between 1786 and 1831 there were more than fifty instances of invention and use of reapers in England, Scotland, Europe, and the United States. Abandoning the stripper, these new inventions cut grain according to one of two patterns of motion by mechanized blades—circular or rectilinear (back and forth).[9]

To little avail, English inventors near the turn of the nineteenth century attempted to employ mechanized circular motion for reaping by fastening blades to a wheel that turned in a plane parallel to the ground. Some also mounted stationary blades into which the moving blades would sweep, thereby shearing the grain. The first patent of an instrument along these lines was in 1799 to Joseph Boyce of Mary-le-bone. His horizontal blades turned around a vertical shaft powered from a ground wheel. In 1805 a man named Plucknet of Deptford designed a similar machine. It had a turning plate with serrated edges to cut the grain, but, like Boyce's invention, it lacked any scheme to gather the stalks into the cutting apparatus or to push the cut grain off the machine in an orderly way. Furthermore, both machines were pushed by draft animals, unlike still another rotary model built by a man named Gladstone at about the same time, which was drawn by a horse hitched to a shaft on one side.[10]

Such experimentation continued over the next decade. From 1811 to 1814 a man named Smith, in Deanston, devised a rotary reaper in which the horizontally revolving blade was at the bottom of a drum that cast the cut grain to the side to form a windrow. Another man named Kerr devised roughly the same machine at about the same time. Donald Cumming, of Northumberland, also contributed a rotary variation, putting a line of revolving disks onto flat bearers, or arms, that extended at an angle into the grain, cutting the grain between the disks as

the bearers advanced through the field. He also worked out a process by which a web on rollers would deliver the cut grain to the side in a windrow.[11]

Trials of rotary reapers continued into the 1850s, but by the 1820s the state of the art in reaper invention had already passed to rectilinear motion. The model was an ordinary pair of hand shears. In 1807 Robert Salmon patented a machine with pairs of shears connected to a bar along the ends of the top blades; the lower blades stayed stationary. Fingers stretched ahead to guide the grain into the shears, and a rake operated by a hand crank swept grain from the platform into piles convenient for binding. The apparatus was pushed like a wheelbarrow. Not much different at first were the efforts of John Common of Northumberland. In secrecy, with trials at night, he constructed a shear-type machine and, with the encouragement of the Duke of Northumberland and the Society of Arts, built two more models, thereby perfecting an apparatus that delivered grain to a windrow along the side by a web moving over rollers.[12]

Common's machines inspired later inventors whose names are better known. Common had at least thought in terms of rectilinear motion. Henry Ogle, schoolmaster of Newham, had visited Common in 1803. Ogle had read of trials of reaping machines and was looking for practical mechanics to assist him in making one. He was thinking of a rotary machine and was having trouble devising a model. Common thereupon discussed the shearing action with him. Common also gave patterns for his machine to Thomas Brown, who ran a foundry in Alnwick.[13]

These disseminations to Ogle and Brown resulted in an important advance in reaper design—the replacement of the rectilinear shear model by a reciprocating sickle, with teeth mounted below or above that extended to hold the grain to be cut. Parties to this later invention disputed how much credit belonged to Ogle and how much to Brown and his son, Joseph. By 1816 the Browns were testing a reaper reported to work satisfactorily that may or may not have incorporated the new principle. By 1820 the Browns were advertising reapers for sale. Ogle, however, later wrote that the essential principles were contained in a model he had given the Browns in 1822. The Browns had then, according to Ogle, built a machine that had a reciprocating knife working under projecting teeth; a reel to push grain onto the knife; a platform to collect grain that might be raked off ready for tying into a sheaf; and a frame into which a horse might be harnessed to draw the machine. Regardless of who was responsible, the machine worked.[14]

Unfortunately, public reception of the innovation was cool. According to Ogle, farmers at first were skeptical of the whole proposition, and even when the cutting mechanism was shown to be workable, they pointed out that little labor would be saved unless a platform was added to collect grain to be raked

off. Even where farmers accepted the machine, a new source of opposition arose. "Some working people at last threatened to kill Mr. Brown if he persevered any farther in it," recounted Ogle. For whatever reason, the Browns emigrated to the United States before public acceptance of their machine in England.[15]

Following on the heels of the Browns was one last notable British inventor of reapers, Patrick Bell, a Scot. Bell invented his reaper in 1825 while he was a divinity student. He believed that he had made an important innovation, and he carried on his trials in great secrecy and excitement, but in truth his machine was built on faulty principles. His inspiration for the cutting mechanism was a pair of garden shears; he did not use a reciprocating knife. After Bell resumed his ministerial studies, manufacturers produced commercial models of his machine, even exporting a few to Australia, Europe, and the United States. This bit of commercial success did not conceal to later inventors that the true theoretical advance had already occurred with the Brown-Ogle machine.[16]

The fruition of that development took place across the Atlantic. This was a logical turn of events, not necessarily because of superior American inventive genius but rather because North America, with its abundant acreage and limited labor, provided a favorable environment for technological invention. Remarking later on the rapid advance of reaping technology in the United States contrasted to that in England,

Philip Pusey, gentleman farmer and member of Parliament, pointed out in 1851 that a variety of environmental and social conditions put England at a disadvantage. The climate was wetter, making the grain more likely to lodge; ridges and furrows necessary for drainage hampered efficient operation of machines; fields were small and hemmed by fences and gates that stopped machines; and harvest labor was relatively cheap.[17]

During the early 1800s American inventors paralleled the British in attempts to make rotary cutters, all unsuccessful. During the early 1830s, however, several Americans, apparently independently, hit upon effective principles. Later British claims that American inventors took inspiration from the Bell reaper were groundless. The American machines resembled in principle the Brown-Ogle invention, not that of Bell, and the American inventors evidently lacked knowledge of either precedent. In 1831 William Manning of New Jersey patented a reaping machine with a toothed blade and dividers. Neither his nor other inventors' machines were so important to the history of reaping as were those of Cyrus McCormick and Obed Hussey. The genius and jealousy of these two men combined with historical circumstances to mechanize reaping in North America, whence mechanization and its principles could be repatriated in the Old World.[18]

McCormick was the son of an inventor, Robert McCormick, whose twenty-some years of tinkering with rotary and

other designs had produced no workable reaper. Young Cyrus built and tested his first machine in 1831. Like the Ogle-Brown machine, it had a straight, smooth-cutting blade, but unlike the English machine, the blade acquired its reciprocation from a crank and pittman (bar attached to a crank or wheel that converts circular to back-and-forth motion). During the next two years, McCormick traveled constantly between Virginia and Kentucky; however, he did come back to Walnut Grove, Virginia, long enough to improve his design. Most important, he serrated the cutting edge of the sickle.[19]

Unknown to McCormick, Obed Hussey, a sailor from Maine who had retired to Maryland, was working along similar lines. In some respects Hussey's machine, which he first tried and patented in 1833, was superior to McCormick's. It had triangular knives (instead of a straight blade) that were driven by a pittman. After McCormick read of Hussey's patent in 1834, two things happened. First, McCormick rushed to patent his own machine, although he regarded such action as premature; second, he initiated a bitter campaign of publicity and letter writing that he and Hussey would engage in for decades thereafter.[20]

For a few years, while Hussey overhauled his design, McCormick was prevented by personal financial difficulties from pursuing his own development. By 1843, however, McCormick had accepted Hussey's challenge for a public competition between their two designs near Richmond, where observers and the judges generally favored Mc-Cormick's machine. Other contests (as well as acrimonious public correspondence and vengeful lawsuits) between the rivals continued and, with abundant press coverage, spurred sales of both models. In 1851 trials held in England in conjunction with London's Great Exhibition carried the reaping revolution back to the Old World.[21]

West, however, not east, was the important direction of change. Whereas Hussey eventually would give up manufacturing and sell his patent rights, McCormick carried reaper manufacturing westward with the frontier of farming. This, more than his technical genius, marked his place in reaping history. American frontier agriculture in his time was poised on the edge of a domain where a machine such as the reaper was more suitable—environmentally, economically, and socially—than it had been anywhere else: the open prairies of the Midwest, with their black soils and relatively favorable climates for reaping.

By the late 1840s McCormick was building fewer than one hundred reapers in Walnut Grove and had licensed several other manufacturers. In 1847, however, he had begun negotiations that would end McCormick reaper production elsewhere and concentrate it under his own management at a new plant in Chicago, gateway to the West. The advertising campaigns and credit sales he then initiated were well suited to the speculative nature of western frontier enterprise. This move west was particularly important to McCormick because in 1848 his original patent ran out. The relocation made him dominant, nevertheless, while a host of manufacturers—including Manny, Ketchum, and Atkins—entered the field, each introducing its own refinements.[22]

During the 1850s reapers led the way toward the mechanization of agriculture on the midwestern prairies. By 1860 more than eighty thousand were operating west of the Appalachians, harvesting almost 70 percent of western wheat. The time was right. The rich soil encouraged production of wheat as a cash crop in conjunction with corn as a feed grain. The Crimean War had pushed grain prices up. The drain of labor into mining rushes in conjunction with increased agricultural settlement of the frontier created a shortage of harvest labor.[23]

Even as the reaper eased the harvesting bottleneck, these same conditions turned the attention of inventors toward diminishing the labor requirement yet more. Harvesting with a reaper still required a good-sized crew—a man to drive the reaper, another to rake off the gavel (cut grain), and a half dozen or more to bind and shock the grain. The driver was not expedient, and shocking was a process difficult to mechanize, but the raking and binding of the gavel could be streamlined.

Earlier inventors in both Britain and the United States had included raking devices in designs for reapers, but until the reaper itself should be perfected, such plans were moot. Moreover, there were several false starts before inventors hit upon the designs that would make the popular self-rake reaper. During the late 1830s and the 1840s American inventors first tinkered with canvas aprons, such as the one Bell had used on his reaper, then with toothed arrangements that reached from above or below to sweep off the grain, and finally with revolving rakes. The problem was more difficult than it seemed, because not only did the devices have to sweep the grain off the platform, but they also had to deliver it to the left side so that the stubble alongside the standing grain would be free of gavel where the horses would walk on the next round.

During the 1850s a combination of inventors' ideas forged the self-rake reaper. A contraption called the Atkins Automation had brief popularity and advanced the cause. It was created by Jearum Atkins, an invalid and a former millwright, who in 1852 patented a device that merely duplicated the action of a human arm and a rake in sweeping off the gavel. This model did little more than demonstrate the advantage of a self-raker, since its principles were not workable and its manufacture ended after being caught in overproduction by John Stephen Wright, editor of the *Prairie Farmer*.[24]

Most important to the development of the self-rake reaper was the collection of patents bought or developed by the firm of Seymour and Morgan at Brockport, New York, which enabled the company in 1854 to market the New York Self-Rake Reaping Machine, or New Yorker, as it was commonly called. The New Yorker incorporated the quadrant principle—the idea that the rake should sweep not straight back or across but in a quarter circle back and to the left.[25]

The New Yorker, however, had only a single rake. The Dorsey, patented in 1856 by Owen Dorsey of Maryland, improved the state of the art by mounting four rake arms on a cam atop a vertical axis. The arms swung low to sweep the platform back and to the left, then swung high around the wheel and gears to the left. This principle, called the pigeon wing or sweep rake, was attributable to a patent in 1852 by a man named Hoffheim. An early problem with the design was that the sweep of the arms did not allow the driver to sit on the machine; he had to walk alongside or ride one of the horses. The company's acquisition of another patent in 1861, however, allowed the arms to avert the sitting driver's head. In addition to raking, the pigeon-wing design had another advantage over earlier models: It eliminated the need for a circular reel to sweep the grain into the sickle. The rake arms swept low enough in front of the sickle to do this. The idea was so successful that McCormick quickly adopted it in 1861. By 1864 two-thirds of the McCormick reapers manufactured were self-rake models.[26]

A mechanism to deliver grain to the stubble was also designed during this period. The dropper, which Ogle had envisioned years earlier in England, put the platform on hinges so that it could be dropped to deposit the gavel. American patents for such a design appeared at least as early as 1849, but commercial production was insignificant until 1869, when Amos Rank accumulated a number of patents and licensed various companies to make droppers. These later models held the grain on slats rather than on a solid platform. At any rate, droppers, although popular in the East, were not used that much on the prairies or the plains. For that matter, neither were self-rake reapers, except in the earliest years of settlement. The reason was that the self-rake mechanism, so painfully developed, quickly became obsolete with the advent of a self-binding device. The invention of an automatic binding device would eliminate fully half of the hand labor incidental to the harvesting of small grains. Not only would the raker be unnecessary but also the men on the ground would be relieved of gathering, packing, and tying the gavel into bundles. All they would have to do thereafter was stand the bundles in shocks.[27]

Although the chief, unavoidable obstacle faced by all inventors of binding machines was the conception of a device that could tie a knot to bind the gavel, they first tackled a lesser problem: the movement of the gavel across to the left side of the platform, over the wheel, and onto the far left side where it might be tied up and dropped. The solution was achieved by the Marsh brothers, Charles W. and William W., Canadians who had moved to Illinois. In 1858 they patented a machine that came to be known as the Marsh harvester. Other inventors, such as Bell, had used an endless apron of canvas to carry grain off the platform and to elevate it over the wheel. The Marsh machine, however, intended this motion not just to drop the grain onto the stubble but also to make it available at waist level to men riding on the harvester, who would tie it into bundles as they rode. The grain fell from the canvas into a box, from which the men lifted it and tied bundles with straw bands. The Marsh harvester was itself a notable innovation for the harvest. By 1870 the Marsh firm was building more than one thousand a year. More important, however, were the binding mechanisms that would be attached to their machines, replacing the hand tiers with a practical automatic binder.[28]

The first successful binders that developed from the Marsh model tied bundles with wire because iron wire cost about half as much as twine. C. A. McPhitridge of St. Louis had in 1856 already patented a device that fed wire from a spool, encircled the gavel, twisted the wire around itself, and cut it off. In 1861 W. W. Burson of Yates, Illinois, put such a device on a Marsh-type harvester and on Manny reapers. Other inventors worked along similar lines during the 1860s, and in the early 1870s several companies came out with satisfactory wire binders. James Gordon mounted his packer-binder on Marsh harvesters at the Marsh works in Plano, Illinois; Sylvanus D. Locke put his similar device on a Marsh-type harvester built by another firm. These two men popularized wire binders early; before long the big companies also stepped in. McCormick, for example, began making wire binders in 1876.[29]

Various people, however, objected to the use of wire for binding. Millers feared wire fragments would get into their machinery or pass through into the flour; threshermen complained of wire lodging in their machines; stockmen attributed the mysterious deaths of their cattle to their presumed consumption of pieces of wire and development of hardware disease. Manufacturers of wire binders did their best to stem the swell of popular opinion against wire, but inventors turned it to their advantage.

Devices for tying knots automatically in twine already existed, and as twine became less expensive and iron more suspect, they were implemented. John P. Appleby in 1858 had invented a knotter with a bird-bill arrangement that gripped the twine, rotated it, and then pulled it through itself to make a knot. An invention patented in 1864 by Jacob Behel refined this design. During the mid-1870s Appleby again turned his attention to knotters and, with the backing of William Deering, finally perfected one. Deering, McCormick, and other major companies knew what was coming. They immediately purchased rights to knotters and began producing twine binders. The 1880s saw the complete abandonment of wire as well as great sales of twine binders.[30]

Thereafter, the basic mechanical principles of the automatic binder were in place, although improvements continued to be made. Binders composed predominantly of wood, for instance, were heavy—the McCormick was sometimes singled out as a horse killer. Steel frames introduced in the mid-1880s eliminated this problem. In the 1890s major companies lowered the binder mechanism so that the machines would be less top-heavy. They also put a wheel under the hitch to take weight off the necks of the horses. In all, the companies made the changes that brought binders to near maximum efficiency in the age of horsepower. Further technological gains awaited the introduction of the tractor.[31]

Binders cut a considerable amount of straw with the grain, which was an advantage to those who could use the straw for fuel or bedding. This method also allowed the grain to ripen fully and evenly in the shock without heating. However, to the cash-grain operator, the straw was of little value. It made extra bulk for hauling and threshing and required binding for handling.

The solution to this problem lay in the header, a device that cut heads of grain with little straw attached. Since the time of Pliny, developments in harvesting technology had progressed from the handling of loose, headed grain toward the handling of tied bundles. Until the 1840s, no North American inventors or manufacturers produced headers of greater than local use or renown. The machine that forged this new road in technology was invented and patented in 1849 by Jona-

Binder on the Peter Thielen farm, central Kansas, July 12, 1912. Although Thielen bound his oats, the stacks in the background indicate that his neighbors were harvesting wheat with a header. (Halbe Collection, Kansas State Historical Society, Topeka)

than Haines and then manufactured by Barber, Hawley and Company in Peking, Illinois: the Haines's Illinois Harvester. It tied no bundles, and its cutter bar and reel were longer than those of a binder, thereby enabling it to take a bigger swath. It cut the grain close to the head, leaving most of the straw standing as stubble. An apron of canvas carried the grain to the left side, as on a binder, and elevated it over the wheel; but instead of delivering the grain to a binding mechanism, the header dumped it off the elevator into a wagon pulled alongside by horses. The header, because of its wide swath and unbalanced weight, was pushed, not pulled, by horses. The driver sat behind the machine and steered it by moving the rear wheel with his feet. By 1862 the company had made more than four thousand Haines's Harvesters. Other companies entered the field during this decade. As various patents ran out during the 1890s, still more companies manufactured headers, which gradually increased in size. This increase was particularly important to drier regions of extensive farming, such as the Great Plains, California, and the Pacific Northwest.[32]

Although the combined harvester, or

Header on the George Bretz farm, western Kansas, 1915. The header, pushed by horses, elevated the cut grain up a canvas into the header barge alongside. (Courtesy of Guy Bretz)

combine, was implemented on the Great Plains much later than binders and headers, its development predated settlement of the region, and it was used elsewhere early in its history. The invention of the combine in Michigan during the 1830s, its proliferation in the Far West, and its manufacture by Best and Holt became pertinent to the agriculture of the Great Plains only after the turn of the century, when particular circumstances resulted in the combine's introduction there. Until that time, harvesting and threshing on the plains remained sequential, distinct operations. Like harvesting, threshing on the plains inherited a network of previously used systems and technology.

The earliest developments of threshing technology predated historical record. The earliest archaeological sources showed a mixture of methods, including beating and treading, with progressive refinements in each. Classic images of ancient Egyptian methods depicted animals treading on an outdoor threshing floor, men forking out the loose straw, and pairs of workers using winnowing scoops to toss the threshed grain into the air as the wind blew out the chaff. Later depictions, however, showed men clubbing sheaves with sticks, a cruder method. Biblical sources, especially Isaiah, also mentioned both treading and beating.[33]

Ancient peoples developed a variety of sledges to improve upon simple treading by animals. Archaeologists pronounced images on an urn in Iraq dating from 3000 B.C. to be a threshing sledge, but written documentation of such devices began with the Romans. Marcus Varro wrote that threshing in his time was done on an open floor with either a *tribulum* or a *plostellum poenicum*. A tribulum was a weighted sledge with pieces of stone or iron embedded in the bottom to rub out the grain. A plostellum poenicum (Punic cart) was an axle, fitted with low wheels, upon which the driver could sit; it was used in eastern Spain and in neighboring regions along the Mediterranean. Sledges and rollers remained in use to modern times in the Middle East.[34]

What rollers and sledges were to treading—that is, improvements in device but not in concept—the flail was to beating. The flail consisted of a handle about five feet long and a beater about three feet long joined with leather or metal. Although Pliny mentioned it, and Columella thought it the best method of threshing, the origins of the flail are murky. It was certainly used in England and Europe before the Middle Ages, and its use in China and Japan probably predated that period.[35]

What all of these methods had in common was the direct application of human and animal power in linear fashion. The story of modern threshing machines, however, was the development of processes of circular motion in a confined area, processes that could then be converted to other sources of power.

Until about 1830, there was more progress in the development of threshers in Scotland and England than there was in North America. As with harvesting implements, early attempts were designed to imitate known motions, and it took some time to break away from these principles. Early threshers replicated the motion of a flail. Efforts of inventors in England and Scotland during the early 1700s produced little. Not until late in the 1700s did a Scot named Andrew Meikle finally build several important machines; his first patent was in 1788. Grain was fed into Meikle's machine headfirst between two rollers so that the heads intruded into the path of four scutchers (bars mounted on an axis to be spun around). Threshing occurred when the scutchers pounded the heads. The process was enclosed within breasting, but this breasting did not operate as a concave, one of the frictional elements in later threshers. Although the scutchers moved in a circle, their threshing was still done in beating, linear fashion. However, Meikle's work, especially because he applied water power to his machines, was important. He and his son, George, sold machines commercially, and numerous other inventors of the 1790s copied their designs.[36]

In fact, the Meikle design set the course for the development of what would come to be known as the "Scottish" design of threshing, characterized by the beating action of the scutchers. This action did not fully exploit the advantages of circular motion, however. John Ball of Norfolk remedied that in 1805 with a design that set the pattern for the "English" thresher. This model had no rollers; grain could be fed in any fashion. A concave was set close to the moving bars, which were not just beaters such as Meikle's scutchers but were designed to pass near the concave, separating the grain by rubbing it in a circular motion around the circumference. The English design proved superior and was eventually revived on the western shore of the Atlantic after being improved in 1848 by John Goucher of County York. His threshing bars were rasped rather than flat, with grooves to produce greater action on the grain.[37]

Early threshing machines knocked the grain loose from the chaff, but they did not expel the chaff from the grain. This step was done separately with a fanning mill. Since antiquity, when winnowing had been accomplished by natural wind alone, the development of the fanning mill had gone through a strange course. In China, by the time of the Han Dynasty, the Chinese were using a human-powered rotary fan to blow the chaff from grain. Centuries later, European traders in China, especially Dutch traders, observed this process and brought the idea back to western Europe, where the first rotary fanning mills, closely modeled after those of the Chinese, appeared in the 1500s. Subsequently, James Meikle, father of the Andrew Meikle who was to greatly advance the technology of threshing, traveled to Holland in 1710 with the backing of an English patron. He brought back the technology of fanning mills, and these mills were fit-

ted on some of his son's threshers. Local clergy, who favored the use of natural wind and could even approve of waving barn doors to aid it, condemned the use of Meikle's "Devil's wind"; but the fanning mill was a major advance, especially when coupled with a sieve for separation. In 1761 William Evers patented the process whereby the fanning mill forced air through the threshed grain and blew out the chaff and light straw. The grain and heavier straw fell upon a sieve that excluded the straw.[38]

In Scotland and England lay the scholarship and the scientific and mechanical abilities to devise basic principles of threshing, and there they developed. In the isles, however, threshing mechanized slowly because there was not the pressing need for such innovation as was present in North America. During the early nineteenth century, as the hierarchical society of British agriculture was transformed by an international cash-grain economy, a labor surplus prevailed. Farm laborers, hired by the day or week, were reduced to reliance on the Poor Laws. When certain farmers, more for efficiency than for economy, proceeded to adopt machine threshing, they encountered considerable social resistance. This opposition came to a head in 1830 with the Thresher Riots. Farm laborers, seizing on the mechanical symbol of their economic troubles, destroyed nearly four hundred threshing machines. Other tactics of the hard-pressed workers included setting fire to ricks and barns and sending threatening letters, signed by "The Swing" or "Captain Swing," to landowners. The Swing, which began as a local protest against threshers, developed into a general movement for regular employment and a living wage. Magistrates enlisted the aid of troops and large posses of temporary constables to quell The Swing; special commissions moved from county to county and tried the rioters. Nineteen were executed, and some five hundred transported to Australia or Van Diemen's Land. Nevertheless, public sentiment largely favored the cause, if not the incendiary tactics, of The Swing. The Swing, the sentiment that supported it, and the labor surplus combined to retard, but not stop, the proliferation of threshing machines.[39]

In North America there were few such social constraints. Agriculture was expanding, labor was relatively scarce, and technical advances were hailed as freeing men from hard labor, not displacing them. The colonists brought with them English and European ways of threshing, modified somewhat by environment. Generally, threshing in New England, following English and Scottish precedent, was done with a flail in the barn. Old-World style flailing also prevailed among the culturally conservative Pennsylvania Dutch, effecting the distinctive designs of their barns. In other wheat-growing Middle colonies and the states that developed from them, treading was an accommodation to more expansive operations producing cash crops. In the same area during the early nineteenth century, there developed a special roller in-

tended for indoor use called a porcupine (or groundhog, or Tumbling Tom). It consisted of an oak log trimmed hexagonally; pegs driven into it, the pegs longer at one end than at the other; and a shaft running down the middle. The end with the shorter pegs was attached by the shaft to a post in the center of a barn threshing floor, and the whole porcupine was pulled in a circle around the post by horses. Fanning mills were also used in this region before the Revolution, although most farmers winnowed with a sheet or a wicker fan. As threshing methods extended into the Midwest, farmers continued to choose between flailing and treading according to a complex of circumstances—ethnic background, available markets, grains raised, barn styles, the need for straw to feed and bed animals. The material culture of threshing, especially flail design, displayed the rich variety typical of dynamic folk cultures.[40]

The first mechanical threshing machines used in the United States were imports, beginning with a Scottish model, probably one of Meikle's, which arrived in New York in 1788. Thomas Jefferson of Virginia imported a threshing machine in 1796. Scottish and English threshers were imported in numbers thereafter, at first mainly into the mid-Atlantic states. The first American patent for a threshing machine was in 1791 by Samuel Mullikan of Philadelphia, and the first thresher built in the United States was by a Colonel Anderson, also of Philadelphia, in 1792.[41]

Thereafter more American manu-

The peg drum and concave, an American improvement in thresher design. (From American Thresherman)

facturers produced home products to compete with the imports. This trend was true especially after 1822, when A. Savage patented a distinctively American improvement to thresher design—the peg drum and concave. In this design the threshing was accomplished, not by rubbing the bars against the concave, but by striking the grain between two sets of meshing teeth. These pegs protruded from both the drum and the concave and were set to pass close to one another as the drum turned, thereby striking out the grain. These early peg or toothed machines were called groundhog threshers, some said because they were staked to the ground, and others said because they looked like they were digging into the ground like a groundhog. The ma-

chines were built low, perhaps four feet high at the top. They were powered by horsepowers, and early ones threshed perhaps one hundred fifty bushels of grain a day. The grain was often passed through a separate fanning mill as well, especially if it was to be used for seed.[42]

Combining a threshing machine with a fanning mill to create the combined thresher and fanner was the achievement of Hiram A. and John Pitts of Maine. The Pitts brothers did custom threshing with a groundhog thresher during the 1820s. In 1830 they patented and began producing their own horsepower thresher, and by 1834 they were selling a combined thresher and fanner. In their machine the grain passed through a peg drum-and-concave threshing chamber and was carried to the fan by an endless belt of wooden slats fixed on two chains. The grain fell between the slats while the fan blew out the chaff and light straw. The larger pieces of straw were delivered to a raddle, a vibrating table with spikes inclined up from the endless belt, that carried the straw away. An improved patent in 1837 substituted an apron conveyor for the endless chain.[43]

In 1847 the Pitts brothers—following the wheat frontier west, as had McCormick—moved to Alton, Illinois, and shortly thereafter to Chicago. Hiram Pitts produced the Chicago Pitts thresher there, while his brother, after working temporarily in Ohio, went back east to Buffalo, joined in partnership with Joseph Hall of Rochester, and began producing the Buffalo Pitts thresher.[44]

Two other men—George Westinghouse and J. I. Case—were also prominently associated with the manufacture of threshers during this period. Beginning in the early 1840s, and continuing past 1900, Westinghouse and his company built threshers at Schenectady, New York, on the patents of Jacob V. A. Wemple. The Westinghouse threshers used canvas aprons in place of wooden slat belts for moving straw, and they improved the design of the raddle. Case, a native of New York, ran a groundhog thresher near his home as a teenager. In 1842 he bought six machines on credit and took them to Racine, Wisconsin. There he sold five and started custom threshing with the sixth while making improvements on the design. In 1843 he began to manufacture

and sell threshing machines in Racine.[45]

One more major improvement came prior to the Civil War. Following a pattern patented as early as 1829 in England but little used there, Cyrus Roberts and John Cox of Belleville, Illinois, in 1852 patented a machine that did away with both raddle chains and canvas aprons. Their machine, which Roberts produced for market, incorporated straw walkers, or, as they were called then, "vibrators." The Nichols and Shepard Company of Battle Creek, Michigan, soon improved the original design and marketed a machine under the name Vibrator. By 1859 this company had put in double shakers, the reciprocal actions of which balanced one another, thus preventing the machine from crawling along the ground. Case's company waited until 1880 to adopt the straw walker principle and then called its machine the Agitator.[46]

Throughout the antebellum years there echoed various objections to the use of groundhog threshers. In addition to harboring general distrust of machines and fear of the capital investment required, many eastern farmers maintained that the grain did not come out as clean as it did when they flailed and fanned it themselves, and that the straw came out broken up and likely to spoil if moist. Developing agricultural conditions and technological improvements swept these objections aside, however. The settling of the prairies and their planting to wheat, coupled with the perennial shortage of labor on

Treadmill threshing near Duck Lake, Sask., 1907. (Saskatchewan Archives Board, Regina)

the frontier, required mechanization in threshing just as in harvesting and other agricultural operations. By the 1860s groundhog threshers were regarded as reliable and could thresh up to two hundred bushels a day when powered by two horses. One man was needed to feed in bundles, one to pitch away straw, and a third to bag grain. Few machines were portable (mounted on wheels); so farmers either bought their own machines or, more often, hauled their grain to the threshing site of a custom operator. The Chicago Pitts machine was already on wheels, which facilitated custom work and made the machine even more popular on the prairies. By 1866 the United States commissioner of agriculture was able to report that "threshing machines are as perfect as they can be made" and

that custom threshing, with each machine handling up to three hundred bushels a day, was ruling in the West.[47]

The development of threshing on the prairies had truly been rapid and amazing. By the time of the commissioner's report the main difficulty holding back further technological progress was not the mechanism of threshing but the application of power, which was still largely limited to horsepower. There were two common ways of converting the linear motion of animals into the circular motion of threshers. One was a treadmill, composed of an endless belt of chains and slats, which was sometimes made portable by mounting it on wagon wheels. There were several technical problems with treadmills in threshing. For example, the mill tended to run away if the load

Horsepower threshing in Saskatchewan; six teams are on the horsepower. (Saskatchewan Archives Board, Regina)

was lessened or if a chain broke, forcing the poor horse to either gallop or fall. The addition of governors and flywheels corrected this problem, but the fact remained that the great number of moving parts in a treadmill dissipated much of the power applied to it. Furthermore, that power was limited to the efforts of one horse.[48]

Consequently, the more popular method of applying horsepower to threshing was with sweeps, sometimes called booms. Sweeps were horizontal beams that stretched out from a vertical axle. At the outside ends were hitched teams of horses. The axle transferred power through a series of gears to a tumbling rod, which ran out from the circle to connect with another gearbox on the thresher; power was sometimes applied directly from the gearbox to the thresher, often by means of an endless belt. During the 1840s inventors put such devices on wheels, constructing the beams so they could fold and thus be portable. A popular sweep horsepower was the Pitts-Carey, developed by Hiram Pitts and marketed in portable form in 1856. This horsepower had a variable number of sweeps to accommodate up to five (later six) teams. Another popular sweep was the Woodbury and Dingee, manufactured by Case in Racine. Horsepowers continued in common use throughout the nineteenth century. By 1905 fifty-seven manufacturers offered them for sale. By that time, however, they were already a technical anachronism. The age of steam had begun.[49]

The adoption of steam power for threshing was slowed by a number of fears. Explosions were common because the pressure in boilers could reach one hundred pounds per square inch. The fire maintained under the boiler was dangerous around straw and farm buildings, so much so that insurance companies at first refused to insure buildings on farms where steam was used. Still, horsepower was not without its disadvantages, either. First, horses were needed for other farm work, and threshing not only occupied them for the duration of that job but also generally wore them down, because threshing sweeps were hard on their necks and shoulders. Second, the power delivered by teams was often uneven, for horses were likely to stumble or fall down. And, last, after the Civil War, there was a temporary shortage of animals as agricultural expansion resumed.[50]

As early as 1784 James Watt, in England, had acquired a patent on a portable steam engine applicable to threshing, and many people had used steam for threshing through the next several decades. In 1814 William Lester patented a portable steam engine designed specifically for threshing. By the 1830s portable threshers and engines operated by custom outfits were fairly common on large estates in the eastern counties of England. In North America, however, although Horace Greeley of the *New York Tribune* had reported use of steam for threshing in 1850, its employment was insignificant until after the Civil War. The large-scale implementation of steam threshing awaited further technological advance and the development of a greater need for it. The impetus was to come with the agricultural settlement of the Great Plains.[51]

Through centuries of trial and experimentation, farmers and inventors had struggled to reduce the labor involved in harvesting and threshing. Labor was the central question, and it was seasonality that made the question sticky. Harvesting and threshing required intensive labor for short segments of the year; harvesting and threshing were by nature the bottlenecks in the production of small grains. The employment of itinerant labor for the harvest was an expedient dating from the ancient Egyptians, but it was an expedient nevertheless. The hope for eventual resolution of the seasonal problem lay in technology. Hence the continual efforts of inventors.

Progress, however, was halting. Sometimes this was due to negative constraints on innovation (for example, popular discontent, unfavorable environments, or economic problems) and sometimes to the absence of positive incentives (for example, the opening of new agricultural lands). Given the right conditions, however, innovation flourished and often in such flurries that it was impossible to trace individual achievements. Progress sprang from many heads and hands at the same time. Implementation of the resulting improvements was then rapid, moving small-grain farming in the direction of capital intensiveness, that is, into the Machine Age. Custom operators eased the demands of capital intensiveness on farmers by making machines available for seasonal work.

The technological progress of harvesting and threshing prior to the settlement of the plains had prepared North American farmers to enter the region. They carried a substantial yet dynamic technology as well as a body of customs that had filled the prairies and were ready for the plains. The technology was to enter a new phase of development as it responded to the still more expansive and distinctive agriculture and environment of the plains, just as it had with the earlier advances of geographic frontiers.

The new agriculture of the plains was to be not only expansive but also expanding. In westward migration from the Atlantic coast, wheat followed the frontier, but there was never a wheat frontier like the plains. This frontier was on the move continually (not continuously, for economic conditions interrupted it several times) from the late 1860s through the mid-1920s. The Golden Belt of central Kansas, the heart of the winter wheat area, was

settled during the 1870s, but beyond it lay the increasingly marginal lands of western Kansas, western Nebraska, western Oklahoma, west Texas, and eastern Colorado. Thus the plow-up continued. The Dakota boom dated from 1878, but after the level Red River Valley and other parts of eastern Dakota were filled with settlers, beyond stretched the West River country, and beyond that the tarpaper-shack frontier of Montana. To the north was the Last Best West of Canada, where converged streams of settlements from the American midwestern states, the Canadian middle provinces, and, as was always the case on the plains frontier, the European nations. The accessibility of railroads, the voracity of European markets, and the environment of the plains compelled farmers to emphasize small grains and encouraged, in vast areas, virtual wheat monoculture—a cash-grain farming that was strikingly different from the more diversified, self-sufficient agriculture of earlier frontiers.[52]

The expansion of grain farming onto the plains was concurrent with a flowering of farmers' receptivity toward technological innovation. Notwithstanding popular and historical images of farmers as "reluctant" or "troubled," the agriculturalists of the late nineteenth and early twentieth centuries were innovators—not just adoptors of innovations but adapters and even originators as well. Farmers as a whole did not lunge after every new contraption that came along, but among the people on the land, certain

individuals—often custom machine operators—acted as the leaven in the
meal. A historian of power farming in
the United States has concluded that
"to the American farmer, change was
traditional"; a historian of western
Canada has termed his region a "mechanical agricultural frontier."[53] It is
the idea of a tradition of change that
makes the wheat culture of the plains,
especially its harvesting and threshing,
comprehensible. Such a regional culture might evolve continually, adjusting
to complex forces, and still retain
enough overall regional integrity to
constitute a recognizable culture.[54]

New technologies, whether from private invention or from public research,
would take shape according to the
needs of the region. Into the Great
Plains, agriculturalists carried their
technologies and customs, some of
which worked well, at least initially,
while others seemed inadequate. Rapidly, those ways not suited to the environment of the region would be replaced by ways more appropriate. This
process was to require ongoing technological innovation. The accommodation
of technology and custom to environment, however, was not to take place in
static, insulated circumstances. Mighty
forces from outside the region, such as
international economic trends and national governmental policies, would
have their effects as well. Technological
heritage, environmental adaptation,
technological innovation, and the effects of outside forces would combine
on the plains to create a vital culture
devoted to the harvesting and threshing of small grains.

CHAPTER TWO.
HARVESTING

The technology and culture of farming evolve in curious disregard of North American federalism. The experiment stations, agricultural colleges, extension services, and similar institutions of the United States and Canada define their territories according to political lines irrelevant to agricultural practice. That is why the publication of "Farm Practices in Growing Wheat" in the United States Department of Agriculture's *Yearbook* of 1919 was so remarkable.[1] In the article, the authors, J. H. Arnold and R. R. Spafford, presented information they had gathered by questionnaire from about seven thousand wheat farmers. They organized the grass-roots data geographically; state lines meant nothing in their analysis of tillage, planting, and harvesting. They viewed such practices as if from a satellite, with at least a national, if not a continental perspective, and as they did so, patterns appeared on the landscape, patterns they could map. This broad view, they said, showed that farm practices should be analyzed and evaluated "by considering them in the light of the climatic, soil, and topographical features of the area where they have been developed." It was obvious, they observed, "that practices suitable for any given area can not be transplanted unmodified to another."[2]

The Arnold-Spafford approach was astute in that it outlined the relationships among environment, technology, and culture. It was limited, however, in that it studied these things at only one point in time. A historical approach to some of the same phenomena Arnold and Spafford studied in 1919 not only confirms their findings but also adds recognition of the evolution of practices through time, an evolution deriving from causes other than environment. Such, at least, is the case with the history of harvesting small grains on the Great Plains of North America. There were patterns such as those Ar-

Doukhobor women harvesting with sickles in western Canada, ca. 1900. (Provincial Archives of British Columbia)

nold and Spafford saw, but they were dynamic patterns only partially portrayed on a static, two-dimensional map, and they derived, as had been so since antiquity, from a complex of forces.

Although the patterns of harvesting practices took shape rapidly on the plains, the earliest settlers in any particular area often temporarily employed anachronistic technologies. Until railroads should connect them to implement manufacturers and central markets, these pioneers fell back upon previous cultural or ethnic experiences to handle small crops. "Harvesting and threshing in the early years was accomplished in many instances by what now seem primitive means," reported the compiler of a survey of pioneer farm practices in western Canada.[3] Old-timers on those northern plains re-

called common use of cradles, scythes, and even sickles. Ukrainians and other eastern European immigrants were accustomed to using sickles and hand-tying sheaves in their homelands, and they transplanted such customs to Canada. Sickles were scarce (as were eastern Europeans) on the American plains, but cradles were common pioneer implements. A Kansan recalled cradle harvesting at the rate of one-half acre to two acres per day, "depending upon the man who was swinging it," and then tying bundles with straws selected from the piles of grain the cradler had left. Reminiscences from Washington County, Kansas, confirmed that when residents harvested their first wheat crop in 1861, their only implements were two cradles. Pioneers of the Texas Panhandle, too, cradled grain. Some also, before they obtained

Binding wheat on the Oleson farm near Brookings, S. Dak., 1898. (South Dakota State Historical Society, Pierre)

binders, used reapers or mowing machines to cut loose grain and even rigged up clever devices of cowhide or other material to collect the grain into piles.[4]

Plainspeople were no antiquarians, however, and as soon as possible they imported what they considered respectable, up to date harvesting implements—binders. "The farmer used the binder as it came to him," wrote James C. Malin, Kansas' premier historian of the plains, "without modifying it through new inventions, or through adaptation to new uses."[5] At least as early as 1876 farmers in the Golden Belt of central Kansas were getting Marsh and Wood wire binders from local dealers, and by 1880 they could buy twine binders. To the west, in Pawnee County, a farmer-diarist recorded that settlers in his locality harvested their

first wheat crop in 1875 with his binder.[6]

As in Kansas, so it went throughout the North American plains: Binders constituted a universal stage in development that would make historians of the successive-frontiers school, concerned with the successive stages of frontier development, proud. In large subregions of the plains, however, settlers took measure of this humid-area implement. Where winter wheat culture challenged the more arid parts of the region, farmers found the binder wanting and turned instead to the header. The binder, they said, cut too narrow a swath (seven or eight feet), missed bundles on rough ground, and, worst of all, performed poorly in the short crop of a dry year. Some might object that grain stacked directly from heading rather than first shocked was

*Heading wheat on the John Thielen farm, central Kansas, July 9, 1909. The header was the machine
for big farms in the winter wheat region. (Halbe Collection, Kansas State Historical Society, Topeka)*

likely to spoil; but on the dry plains, this problem seemed remote. As Malin found, "The dry years 1880, 1881, confirmed fully the dominant position of the header as the necessary Plains harvesting machine."[7] The header, like the binder, was available to farmers on the plains almost from the outset, and, given the choice, farmers made the environmentally sound decision. The header handled short crops just fine. Furthermore, it missed no bundles because it tied none; it took a wide swath (commonly twelve feet) with no side draft because it was pushed from behind; and it saved the labor of shocking, a decided advantage inasmuch as labor was chronically scarce on the plains.

Arnold and Spafford in 1919 charted the areas where the header had displaced the binder as the predominant wheat harvesting implement. Their maps were inexact but clear: Although the binder predominated over most of the country, in certain parts of the plains, farmers much preferred the header (see Figures 2.1 and 2.2). The three concentrations of header preference were (in order of magnitude) the western reaches of the winter wheat belt on the southern plains, comprising the Texas Panhandle, northwestern Oklahoma, western Kansas, northeastern Colorado, and southwestern Nebraska; the heart of the spring wheat belt in the central Dakotas; and the winter wheat area of central Montana. "The header in particular adapted to areas where wheat usually develops a short, stiff straw and where the harvesting season is normally dry," observed the two authors.[8]

Whereas Arnold and Spafford provided the big picture, students of harvesting and threshing in the individual

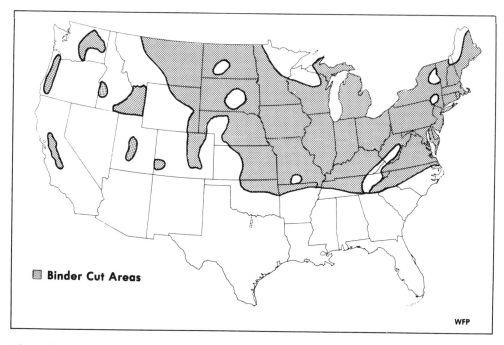

Binder Cut Areas

WFP

Figure 2.1 Areas Where Wheat Was Cut with Binders in 1919. *Source:* Data from J. H. Arnold and R. R. Spafford, "Farm Practices in Growing Wheat: A Geographical Presentation," *Yearbook of the* [U.S.] *Department of Agriculture* (Washington, D.C.: GPO, 1919), pp. 123–50.

states chronicled local conditions. A report from the Kansas State Board of Agriculture in 1920 divided the state into three sections—eastern, central, and western—and recorded relative use of headers and binders in each. In eastern Kansas 99 percent of the farmers preferred the binder over the header, but in central Kansas 62 percent preferred the header, and in western Kansas 96 percent preferred it. Although a clear trend existed, it had a slight deviation: It was common to begin cutting green wheat with binders and then to switch to headers as soon as the grain was ripe enough. Already

in 1910 a federal bulletin had reported this practice throughout header country in Kansas, Nebraska, and the Dakotas. Obviously, farmers with binders did not scrap them when they got headers but rather used the binders to get a jump on the hectic harvest. Another consideration in the binder-header decision was the size and nature of the operation. As cereal scientists observed in Montana in 1916, large farms devoted mostly to small grains had the greatest use for headers, whereas small farms with diverse crops had the least. Such differing operations might exist side-by-side in the same lo-

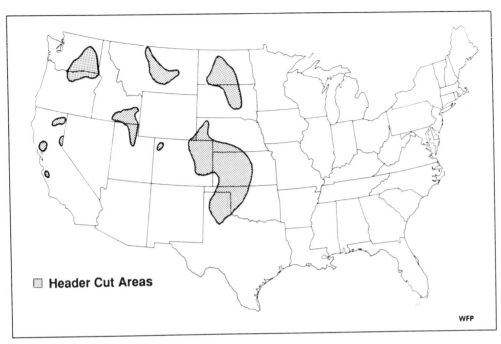

☐ **Header Cut Areas**

WFP

Figure 2.2 Areas Where Wheat Was Cut with a Header in 1919. *Source:* Data from J. H. Arnold and R. R. Spafford, "Farm Practices in Growing Wheat: A Geographical Presentation," *Yearbook of the* [U.S.] *Department of Agriculture* (Washington, D.C.: GPO, 1919), pp. 123–50.

cality, thus blurring the distinction between binder country and header country.[9]

Such lessons in agricultural geography were commonplace to farmers of the plains, who observed them through space and time. Michael Ewanchuk, a native of Gimli, Manitoba, confirmed the universal use of binders in the locality but also said that people knew about headers and considered them characteristic of points west, out in Saskatchewan, perhaps. Farmers in central Saskatchewan, however, had little use for headers. In twenty years of farming just south of Moose Jaw, from 1909 to

1928, Alexander Boan never recalled anyone using headers: "The crops were good enough that we didn't need a header," he explained, implying thereby that only a poor farming country required headers. The header country of western Canada lay west of Boan's land, from Swift Current into eastern Alberta.[10]

George Hitz grew up just east of the header area of North Dakota, and his recollections showed the capacity of farmers to weigh the merits of the two implements. "My folks farmed ten miles west of New Rockford," he said. "We always used binders, but at times they were a headache when trying to have them make a decent bundle when grain was leaning badly or broken down. Durum wheat was bad when put on rich soil like summer-fallow. It practically all lodged down. Some years when the crop was on the lean side, especially barley, there was quite a bit of waste where a header would of been better." From nearby Cathay, William J. Lies knew of the headers used in "drier territory" but expressed the local sentiment that "to cut with a binder and make bundles was a better process in particular if you got any rain, as the bundles stood upright and would dry out better than if there were just heads of grain stacked." Use of the straw was another issue he raised: The straw saved from threshing bound grain was good bedding and even feed for livestock.[11] (A counterargument, naturally, was that the header left the straw in the field to return organic matter to the soil.)

The testimony of three Kansas natives also produced clues about folk attitudes toward the harvesting implements. Ernest Claassen, born in 1895 in the Mennonite country of Harvey County, Kansas, recalled (and recourse to personal diaries confirmed) that in his youth, his family and all the neighbors bound their grain. It was, however, a matter of local and recent preference; old, unused header barges standing around testified that an earlier generation had used headers. Harvey County was near the border between header and binder country in central Kansas, and evidently prefer-

ences there vacillated. Milo Mathews, who was a few years younger than Claassen, grew up around Waterville in north-central Kansas. He recalled that all of his neighbors also used binders, and he, too, thought of the home of the header as somewhere to the west. He subsequently followed the harvest and did custom threshing in the Dakotas; there he saw plenty of heading. Still, he observed, many farmers kept their binders, and in wet years, the header stood idle. A third, western Kansan, Guy Bretz, provided an antidote for the backhanded folk attitude of binder users that headers were machines of the poor hinterland. "In 1915 we had a good crop," he recalled. "A little too much rain, but I think Father had the largest crew that was ever assembled on one farm. . . . It consisted of 3 headers, 6 barges, 18 men and 30 head of horses and mules." Header users, in other words, were big-time farmers.[12]

The conservative inclination of many farmers to want both headers and binders available for use, depending on how the grain ripened and if the weather cooperated, was the rationale for the push binder, an implement offered by manufacturers during the 1910s. This was a binder of wide platform (ten to twelve feet), giving it the same economy of scale as the header but also requiring it (as with the header) to be pushed from behind by horses. Richard Goering of McPherson County, Kansas (in the central-Kansas transitional zone between binders and headers), recalled the International

The push binder is used for either binding or heading. This one is on the George Eslinger farm, central Kansas, June 29, 1912. (Halbe Collection, Kansas State Historical Society, Topeka)

push binder his father bought in 1914. Hitching six horses (three on each side of the main beam extending back from the platform) with a six-horse evener, the farmer piloted the push binder into the field when the grain was still green but full. As the grain ripened, the farmer would notice the packer arms of the binder shelling out grain and would decide when it was time to cease binding and begin heading. To do this, he removed the binder apparatus—this required only the pulling of four pins—and attached a grain elevator in its place to dump the loose heads into a barge.[13]

The push binder was a response to the needs of farmers in certain transi-tional areas or times. Other mechanical adaptations, however, were peculiar to areas whose needs were those of ex-tremity, not transition. In the spring wheat areas of the northern plains, there were many big farmers who wanted mechanization to eliminate much of the hand labor associated with binder harvesting but who still consid-ered the header unsuitable. Their grain ripened too unevenly for header harvesting, and, moreover, during a fall harvest it was important to get the grain cut before the snow flew. Many, therefore, embraced the sheaf, or stook, loader to use in conjunction with the binder. Like push binders, sheaf loaders appeared during the 1910s; the

A Stewart sheaf loader near Yorkton, Sask., ca. 1915. (Saskatchewan Archives Board, Regina)

best-known model was manufactured by the Stewart Sheaf Loader Company of Winnipeg. The Stewart brothers shipped their first loader to a farmer at Belcarres, Saskatchewan, in 1910 and subsequently marketed the machine on both sides of the Forty-ninth Parallel. "The Hired Help Takes the Cream Off the Harvest," mourned advertisements for sheaf loaders, but with loaders there was "No Army of Men and Teams to Board." Advertisements continually emphasized that manufacturers recognized the special "need" of big spring-wheat farmers and had designed this contraption especially for them. Most sheaf loaders were drawn by four horses and consisted of a platform, or pickup, that scooped stooks up from the ground and an elevator that dropped them into a barge pulled

by another team alongside. Some sheaf loaders were combination loader-carriers that scooped and elevated the stooks directly back into their own carrier beds.[14]

If the companies producing sheaf loaders got their ideas from ordinary farmers, they never admitted it, but farmers were themselves tinkering with machines along similar lines at the same time. Around 1915 a man named Paulson, near Emerson, North Dakota, devised a shock bucker to carry several shocks at a time to a stationary separator. The Paulson shock bucker was essentially a heavy-duty hay buck, or buck rake, fitted with a frame along the sides to hold the bundles after the protruding buck teeth swept them up. Researchers in North Dakota said that the Paulson machine was "a decided ad-

Harry Tuttle harvesting with a header stack-barge in Edwards County, Kans., 1913. The barge is dumping a stack. (Edwards County Museum, Kinsley, Kans.)

vance over the Stewart bundle loader, as it supplies the threshing operator with the shocked grain much more economically."[15]

About three years later, another North Dakotan named Fisher, near Grand Forks, motorized the sheaf loader. He mounted an ordinary hay loader, a pickup device commonly used to elevate loose hay into a rack, onto the front of a motor truck and engaged it to run off the truck engine. On the back of the truck he mounted metal-frame and chicken-wire sideboards to hold a good-sized pile of bundles. He then ran the bundle truck through the grain field, scooping up shocks and carrying them to the separator.[16]

While these men tinkered with devices to complement the binder, others sought to improve the header. The improved models would eventually be known as header stack-barges, or, in

the Canadian plains, simply as header barges. At first, however, they went by various names. All were creations of folk technology.[17]

In 1915 a farmer named Winifred Jacobs, near Dodge City, Kansas, built a prototype header stack-barge that he called a stacker wagon. His original idea was to construct a wagon that could be drawn alongside a header in operation and that would accumulate and carry a full-sized grain stack, all without the pitching of harvest hands. Stacks so built could be threshed later in the field.[18]

The Jacobs stacker wagon was about twenty feet long, nine feet wide, and eleven feet high; its bottom sloped eighteen inches to the center in a gentle V shape. Its sides, of wooden studs, ran vertically for about six feet and then angled up and in so that the wheat piled highest in the center. Men riding the wagon forked the wheat around and tramped it. When the wagon was full, they opened a rear gate and dropped four skids from the rear of the wagon to the ground. Next they drove a stake into the ground behind the wagon, and to that stake they tied a rope that ran under and around the wheat in the wagon. They then shouted for the driver to pull ahead. The result was a well-formed stack on the ground. The outfit was mechanized, with the header and wagon pulled in tandem by a tractor. The stacks, piled high in the center, shed water and kept well until threshing. By 1920 stacker wagons not only were common in Jacobs's neighborhood but also were used in Rice County, Thomas County, and probably elsewhere in Kansas.

Jacobs's idea must have been a good one, suited to the region, because not only did neighbors copy it but also other folk inventors came up with roughly the same device independently. Invented in 1913 by two men named Graham and Roach, and used contemporaneously with Jacobs's model, was a smaller stacker used near Carrington, North Dakota. This region was binder country; thus the implement used to pile grain into the Graham-Roach stacker was a binder with the knotter removed and an extension elevator attached. The stacker was ten to fifteen feet long. A man on top formed the high-centered stack. When the stacker was full, a rear gate opened and the wagon bottom, composed of rods running parallel to the

direction of travel, dropped to the ground so that the stack slid off. The stacker was drawn by a team of horses or pulled in tandem with the converted binder by a tractor. Hands followed to tie down the stacks with binder twine run through with a long needle.[19]

A folk invention closer in design to the Kansas model than the Graham-Roach stacker was the header barge built by C. W. Hart, near Hedgesville, Montana, around 1918. Used with a header and pulled in tandem by a tractor, the Hart header barge was eighteen feet long, twelve feet wide, and twelve feet high. Its sides were similar to those of the Jacobs stacker, as was its unloading process, which could be completed in fewer than five minutes.[20]

In Walworth County, South Dakota, a farmer named Jake Rabenberg in 1926 built a header stack-barge similar to those of Jacobs and Hart. Rabenberg's model differed from the others, however, in that its rear gates hinged from the sides, which were completely vertical. It was twenty by twelve by twelve foot in size, but his neighbors, who had smaller tractors, decided to build smaller barges as well.[21]

Undoubtedly the most fertile, if not the first, field for early header stack-barge invention was the plains of western Canada. Henry Schwindt of Perry, Saskatchewan, said that he began using a stack-barge in 1919. Albertans traced the origin of the device in their province to farmers, particularly a Mr. Hellam, near Acadia Valley. As the header stack-barge (called the header barge by Canadians) proliferated in western

Bundle racks deliver bundles to the stacks on the P. J. Larson farm near Salem, S. Dak. The women do not appear dressed for stacking. (South Dakota State Historical Society, Pierre)

Canada, however, its use, surprisingly enough, was to be associated more with the combined harvester than with the header or the binder.[22]

Despite the efforts of these farmer-inventors, most grain farmers on the plains accepted the harvesting devices presented to them by implement manufacturers and used them with harvest labor in a generally conventional fashion. Even when they did so, however, it was still up to them to supply, through their own construction, certain additional, necessary devices—that is, bundle wagons or header barges to transport their grain to the thresher or stack.

Seldom were bundle racks intended for bundle hauling only; most were general farm racks, but because bundle hauling was the most intensive use for them, that function heavily influenced folk design. Certainly such was the case with A. P. Murphy of North Dakota, a farmer-thresherman who in 1928 described his bundle racks for *American Thresherman.* "It seems queer that so many so-called farm racks are made on no particular plan," he remarked. "They are usually heavier than is necessary, far too clumsy, and nearly all require too much labor to load and unload."[23]

Murphy then described how his racks were built. They were eight feet by sixteen feet, although other farmers commonly used smaller, seven by fourteen racks. Murphy's plans were de-

tailed, precise, and aided by draw-
ings—a testimonial to the potential
expertise of folk technology. The backbone of the rack, Murphy said, was its
sturdy, lengthwise sills of three-by-
eight-inch lumber (which projected a
little in the rear to hold a feedbox).
The sills, spaced with two-by-sixes,
were the base for the two-by-six cross-
sills. Onto the cross-sills went a floor of
"common rough boards not laid tight
or matched," showing daylight between. A rim of flat two-by-fours outlined the floor and was bolted through
to the cross-sills. From each corner rose
four-foot corner posts, which were also
bolted to the cross-sills. The front and
back walls of the rack consisted of one-
by-sixes spaced a few inches apart and
nailed horizontally to the corner posts;
the walls were then braced by diagonals. Also in the front, bolted to the
front cross-sill, was a vertical two-by-six
standard piece by which the driver was
to stand. A V-shaped cut in its top end
served as a holder for lines or as a
handhold for the driver climbing
aboard. Side boards consisting of one-
by-sixes and two-by-fours ran diago-
nally down from the tops of the corner
posts to the midpoint of the floor
length. Murphy estimated the cost of
one of his bundle racks, eight of which
he had used for years, at twenty-five to
thirty dollars. An account such as his
provided impressive testimony to the
folk engineering necessary to complement manufactured machinery.

Fellow North Dakotan William Lies
described a shorter, eight-by-twelve-
foot bundle wagon. "A rack was always
a home made job," he confirmed, with
the two rear wheels always a little
larger than the two in front. The
height "varied depending on what
other uses it may be put to," but it was
generally four to five feet. The sides, as
drawn by Lies, were similar to Murphy's. Down in the binder area of eastern Kansas, F. M. Redpath recalled an
outfit of twelve slightly different, slant-
sided bundle racks, "eight by sixteen
feet at the bottom, and about ten by
sixteen at the top." Although most
bundle wagons captured in photographs appear unpainted, these twelve
were painted—six red and six yellow.[24]

The variation among bundle racks
was largely of scale and detail, not of
concept, as is evident from the many
that have been photographed. This was
generally true among header barges,
too, although these more specialized
devices also differed in material and
appurtenances. Typical header boxes
were, as a bulletin put it, "built especially for use in heading wheat," not for
general farm use. They also were "inexpensive, since they usually [were]
made on the farm from cheap lumber;
$8 per box probably [was] a fair aver-
age cost."[25] Most boxes, the same study
observed, were cheap to maintain because they could be fixed with scrap
lumber, were unpainted, rested on running gear that could be taken off and
used for other things as well, and
lasted for about ten years in the dry climate of the plains.

Operators in the header country of
Montana refined the header box further for their large-scale operations.

Typical homemade header barges on the Peter farm, Barton County, Kans., ca. 1910. (Courtesy of Rollie Peter)

The standard box there, a bulletin said in 1924, was seven and a half by sixteen feet, with slightly spreading sides and a partition in the center that separated the front of the box from the back. At the bottom of each of the two compartments lay a sling, either store-bought or homemade, that was used to unload the spikes (grain heads) onto the stack.[26] The sides of a header box, unlike those of a bundle rack, had to hold loose spikes. Most, therefore, as shown in photographs, were of solid board construction. A few employed wire mesh or netting on the sides, thereby easing the work of the teams pulling them.

The folk artistry exhibited in bundle wagons and header barges emphasized how important it was for agricultural-ists to work methodically and well at all tasks associated with binding and heading. Like dignitaries, the binder and the header occupied prominent places in the host of customs and technologies that accomplished the harvesting of small grains on the Great Plains. They were the central elements, the key items of capital that characterized the harvest in their respective technological domains. Upon them, however, there developed networks of tools, tasks, and organizations that completed the harvest. These constituted the culture of small-grain harvesting on the Great Plains prior to the advent of the combine.

The operation and support of a binder in a wheat field required a certain organization of people and tasks.

The vertical staves on the sides of this header barge were a fairly common alternative to horizontal planks. This one is on the Estan Allen farm in central Kansas, July 8, 1912. (Halbe Collection, Kansas State Historical Society, Topeka)

It was essential that the binder be kept running steadily for a long workday, from first light until dead dark; indeed, in the more expansive wheat farming regions it was not uncommon for the binder to operate after dark, a lantern, tied to the whiffletree of the horse nearest the standing grain, providing adequate light for the driver to continue his work. The binder driver had to be skilled and reliable, and working such long days he had to have relief, either through a regular shift change or through someone just occasionally taking the reins to let him rest.

Likewise the horses on the binder in intensive operation needed rotation, although in more relaxed operations one team might work the full day. Ordinarily three horses were enough to pull a six foot binder at an appropriate speed. Where the ground was soft or hilly, some operators would hitch four horses. A seven-foot binder required four horses for best operation, and an eight-foot binder put four horses to their most efficient use. During the era of pioneer settlement, farmers sometimes used a variety of animals to draw the binder, occasionally even oxen, but once farming operations were better established it proved more efficient to put quality horses or mules on the binder.

Working with the driver and his animals was the infantry of binder harvesting, the stookers or shockers, who picked up and set up the sheaves or bundles. Economists studying harvesting operations during the binder era confused rather than clarified the relation between binding and shocking. The main reason for this was that the economists habitually calculated the labor of both the binder driver and the shocker at the rate of ten hours per day, whereas no such standard days existed, and the expected length of the workday for the two types of labor was different. The binder started at first light, whereas the shockers came to the field later in the morning. The shockers quit sometime around dark, whereas the binder often worked longer. Nevertheless, the studies were adequate to show that the harvest required more shockers than binders; the number varied according to the size of the binder and the work habits of the crew. Usually from two to four shockers supported the binder. The only agency ever to report the combination of horses and men required to accomplish binding and shocking, according to how operations were conducted in the field by farmers, was the Kansas State Board of Agriculture in 1920. Its report of "standard outfits" showed that typically the driver of a binder handled four horses and covered from ten to fifteen acres per day—fewer in the eastern part of the state and more in the western part. The typical shocking arrangement was for two shockers to complement the binder, and their capacity was about equal to that of the binder.[27]

The product that these men were handling and the tasks in which they were engaged were called by different names in different parts of the plains. The straw and grain knotted together by a binder was most often called a bundle; it was also called a sheave. "Bundle" prevailed throughout the plains of the United States and was common through much of the plains of Canada, which was to be expected, given the preponderance of American settlement in much of western Canada. However, the British "sheave" rivaled "bundle" in usage and probably predominated except in areas where Americans were numerous. The prevalence of "shock" (or "shocking") and "stook" (or "stooking") was also determined by settlement patterns. Throughout most of the wheat-growing region, harvest hands engaged in shocking and built shocks. These terms were unfamiliar in the Canadian plains, however, where harvest hands engaged in stooking and built stooks. That "stook" was of Norse and Scottish origin explained why it was current in the Canadian plains and also, considering patterns of ethnic settlement, why it rivaled usage of "shock" in the spring-wheat growing areas of the Dakotas.[28]

Farmers and agricultural scientists agreed that inasmuch as the binder was a central implement in harvesting, it had to be kept in running order. Farmers and scientists disagreed among themselves, however, about how this could best be done. The basic disagreement was whether farmers were capable of repairing and refurbishing a binder worn by heavy use. Some agreed with the authors of a Montana bulletin who said, "Where the farmer has a large acreage to cut he must have binders that are dependable. He will find it more profitable to discard binders as soon as they grow old enough to become undependable."[29] Others contended that careful maintenance and routine repair were within the ken of farmers, who should be able to use their binders for years. "The binder is a more complicated piece of apparatus than even the mower or reaper," wrote an authority in 1918. "Yet by a little systematic study of the various parts and the relation to each other, an intelligent mastery of this machine is acquired readily."[30]

Those who believed that farmers could maintain their binders pointed to the need for beginning long-term maintenance as soon as the harvest was over. The binder should be housed, not exposed to the elements. Immediately upon shedding the implement, the owner should prop up the tongue so that it would not acquire a sag; clean the cutter bar and probably detach it to store in a dry place; remove all accumulations of debris, especially vegetable matter, from the machine's parts; and apply oil and grease where needed. Then, through slack seasons of the year, the farmer should systematically refurbish the machine in preparation for the next harvest. He should

check the alignment of the cutter bar, not just by eyeballing it but by stretching a string along the surface. He should slide his hand down the bar to make sure that the guards were properly aligned and would not interfere with the cutter bar. He should check over each sickle section on the cutter bar and on the extra cutter bar and replace the bad ones (by shearing the rivets, not by knocking them out). He should check, service, and, if necessary, replace bearings, particularly the pittman bearing. He should clean the enclosed gears and refill them with grease and graphite and clean and refill the oil cups. He should preserve the wooden pittman with linseed oil and repaint other exposed wooden parts. He should take off the canvas, check the alignment of the canvas rollers by measuring the diagonals between the ends of the rollers, and put the canvas back on. He should check and lubricate all chains. He should test the reel slats and replace any that were cracked or sprung. After these and other tasks, he would still have the most ticklish job—working over the knotter. Most knotter adjustments took place under field conditions, but certain bits of maintenance, such as sharpening the twine knife and replacing bad knotter parts, could be done in the shed. The idea was to have long-term maintenance done long before it was time to wheel the binder into the field again.[31]

Obviously, the time of harvest varied in localities of the plains with latitude, altitude, and other conditions from early May in the far south to September in the far north. What most concerned the individual farmer was how to tell when he should begin to bind his own wheat. A good amount of neighbor watching went on, and thus farmers were influenced by one another's actions; but the great determinant was the condition of the wheat in the field. Generally, the wheat was ready to bind a week or ten days before it would have been ready to be cut with a header (or, later, a combine). Color was the first and obvious consideration: The wheat should look yellow-white, with no visible green except in low spots. The turning of the wheat brought the farmer into the field to pluck a few heads and examine the seed. Kernels of wheat ready for binding would be starting to harden; they would no longer be "milky," as farmers put it. They tested this by pressing a thumbnail into the kernels and putting them into their mouths. One more consideration, particularly with winter wheat, was the angle of the heads on the stalks. If the head stood vertical, then it was not quite ready to bind (or else there was no grain in the head, which was worse). When the wheat was ready to bind, the heads would begin to bend. Impatient farmers would be in the field by this time, but others would wait to make sure that the grain had full opportunity to fill in the head. Richard Goering's uncle used to tell him when he was impatient to begin binding that if "you go and look at your wheat and you think it ought to

be about ready in a day or so, go fishing for three days and then come back, and your wheat will be ready to go." [32]

Having decided to bind, the farmer would road-hitch the binder and haul it to the field. At the field he would unhitch the horses and prepare the machine for work. This meant he had to disconnect the road hitching and adjust it for fieldwork, lower the platform wheel and bull wheel, make final lubrications and adjustments of mechanisms, and then rehitch the team. He would then be ready to open the field. [33]

Some farmers began with the back-swath. The back-swath was the swath of grain that stood closest to the edge of the field. In some areas, such as most of the Canadian plains, this posed no problem because there were few fences along field edges and few other crops bordering wheat fields to be trampled; the binder operator would merely commence cutting the field in the usual clockwise, round and round procedure, starting from the outside edge, with the horses walking outside the field of standing grain. In many other areas, by contrast, the binder operator might begin with a counterclockwise round, with the horses walking through the standing grain and the platform extending to the edge of the field. After this back-swath the driver would turn around and cut the rest of the field clockwise. More commonly, however, the driver would begin by cutting a clockwise round and leaving a small swath of grain, perhaps six feet

L. G. Brown has just opened a field on his farm in central Kansas, June 29, 1912. (Halbe Collection, Kansas State Historical Society, Topeka)

The binder operator has laid the bundles down properly for efficient shocking on the John Erickson farm in central Kansas, June 29, 1912. (Halbe Collection, Kansas State Historical Society, Topeka)

wide, standing along the edge of the field. He would then turn counter-clockwise and cut the back-swath before turning again and cutting the remainder of the field clockwise. While he cut the back-swath, someone, probably a boy, would walk into the standing wheat to the right of the first clockwise swath and toss the bundles that the binder had dropped into the stubble, clearing the way for the driver's return to the clockwise round. If the driver did not cut the back-swath before proceeding with the rest of the field, the boy would have to hurry to stay ahead of the binder.[34]

The binder operator tried to lay the bundles on the stubble in a pattern that would make it easy for the shockers to do their work. Early binders dropped single bundles, which were scattered evenly throughout the field; but from the mid-1890s on, most binders were equipped with bundle carriers. The bundle carrier held four or more bundles and released them only when tripped by the driver. The driver intended to leave the piles of bundles on the stubble close enough to one another so that they might be combined into shocks without excessive walking by the shockers. Thus as much as he could, the driver would trip the bundle carrier at about the same points in each round of the field. If he succeeded, the piles of bundles, after he completed the field, not only would be in lines following the progress of the binder around the field but also would be in perpendicular lines stretching from the center of the field to the edges (except

that the shockers were probably working in the same field and thus had shocked up the pattern as it was laid down).[35]

Obviously, as one harvest laborer observed, "no man has a right to point to himself with pride as a binder-operator if all he knows about the job is to hold the lines over four horses."[36] Besides watching where the dumped bundles landed, the driver had to see that he took a "full cut" but did not move over too far to the right so that he left heads standing on the left. He had to regulate simultaneously the height of the sickle and the position of the straw as it entered the binding mechanism. Regulating the height of the sickle ensured that enough straw was attached to each head so that the binder could tie good bundles; regulating the position of the straw as it was bound ensured that the twine would wrap around the middle of its length, not around the end, where it could slip off. This was particularly tricky when the height of the grain varied within a field. Every time the driver adjusted the height of the sickle, he also had to check the position of the twine on the bundles. Beginning binder operators, such as Richard Goering, received little maxims from their fathers: "Regulate your binder according to the length of your straw"; or, one should adjust the reel "so that the reel would hit your full head." The reel should be low enough to strike each head but not below the head. The binder operator continually checked to make sure that he was tying good bundles. He watched to see that he did not run out of twine; he watched for wear on the knotter; he watched to make sure that each bundle was tied. He noted the supply of twine coming through the tension rollers: If it was too loose, the twine would snarl; if it was too tight, it would break.[37]

Meanwhile, was the canvas running evenly on the rollers? Were there any strange sounds that might indicate lack of lubrication or bad alignment? Even if all appeared to be running smoothly, the binder operator could not get too comfortable on his seat. He had an oil-can ready to squirt troublesome parts. There were thirty or more zerks to grease on many binders, and some of them, such as the pittman, had to be greased many times during the day, depending on how dry and dusty it was in the field.[38]

The best driver had trouble turning out good bundles if his twine was of poor quality. "Take the matter of twine now," one laborer complained. "Some folks seem to believe that all they need is a string that will not pull in two every so often. 'I ain't buying for style,' the farmer says."[39] Harvesters needed good twine of even gauge, and they needed it in quantity; it took two pounds of twine to bind an acre of twenty-bushel wheat, and barley or oats required even more per acre. Most farmers bought their twine from their implement dealers, but they complained chronically about both the quality and the price of the product supplied by these "trusts," as they called them. Several state governments therefore manufactured their own binder twine,

using penitentiary labor. In Kansas in 1914, with estimates saying farmers would need 8.2 million pounds of twine that year and with a private dealer cost of eleven cents per pound, authorities at the state penitentiary in Lansing had ninety men working thirteen hours a day making twine. Still, the prison authorities refused all orders received after March 20 of that year. "Generally," reflected one North Dakotan, "twine manufactured by the state penitentiary usually ran uniform, more so than twine that was made by commercial companies." Consequently, farmers would pool their orders early and buy their twine in carload lots from state prisons.[40]

A chronic problem with binder operation was the extra power required from the bull wheel to run the knotting mechanism to tie bundles. In most areas where the ground was muddy or sandy, the bull wheel would slip when the binder tried to tie a knot, and an untied bundle would be kicked out. A common folk remedy was to mount a beer barrel on a frame atop the binder. The barrel could be left empty when there were no slippage problems but filled when needed, thereby providing extra weight and preventing the bull wheel from slipping. Another solution, more expensive but also more dependable, came during the 1910s with the advent of Cushman and similar small engines. Farmers in the Red River Valley of North Dakota and Minnesota at least as early as 1904 obviated bull wheel power by mounting small gasoline engines on their binders; in most places, however, this practice was adopted several years later. During the early 1910s *Canadian Thresherman* carried many advertisements for Cushman engines to mount on binders. "I sold three of your engines here for binders and attached same," testified one dealer in Alberta. "They are doing splendid work. The land is so soft that they can't get their grain any other way." Goering recalled buying a Cushman engine and disconnecting the bull wheel in 1919 or 1920.[41]

"The shocking of wheat that has been cut with a binder is universal," asserted the Kansas State Board of Agriculture in 1920. That was true insofar as Kansas went, but for the Great Plains at large, as a federal bulletin pointed out, the practice of shocking bound wheat was merely "almost universal."[42] Occasionally, the grain being bound was already in the dead ripe stage, and a threshing outfit was on the scene ready to thresh; in such cases, the bundles would be loaded directly onto wagons from the piles on the stubble and threshed immediately. In other circumstances, such as were noted in Montana in 1924, labor shortages could cause farmers to leave bundles lying on the stubble for an extended time without shocking, but this exposed them to serious damage from weather and increased the amount of labor required at threshing time. Occasionally, too, dry bundles might be hauled directly to a stack instead of being set up in shocks. Most bound wheat could not be so handled, however. "An opportunity must be given

for the grain to completely ripen and for the straw to dry out before the bundles are stacked, to avoid heating, or 'burning,' in the stack," explained the Kansas State Board of Agriculture. "For a time, while the wheat is in the shock, the sap continues to flow from the straw into the head, resulting in greater plumpness and better quality in the berry. Wheat should stand in the shock not less than forty-eight hours, and would be better for standing as long as ten days before it is stacked or threshed."[43]

In the techniques of shocking there developed an accommodation between tradition and environment. One example was the way in which farmers decided the number of bundles to put into a shock. From previous experience outside the plains, farmers had an idea how big a shock should be—usually eight or ten bundles. But when the Kansas State Board of Agriculture surveyed practices across the state in 1920, it found 106 farmers who advocated eight to ten bundles per shock; 97 who favored ten to twelve; 233 who said twelve to sixteen; and a few who believed a shock should contain twenty-five, thirty, or more bundles. The reason for the much larger shocks was the south wind, which dried large shocks effectively and blew small ones around. The farther west a location was on the windy plains, the larger were the shocks. Milo Mathews observed this bit of agricultural geography in the course of his working life. As a boy in Iowa, he made small shocks, eight to ten bundles; however, later, as a custom

Capsheaves top these stooks on the Al Boles farm near Gladstone, Man., ca. 1906. (Glenbow Archives)

thresher in the Dakotas, he saw much larger shocks.[44]

Another eastern practice called into question by plains farmers was the use of capsheaves atop shocks to turn the rain. To make a capsheave, the shocker held a bundle between his knees or over his leg and spread both ends in a fan shape. Mathews recalled that although some old farmers in northern Kansas wanted capsheaves, they were of little use because the wind blew them off. Guy Bretz said of practices in western Kansas, "We never used a cap sheaf. Didn't think it was necessary in dry western Kansas." Richard Goering said only a few of his acquaintances used capsheaves, and many said that instead of turning water, capsheaves held it in the shock. "It wasn't customary around here at all," agreed Ernest

Claassen. "One year my father was out, and we had started to shock, and he suggested that we try capsheaves. We went to doing that on each shock. And he would sort of break each bundle over his knee so the straw wasn't stiff and straight there, and turn it over so that both ends hung down. But, especially if it had been dry when we were shocking, the bundles were bushy, and the Kansas wind was working on them day and night, and we only tried that once." If it did rain on capless shocks— as happened in 1914, Goering recalled—some farmers would just turn them so that they dried.[45]

To the casual observer shocks of grain were just amber piles, but in each shocker's mind was a pattern of how a shock should be constructed. The patterns varied with circumstances, of

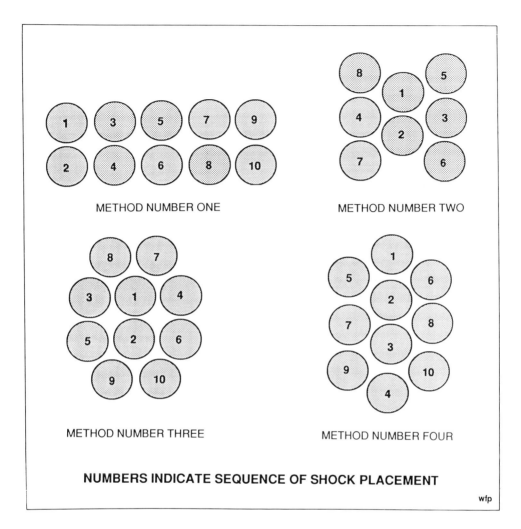

METHOD NUMBER ONE

METHOD NUMBER TWO

METHOD NUMBER THREE

METHOD NUMBER FOUR

NUMBERS INDICATE SEQUENCE OF SHOCK PLACEMENT

wfp

Figure 2.3 Sheaf Arrangement in Shock Formation.

course: Thin or thick wheat affected the distance between the piles left by the binder, and the time of tripping the bundle carrier affected the number of bundles in a pile. Despite these constraints, the patterns were clear and persistent enough to be recorded or recalled. The shocker possessed a sense

of order, and his product gave him a sense of accomplishment.

This craftsmanship was so taken for granted by farmers, however, that the only agency to document it with any care was the Kansas State Board of Agriculture. The board identified and sketched four patterns for shocks (see

Figure 2.3).[46] Pattern 1, a "somewhat common but inferior method," was simply to stand pairs of inward-leaning bundles in a line. Although this position allowed good aeration of green wheat, it also blew down easily. Pattern 2 used capsheaves. The shocker first leaned a pair of bundles against one another. He then leaned another pair into the slot of the first two, and finally four more into the slots ("corners," shockers would say) between the first four. Two capsheaves made this a ten-bundle shock that stood up well and shed rain.

Pattern 3, a more common type, began, as did the others, with one pair set up. The shocker would then set two more pairs on either side of the first to make a row of three pairs. Last, he would put a bundle in each corner of the row. Two capsheaves made this a twelve-bundle shock. Pattern 4, "perhaps the best" form of shock, was unusual in that it placed the first two pairs of bundles in a four-bundle row. Six more bundles were then laid in the corners; with two capsheaves, this became a twelve-bundle shock, usually set up with its long axis parallel to the binder's direction of travel. This shock stood wind better than most as well as provided good curing of the grain.

There was more to it than this, however, as old shockers recalled the process. First, there was the question of how to pick up and hold a bundle. Men usually lifted bundles by the twine and carried them in each hand. When setting the starters, however, it was important to plant them firmly on the ground and not leave them tipsy on the standing stubble. The shocker therefore would wrap his wrists and arms around them and even hold them tightly against his body, with the heads up and the butts down, before he plumped them down hard with his body weight.[47]

Ernest Claassen said, "Someone who was really going to shock picked them up under his arms, and then he would come down solidly in that stubble so that it was setting on the ground, not teetering on the stubble." Then came two more bundles in the slots; then four more in the corners of the first four; then, "if the bundles were fairly handy, you'd set one at each side so they totaled twelve. Shocking the grain that had just been cut and was still a little on the green side would work very nice, the bundles would fit smoothly together. But if it had lain there twenty-four hours in a dry wind, that was stiff and bushy and you really had to push it hard to get that solidly together."

"I would pick up two sheaves—one under each arm—and place them on the stubble, joining them at the top," explained Michael Ewanchuk. "Then I would add two more sheaves, two on each side, and complete the operation by placing a sheaf at each end." If the wheat was green and flexible, he would put on a capsheave. Guy Bretz thought that shocking was "very easy," but in western Kansas the stubble was thinner and less liable to tip the bundles. He set his starters, laid another pair into the slots, and commenced setting into

*Arthur Schmidt, shocking on the Peter U. Schmidt farm, Marion County, Kans., sets the bundles
firmly down on the stubble. (Courtesy of Franz Goossen)*

the corners until it was too far to fetch more bundles. "The size of the shock depends a lot on how thick the bundles are on the ground," he noted. "Put them in a straight line [for later con-venience in loading] and judge how many you put in a shock so it will be the least number of steps." This ap-proach was much like that of Texan Ned McKinney, who described his shock as similar to an "Indian wig-wam."

Grains other than wheat required special consideration—especially barley, mainly because it was so scratchy but also because its short sheaves tended to slip in the twine. Shockers preferred to handle it with a fork and generally put more bundles into a shock than they did with wheat. Ewanchuk described the typical method in his area as setting up a first sheaf (not a starter pair) and then just ringing this first one with others leaning in. Rye was a different problem, Milo Mathews recalled. With its long bundles, seldom tied at center, the shocker had to carry one at a time, putting one hand around the bundle and one in the twine. For oats, the shocker grabbed the bundle near the head, not by the twine. As Claassen described it, he would then set up a simple line of pairs, as depicted in Kansas State Board of Agriculture wheat shock pattern 1.[48]

What particularly annoyed serious shockers was to find the loose grain of an untied bundle. They were supposed to gather the loose grain, twist some of the straw together into a band, and use this band to retie the bundle before setting it into the shock. This was just a revival of a skill from the days of the reaper, but the hands considered it good cause to cuss the binder operator. Some farmers, too, were picky about loose grain. "My father had a rule, there should be a string for that loose bundle," recalled Ernest Claassen. "It may have gotten pushed off the knot-

ter, but it should be there, and see whether you can find that. And if you can't find that, then you would bind it with straw and he showed us how. He could do that very swiftly, he'd seen it done in Germany, so we learned to make straw bands."

If shocking bundles was full of subtleties, stacking bundled grain was even more so—people commonly referred to it as an art. "Good stacking is an art," wrote a correspondent of *American Thresherman*, "and few there be who know it." When possible, farmers preferred to leave their grain in the shock until threshing time; but sometimes the interval between harvesting and threshing was so long that they thought it necessary to get the grain out of the shock and into the relative security of stacks. Just how long the bundles might remain in the shock without stacking was a matter of discretion influenced by circumstance. Good stackers were scarce, and even if skilled labor was available, the extra step of stacking added to the total cost of harvesting. In Kansas by 1920, therefore, the State Board of Agriculture reported "that a very small percentage of the bundled wheat is put into the stack." At about the same time, however, the United States Department of Agriculture reported that the stacking of bundled grain was "very common" in parts of North Dakota. Even within particular localities, such as McPherson County, Kansas, another bulletin reported, neighbors differed as to whether they usually stacked their

Beginning a round stack of sheaves near Lebret, Sask., ca. 1903. One man pitches sheaves from the rack; a second delivers these sheaves to the stacker, who then places them. (Saskatchewan Archives Board, Regina)

bundles or not. The overriding consideration was whether a threshing machine would be available promptly.[49]

Stacking of bundles on the Great Plains, when and where it was done, proceeded somewhat more hastily than in the eastern states. In the East, when loading bundles onto wagons from the shock in the field, one man would pitch bundles into the wagon while another in the wagon would arrange them. In the West, by contrast, both men remained on the ground and pitched bundles into the wagon, which was generally somewhat larger than the one used in the East. After the wagon was loaded, both men would ride to the site of the stack, where one man would pitch the bundles from the wagon to the other man on the stack, who would

then arrange the pile. A shortage of skilled stackers, however, might alter this ideal pairing.[50]

The first step in stacking bundled grain was to select an appropriate site. This selection entailed a number of considerations, foremost of which was drainage. Many farmers chose high ground in a field for a stack, whereas others put the stacks on sloping ground. The point in either case was to avoid damp ground and standing water. Sandy ground was a better base than black dirt or clay. A second consideration was that some farmers used straw for feeding; thus they located their grain stacks so that the straw stacks threshed from them would be near the feedlot. Finally, other things being equal, the farmer located his

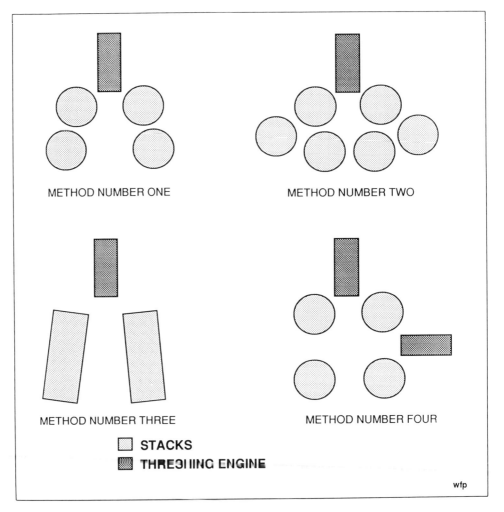

METHOD NUMBER ONE

METHOD NUMBER TWO

METHOD NUMBER THREE

METHOD NUMBER FOUR

▢ STACKS

▨ THRESHING ENGINE

wfp

Figure 2.4 Stackyard Arrangements. *Source:* Data from Kansas State Board of Agriculture, *Thirty-seventh Biennial Report* (Topeka: State Printer, 1949–1950), p. 519.

stacks in a place convenient for the threshing run to minimize travel for the threshing outfit.[51]

Again for the sake of efficient threshing, it was customary to locate stacks in groups of two, four, or even six. Such a group was called a stack yard, or, to the thresherman, a set (see Figure 2.4). If just two stacks were set together, they would be long, oval ricks extending north and south and spaced so that the separator could just be pulled between them at the north ends, but with more room at the south ends.

If four round stacks were in the stack yard, they could be placed according to one of two plans. The first was to set up two closely spaced stacks east and west, as if they were to be the only two in the stack yard. Next, two additional stacks would be added to the south of the first pair; the second pair would be lined up east and west but farther from each other than the first pair. This second pair would, however, be quite close to the first. This trapezoid pattern was designed to give the engineer room to manipulate the angle of his belt on the separator. The second way to position a group of four stacks was to set them as the corners of a square, all of them far enough apart to admit the separator between them. Then the separator could be pulled up to any two of the stacks on either an east-west or a north-south alignment. If six stacks were to be in the stack yard, they would usually be set as the corners of two triangles. The adjacent, parallel sides of the two triangles would run north and south, and between the two stack-triangles there would be enough space to pull the separator on a north-south alignment and to manipulate the angle of the belt a bit. (The six-stack yard was unpopular with threshermen, however, because the distance between the outside stacks made pitching bundles to the separator difficult.)[52]

A stack of bound wheat viewed from above was usually round because that shape afforded the greatest storage space in the stack for the amount of surface exposed. Viewed from the ground, the stack was shaped like a mushroom, bulging out a few feet off the ground and tapering to a point at the top. The taper and the bulge were designed to shed water off the stack and away from its base.

The achievement of such a design, although commonplace throughout binder country, was such an intricate process that it taxed the powers of description. Farmers and laborers could build such things, and they could teach others to build them by example, but they could hardly explain in the abstract how to do it. Adequate description was almost beyond even the best writers of agricultural bulletins and periodicals. Professor S. E. Salmon of Kansas State Agricultural College was among those who tried. "One of the best ways to start a round stack is to begin with a shock in the center," Salmon began. "Then keep adding to the shock by placing bundles in rows leaning against the shock, each succeeding row becoming flatter than the one preceding, until the outer row lies almost flat, but still overlapping, so that none of the heads touch the ground." At this point the outward-pointing butts of the bundles formed a circle of twelve to fourteen feet in diameter on the ground.

Salmon continued: "In stacking the second layer begin at the outer edge, laying the first row of bundles on top of the outside row of the preceding layer, butts out, at the same time laying a row inside the butts overlapping the outside row. The stacker walks on the second row, laying bundles ahead of him until he has gone around the stack. When he completes this round he lays a third row, with butts overlapping the second row as before. From this point until he reaches the center of the stack he lays only one row at a time." Stepping on every bundle except those on the outside perimeter was not just a matter of convenience. The bundles had to be packed down solidly at the middle of the stack; otherwise the stack would settle in the middle and the taper at the top would be lost.

"The third layer is much the same as the second except at this point the stacker may begin to push the bundles out a little to get the bulge in the stack," the professor continued. "The stacker may find at this point that he will have to add extra bundles to the center of the stack in order to keep it full. The center must always be full enough so that the bundles lying against it are always sloping downward." Tramping in the center of the stack lowered it, necessitating those extra bundles to keep it high. The desired downward slope of every bundle in each layer was to help direct water out that might penetrate the stack as it went down.

Salmon was not adept at explaining how the stacker "pushed out" the bundles to make the bulge in the stack, or how he "drew in" the bundles to make the taper; instead he skipped to the end of the process: "When the stack is finished the top bundles must be fastened on. This is often done by taking two or three pointed sticks about 6 feet long and running them through the top bundles into the stack.

These sticks are notched at the top and the top bundles are tied to them." Salmon then figuratively backed away from the stack to check its contour: "A stack which slopes uniformly on all sides of course looks better than one that does not, but of greater importance is the fact that if one side slopes more than the other, or is drawn in more quickly, the stack settles unevenly and the bundles on one side may collect water instead of shedding it."[53]

Salmon described the ideal stack well, but, of course, local and individual practice varied. Round stacks ranged in diameter at the ground from ten to thirty feet, although the most common sizes were twelve, fourteen, and sixteen feet. Stacks of standard size contained from one hundred to one hundred fifty bushels of grain. It took anywhere from six to twelve bundle-wagon loads to make such a stack. Most stackers did not use the number of sticks Salmon had mentioned for anchoring the top bundles; they used only one stick per stack. A minority, instead of topping the stack with bundles of wheat, used bundles of grass.[54]

An eastern Kansas farmer named M. H. Heberling also tried to describe the stacking process in writing. He began largely as had Salmon but then varied somewhat after positioning the ground layer. "The next step is to lay a single course around the outside, keeping the butts just off the ground, thus making the bundles lie nearly flat," Heberling specified. "In this operation the stacker works on the stack and uses his fork to place the bundle, and steps only on the heads of the bundles he is laying." The second layer continued with the stacker putting down a "double course" of bundles. "In laying a double course the stacker should lay the bundles side by side and then break joints with a third, and keep this up until he gets around the stack. The stacker should step only on the second or inside course, as this will keep his weight off the edge of the stack." If the straw was slippery, it would not stay in place well without other bundles on top of it; in such a case, the stacker should lay a triple course where possible. "In laying a triple course the stacker should step only on the third course, as this will allow a large bulge without danger of slipping, even with the driest and most slippery straw." The problem with the slippery straw was that as the stacker pushed the outer butts farther out to make the bulge a few feet above the ground, the bundles, because they sloped outward, would continually slip farther out than he intended.

As the stacker positioned his courses where he wanted them around the outside, he could proceed to lay bundles toward the center, "care being taken to tramp around thoroughly to locate soft spots," for where there was a soft spot, "it should have as many bundles as necessary tramped into it to make it solid." Putting the bulge in the stack was a ticklish operation. Heberling cautioned that because the stack would settle with time, the bulge should be started fairly high off the ground, about five bundles up. The sixth course of bundles, then, should be set out on the edge about six inches. Another consideration arose at this point: Each bundle on the butt end had a long side and a short side; because of the angle of cut on the binder, the straw on the butt end was a bit longer on one side. The long side of the butt should be laid up while making the bulge. "It is a good idea to get down and look the stack over several times while putting on the bulge," advised Heberling, to get the right proportion and to ensure "a good-looking stack."

After creating the bulge, the stacker commenced "drawing in" the stack. This part was easier: "Having built the bulge, the most difficult and important stage is past, and the rest of the stack will be harder for the pitcher [than for the stacker] because of the increasing height, and easier for the stacker because he can look down the sides of the stack and see how much it is coming in." As the stacker did the drawing in, he laid mostly single courses of bundles long side up. He kept the middle well tramped and at the same time gradually built it higher than the outside courses with extra bundles. Thus the bundles more and more sloped to the outside to shed the rain.

Nearing the end of this task, Heberling continued, the stacker had to take care that the slope on all sides was the same, or else the stack would settle unevenly. If he saw one side developing differently from the others, he should get down from the stack, lean a ladder

When the stack gets too high for the pitcher on the rack to reach, the stackers will top it off and descend the ladder. Peter U. Schmidt stacking on his farm in Marion County, Kans. (Courtesy of Franz Goossen)

on it, and use his hands to push bundles around until they aligned. At last the stacker stood atop the completed stack and thrust in the tapered stick that had been tossed to him by the pitcher. He should absolutely not slide down the stack to the ground. Instead the pitcher should place against the stack a ladder as tall as the stack itself, down which the stacker could climb, being careful not to disturb the top bundles.[55]

Joe M. Goodwin, a county agent from eastern Kansas, provided instruction that was similar in most respects to that of Salmon and Heberling. He pro-vided two additional admonitions, how-ever. The first concerned topping the stack. Goodwin noted that many farm-ers, instead of using pointed stakes, threw strings or wires over the top of the stack and hung weights from them. Goodwin said the weights ought to be poles, not rocks, because heavy rocks tended to sink into the sides of the stack and not anchor well. Goodwin also pointed out the key role of the pitcher in making it "either easier or hard for the stacker. He should be able to place his bundles accurately at the side of the stacker and in the position desired by the stacker."[56]

Ernest Claassen recalled the stacking of bundles as something his father would do when few threshing machines were yet in the neighborhood. He did it himself, too, only for two years when the threshing machine was particularly late getting to his place. "I had watched my father stack, and the bank here put out a circular giving some instruction on it, and that was an art in itself," he said. His stacking methods conformed largely to those of contemporary writers, but his recollections gave hints about why stacks assumed the dimensions that they did. The diameter of a stack, he said, was about the length of a bundle wagon; the diameter derived from the convenience of pitching from the bundle wagon. The height of a stack likewise was simply as high as a man could pitch with a fork. Claassen topped his stacks with strings and weights.

When Richard Goering stacked bound grain, he departed from the common round form. He began a stack with a long shock of some sixteen bundles. From this shock he laid out courses, resulting in an oval stack. The bundle wagons came first to one side of the stack and then to the other. Atop a stack, he recalled, some farmers put a few courses of bundles with the heads out because they believed it would shed water better.

The concern over building stacks of bundles highlights the elaborateness and sophistication of the harvesting folk life attached to the binder. The folk life associated with the header was, by contrast, not so elaborate. This was

to be expected, inasmuch as the header was by definition a labor-saving device meant to cut down and simplify the job of grain harvesting. Still, header harvesting assumed its own patterns and place in regional culture.

A header outfit was a big operation. One man drove the header, which commonly was either a twelve-foot or fourteen-foot machine. The twelve-foot was usually pushed by six horses, sometimes eight, standing in traces alongside a fourteen-foot beam that extended back from the platform. Fourteen-foot headers generally required eight horses. One man drove the header barge while another stood in the back, arranging the grain as it fell from the header elevator. Each header barge was drawn by two horses. There would also be at least one other man—more often two—doing the stacking. So a header outfit entailed at least six men and ten horses and frequently more of each. Operations that employed more than one header obviously were considerable matters of organization. A variation in the scheme of labor for multiheader outfits was to have the man who rode the header barge also arrange grain, switching from one barge to the next as they pulled under the header elevator; the man who stayed at the stack would serve as a spike pitcher for every load that came. In 1920 the Kansas State Board of Agriculture reported that the average header outfit in the central part of the state harvested seventeen acres in a ten-hour day, whereas the average in the western part of the state

Header outfit near Belpre, Kans., ca. 1914. Decorative boughs lent festivity to the photographic occasion. (Santa Fe Trail Center, Larned, Kans.)

was twenty-two acres. A Montana bulletin in 1924 said that a typical header outfit in that state could handle about thirty acres a day. The differences in the figures stemmed from the heaviness of the grain.[57]

Like binding, heading had specialized terminology. It was common to refer to loose, headed grain as "spikes" and to a man who pitched it as a "spike pitcher." A stack of headed grain might be called a "stack," but because such stacks often were elongate rather than round, many people called them "ricks." The differences in terminology for heading were not as pronounced, however, as were those for binding.

Some concerns about the header were quite similar to those about the binder, including general maintenance (except that the header, of course, used no knotter). A difference at the outset of harvest, however, was at what point the grain was considered ready to harvest—it was later with the header than with the binder. Guy Bretz said, "Break a head off and rub it in the palm of your hand. If it's ripe, it will thresh out easily and the grains will be hard." The Kansas State Board of Agriculture in a survey found 375 farmers who agreed that they began heading when "the grain was fully ripe, mature and hard"; 122 said they began heading when the grain was "dry enough to stack without heating"; 55 began when they thought that "the majority of the heads were ripe"; 23 began with the grain "in the tough dough stage"; 9 were willing to start "when the heads turned yellow but the straw was still somewhat green."[58]

Inasmuch as headers operated largely in open country, header drivers had fewer concerns with transportation and setting up than did binder drivers, but the large scale of the task facing them required a certain amount of geographic organization. The wheat fields of header country often were so large that they had to be subdivided for heading, or else the distance from the heading operation to the stacking site would be too great. The acreage of grain put into one stack yard was called a land. Facilitated, no doubt, by the rectangular parameters of section, quarter, eighty, and forty and unencumbered in many places by natural obstructions, farmers' folk conceptions of lands for heading were at least geometric, if not aerial, in perspective.

The Kansas State Board of Agriculture gathered information on how to "lay out" a land, which "brought out a diversity of opinion." The majority of respondents tried to lay out a land large enough to yield enough wheat to build two stacks. Some wanted larger lands with four stacks in a stack yard, but this was unwieldy if the grain was light, because it would necessitate long trips with the header barges. Some farmers gave ideal dimensions for their lands, such as twenty-by-eighty rods or forty-by-eighty rods, and others stated a range in acreage from ten to thirty. All this depended, too, on the shape of fields and the yield of grain. Univer-

sally, however, the farmers stacked headed wheat in the field where it was cut. Just where in the field was debatable, but the great majority said that they placed their ricks at either end of a larger land; others planned ahead so that one round of the header would make a barge load, thus rendering the exact placement of the yard less relevant; and a few tried to make things easy for threshing by locating all their ricks in the middle of a quarter section. The great majority put two ricks to a stack yard, although four ricks to the yard was fairly common, and six was the practice of a few. Another name for a stack yard of ricks was a lot.[59]

Patterns unrecorded in the statistical efforts of the Kansas State Board of Agriculture emerged clearly from a bulletin by the Montana Extension Service in 1924. It noted two basic patterns of heading, the "circular system" and the "divided strip system" (see Figure 2.5). In either case a rule of thumb was that forty acres of medium grain was about the proper size for a land.[60] In the circular system the header driver first cut his way to the center of a square land. Then he commenced cutting a circle outward from the center, proceeding counterclockwise until he reached the edge of the land. He never had to stop or slow down for corners; the only stops he made were when changing header barges. When he finished his circle he still had triangular corners standing at each corner of the land, but he left these until later. Most of the corners adjoined similar corners of other lands and therefore

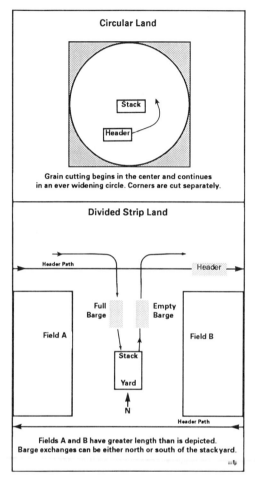

Figure 2.5 Header Land Layout. *Source:*
Montana Extension Service.

strip. These swaths in the middle were
the spaces in which the stacks would be
built. This done, the driver resumed
circling the entire land clockwise. If he
had laid out the land properly, a trip
around one half of it should produce a
barge of grain. Thus a header barge
would pull under the elevator of the
header and stay with it from the cross-
strip halfway around the land back to
the other end of the cross-strip. Hitting
the cross-strip at this point, the header
ran empty for a few feet. This gave the
opportunity for the full barge to veer
off and an empty barge to pull under
the elevator without the header stopping or losing grain. The full barge
had only a short distance to travel to
the stack lot and then, empty again,
from the stack lot to the other end of
the cross-cut strip, where it resumed its
progress under the elevator.[62]

The little seat of the header driver
atop the rear beam was no place for
idle contemplation of the geometry of
the lands. He had quite a few technical
details to take care of. He generally
steered the outfit either with his feet on
a wheel underneath the beam on which
he sat, or sometimes with his hands on
a tiller. He had reins on the horses, but
they needed little guidance; they knew
where they were going. As the bull
wheel of the header, some fourteen
inches wide, smashed down a strip of
stubble, one of the inside horses would
find the strip and follow it. "After two
or three rounds, the horse got the
idea," recalled Guy Bretz, "so the
driver wasn't needed very much except
at the ends turning the corners." This

formed diamonds or parts of diamonds
that might be cut out fairly efficiently
later. The stack lot was formed, or
"raised," at the center of the land.[61]

In the divided strip system the
header driver first cut his way around a
long, rectangular land. After rounding
the land he cut a couple of swaths directly across the narrow middle of the

The seat of the header driver, with a tiller to steer by turning the rear wheel, at the Terning Steam and Gas Engine Show, Valley Falls, Kans., 1981. (By the author)

was good because the driver needed to keep an eye also to the left, where the grain was falling from the elevator into the barge. He had to cooperate with the driver of the barge to deliver the grain at the right place. Ideally, by speeding up and slowing down slightly, they worked to deliver the grain in layers front and back without forcing the man in the barge to step on the grain too much.[63]

The other two main concerns of the header driver were the regulation of the height of the cutter bar and the smooth running of the canvases. He sought to cut just low enough to get all the grain but as little straw as possible. If the grain was lodged, he had to drop down and take more straw than usual. As for the canvases, the header had them not only on the platform but also on the elevator. The driver had to watch for a torn canvas, in which case the header had to be stopped immediately or the loose chains would damage other parts. He checked the canvases in the morning before starting and whenever he stopped. At quitting time in the evening, he took the canvases off and rolled them up to stay dry. Otherwise the dew would dampen them and cause them to shrink; then, after the header had been running a while they would stretch out again and require a halt in operations for tightening.[64]

Handling the header barge while it was receiving grain from the header was less ticklish than driving the header itself. The barge driver kept eye contact with the header driver and

reined in or clucked up his horses to see that the grain was delivered to the right place in the barge. The man in the back of the barge forked the grain around as necessary and tried to avoid stepping on it too much while also trying to avoid bumping his head on the elevator. As the barge filled, he rounded out the top of the load. If the barge was close to the stack yard, the men did not try to load it too full; if it was far, however, they piled on the spikes until they got closer.[65]

The hard work for these fellows came when the barge was full. The driver quickly piloted the barge along the opposite side of the stack from where the previous barge load had been unloaded. He then joined the man in the barge, and each took up his fork. The man on the stack told them where he wanted the spikes pitched. The men in the barge pitched together, inserting their forks into the spikes from opposite directions and heaving them onto the stack. Again, they were supposed to avoid stepping on the grain.[66]

As for the man on the stack, he was, Guy Bretz said, "the most important man out there. The ripe wheat is very fluffy and if not handled right will slide out to one side or the other or possibly a corner slide out, especially if bumped by the corner of the barge." Particular farmers took this job for themselves. "We only needed one stacker, my father took care of that job," recalled Bretz. "He was an expert at stacking wheat, and learned how by experience.

*One stack of headed grain has been completed and another begun on the Peter Thielen farm in central
Kansas, June 30, 1911. (Halbe Collection, Kansas State Historical Society, Topeka)*

Keep it as solid as possible in the
middle, by walking back and forth and
the sides will take care of themselves,
with just a little stomping." At this
point, the spikes required a bit of
tramping, but only so much as was necessary to make the stack solid enough
to stand.

A typical rick of headed grain was
twelve to fourteen feet wide, twenty-
eight to thirty-two feet long at the base,
and as high as the spike pitchers could
throw. If the wheat was not thoroughly
hard, many thought it better to cut
down the dimensions of the stack one
way or another. Milo Mathews recalled
building a smaller rick about six feet by
fourteen or sixteen feet at the base,
then spacing another rick five or six
feet away from the first. This was to
permit better circulation and drying of
the grain. Richard Goering dealt with
the same problem by building long
stacks some thirty feet long and ten

feet high but as narrow as they could
be built and still stand. He recalled
doing this in an extremely wet year,
1919 or 1920. Any stack or rick was tapered from about eight feet off the
ground to the top. Finally, the rick was
topped off with wires or cords thrown
over it and stones or poles suspended
from them.[67]

A few farmers in Montana used
slings and derricks to elevate spikes
from the barge to the stack. This required a header box divided in half
crosswise with a partition. A rope sling
was spread across each of these halves.
The sling was constructed with two-by-
four slats to keep the ropes or chains of
the sling in place. The release of the
sling (the trip) was in the center so that
the load would drop squarely on the
stack. Some farmers made the slings
themselves; others purchased them
from hardware or implement dealers.
Derricks and haystackers mounted on

Philip Grossardt completing an unusual round stack of headed grain near Stafford, Kans., ca. 1917. (Courtesy of Louise Meyerhoff)

wheels were then used to drop the sling loads onto the stack. This method increased the work of the man on the stack but reduced the need for spike pitchers.[68]

In connection with the stacking of wheat, either bundled or headed, there developed an elaborate myth focused upon what was called "the sweat." Elevator operators and millers were great believers in the sweat, a special process of curing grain that produced considerable heat. They knew that threshed grain stored too green or too wet in the bin would heat and be "bin-burnt." They reasoned that green grain also went through this process in the stack but that there the bulk and space of the straw provided enough circulation to prevent the heat from doing damage—

unless the crop had been stacked so wet that it became "stack-burnt." Wheat left in the shock and never stacked, however, was never piled in enough concentration and bulk to promote the special curing associated with heat. Such curing was potentially dangerous in the bin or in a too-wet stack, but under proper stacking conditions, it improved the quality of the grain by safeguarding and even restoring the color of the berry, bringing down the moisture content, and increasing the test weight.

The phenomenon of the sweat received serious treatment in a circular issued by the Bureau of Plant Industry in 1910. "Millers, as well as operators of country and terminal elevators, prefer wheat that has gone through the

Finished stackyards of typically elongated stacks on the Patrick Murphy farm, Lane County, Kans., 1919. (Lane County Historical Museum, Dighton, Kans.)

'sweat,' " wrote Leslie A. Fitz. "The millers invariably hold that sweating of the stack improves weathered grain and is much to be desired." Unfortunately, however, little was known as to exactly what constituted this process of the sweat: "Very little information concerning it can be gleaned from scientific literature," said Fitz. Perhaps, he speculated, there was present in the straw enough plant food to continue for some time the maturation and growing of the kernels, and thus "a chemical or enzymic action within the plant by means of which this nutriment is transferred to the grain and stored as starch may continue for a considerable period. When wheat has been thrashed before going through the sweat, it is probable that a rearrangement of the chemical constituents of the kernels still takes place, and this will account for the sweating of shock-thrashed grain in the bin." The chemical action produced heat, and "this may account for the heat usually generated during the sweating process," which was also related to the percentage of moisture present in the grain. "Wheat cut in the hard-dough, or containing consider-

able moisture, goes into the sweat much more quickly when stacked; straw becomes very tough and a great deal of heat is involved."[69]

Despite this shaky prologue, Fitz went on to test samples of wheat threshed from the stack, which, he reasoned, had gone through the sweat in proper fashion, as well as samples threshed from the stook, all the wheat coming from the same place in North Dakota. He concluded that the stacked wheat had better color; tested better for moisture and weight; stood up better under milling and baking tests; and generally was liable to be graded a level higher than stook-threshed wheat. Whether these differences derived from the sweat or simply from the stacked grain's being better protected from the weather remained unclear.[70]

The Kansas State Board of Agriculture also devoted attention to the phenomenon of the sweat. It asked O. P. B. Jackson, a railroad and warehouse commissioner in Minnesota, whether he agreed with the folk belief that the sweat constituted a "fermentation" in the grain. Jackson replied that it was not fermentation but rather a beneficial process that improved color and lowered the moisture content of grain. His wording was such that it was unclear whether he truly believed in the sweat phenomenon or whether he merely favored stacking on general principles. A chemist from the United States Department of Agriculture, J. A. LeClerc, told the board that sweating "is intimately connected with the life processes of respiration" and was not merely a matter of drying out. He regretted that he was "unable to offer you a conclusion that is warranted by tests and shared in by those who have investigated the phenomenon. I know of no work that has ever been done which will justify definite conclusions." But he was willing to venture that he did not "think it [sweating] is a fermentation in the usual sense." A biochemist from the University of Minnesota, C. H. Bailey, characterized the sweat as "after-ripening" and offered the unorthodox opinion that the grain went through more of a sweat in the shock than it did in the stack. Finally, E. F. Ladd, president of North Dakota Agricultural College, characterized the sweat as "a result of enzymic action that is continued in the kernel. When the wheat is placed in the stack conditions are favorable for this sweating to go on, and wheat so treated and allowed to pass through the sweating state produces a superior bread-producing flour."[71]

The Kansas State Board of Agriculture, determined to discover the truth about the sweat, queried farmers and then announced, "It is customary for farmers to allow wheat to remain in the stack until it has passed through the sweat before threshing." This practice the board attributed to the "generally accepted belief that sweating improves the quality of the grain"; however, farmers disagreed on how long grain should be left in the stack so that it might sweat. After all its inquiries of authorities and farmers, the board concluded that "this investigation developed no definite information as to just what takes place in the berry while it is going through the sweating process."[72]

Thus even though the sweat was much talked about and much written about, it remained dubious whether farmers truly believed there was such a thing. William Lies of North Dakota, for instance, was familiar with the term but thought of the so-called sweat as no mysterious process. "That is merely a drying process it goes through," explained Lies. Ernest Claassen recalled, "There was talk about it, it needed to go through the sweat. I never was sure what the process was supposed to represent or whether it was necessary. At least I didn't worry about the sweat." Perhaps, then, the myth of the sweat arose mainly from the wish of elevator men and millers that farmers should practice good stacking.[73]

Regardless of the merits of the sweat, it was obvious that there developed around the main implements of harvesting—the binder and the header—numerous customs, beliefs, terms, and techniques that in their broad commonality constituted a culture of harvesting on the Great Plains. There was variation from locality to locality, from individual to individual, from time to time, but such variation merely showed that the culture of harvesting was a folk culture, interacting with the environment and evolving through time. It

was based on the high harvesting technology of the time, on existing machinery, but it prospered through tradition and example. As tradition, it was to continue until basic changes occurred in the machinery upon which it centered.

CHAPTER THREE.
THRESHING

The engineer had a lonely job. At perhaps 4:00 A.M. he revived the boiler fire he had banked overnight and began building pressure to power another day's threshing. As black smoke curled from the stack of his machine, he could see similar smudges along the horizon in all directions. When he blew his whistle to bring crewmen stumbling from barns and other overnight shelters, he could hear other engineers sounding theirs, too. Other engineers or engineers' bosses were directing the placement of the separator and the engine next to the stack to be threshed. The hissing engine brought the rattling separator to life, and soon men, machines, and teams functioned as a self-contained unit, oblivious of anything in the surrounding countryside. Until that moment, however, it was evident to any man with active senses, whether in the Arkansas River Valley of Kansas, in the Judith Basin of Montana, or on the Regina Plains of Saskatchewan, that he was part of an extensive system organized to thresh the small grains of the Great Plains. This system, in which custom threshing predominated, not only played a key role in the economy of the Great Plains but also illustrated how agricultural institutions assumed forms peculiar to their region.

Itinerant professional photographers sought to record the system of threshing on the plains and the culture tied to it but found it difficult to do so. Format was the problem: Threshing, figuratively and visually, sprawled across the landscape in proportions that would not fit the dimensions of postcards or even album pages. It required a panorama. What conditions shaped such sprawling systems, and what was the folk life of the threshing culture within them?

The answers depend on a confluence of influences, the first of which was the environment of the Great Plains. The subhumid to semiarid climate of the plains produced a number of peculiar conditions. Among these was an em-

Doukhobor immigrants threshing grain by treading near Carleton, Sask., 1902. (Glenbow Archives)

phasis on small grains as cash crops; a tendency toward agricultural expansiveness to compensate for relatively small returns per acre; a sparseness of population, which meant scarcity of labor; a similar scarcity of capital for development; and, finally, an emphasis on mobility and flexibility as strategies for successful enterprise.

The second influence was the level of technology. As in harvesting, the earliest settlers of the region often had to rely on crude, improvised methods of threshing (such as flails or treading) because of isolation and shortages of machinery. Many pioneers of the Canadian plains, including some after 1900, recalled threshing with flails. Other settlers in the same region, especially those from eastern Europe, used traditional methods of treading. Doukhobor immigrants (communal colonists from Russia), for instance, packed a round

threshing floor in the open and threshed with oxen dragging a wagon and logs. In North Dakota an impoverished German-Russian Baptist woman recalled how even after 1910 she pounded out a threshing ground. Mennonites in Kansas threshed their hard red wheat on packed soil with traditional, corrugated-cylinder threshing stones. Still farther south, in west Texas, John Bell Porter in 1893 threshed his first wheat crop by riding one horse and leading six others over the threshing ground. Even this was a refinement of the earlier method of fellow Texan George D. Harper, who built a pen around his threshing floor into which he turned horses to mill around.[1]

Transportation connections with the outside world, however, brought threshing machines, and with them came custom threshing, at least in a

Horsepower thresher (said to be the first in Lincoln County, S. Dak.), 1886. (South Dakota State Historical Society, Pierre)

limited way. The first stationary separators on the plains were powered by horsepowers. Such rigs were light and portable enough that they frequently preceded the railroad into areas of the plains. The Hudson Bay Company took threshers and horsepowers into the Northwest Territories, and others followed; thus by the fall of 1878, ten outfits were working in the vicinity of Prince Albert (in what was later to become Saskatchewan). When a local farmer invested in a horsepower threshing outfit, he threshed not only his own grain but also that of his neighbors, charging them a set fee per bushel. This was custom work to the extent that the thresherman furnished the separator, the horsepower, some of the teams, and perhaps a few men; but

his farmer-customers supplied most of the teams and men by trading work with one another. The horsepower thresherman, common throughout the settlement period of the Great Plains, was a provider mainly of machinery, not of a complete outfit. T. C. Henry, the wheat king of Abilene, Kansas, reported that such practices were well established in his area during the 1870s. Horsepower threshing was everywhere on the plains at early stages of settlement, and those who experienced it remembered it well. Eugene Barrows recalled that "the thing that impressed me most [about my father's outfit near Fort Benton, Montana,] was the horsepowered 'sweep.' . . . I thought that when I got older I would like to ride up there and drive those horses."[2] Al-

The path is hoof-worn around the horsepower on the Peter Burroughs farm near Tregarva, Sask., ca. 1896. (Saskatchewan Archives Board, Regina)

exander Boan of Saskatchewan, who saw horsepower threshing at home in 1900, could still describe and sketch the details of the operation more than eighty years later—the six sweeps, the twelve horses, the tumbling rod, the platform at the center on which a man stood to handle the horses.

Although horsepower threshing persisted in newly opened localities until after the turn of the century, steam power arrived in many settled areas during the 1880s and almost everywhere during the 1890s. For instance, Regina, Saskatchewan, on the Canadian Pacific Railway, probably received its first few portable steam outfits in 1884, with the purchasers not only threshing their own grain but also taking custom work. Later in the 1880s other operators on the Regina plains still bought and used sweep horsepowers and even treadmills. The transition from horsepower to steam took most of a generation: Even by 1899 the Department of Agriculture of the Northwest Territories said that of 402 threshing rigs in the territories, only 65 percent were steam powered. The advent of traction, however, made steam irresistible: Steam traction engines disembarked from flatcars and rolled onto

One of the earliest portable steam engines used for threshing in Saskatchewan, Moosomen District, 1886. (Saskatchewan Archives Board, Regina)

the flatlands during the 1890s. The reign of steam engines on the Great Plains lasted roughly into the early 1920s, when gasoline and other internal combustion engines displaced them. Belted to the steam engines were stationary separators, or threshing machines—wooden ones equipped with straw elevators until a few years into the twentieth century, when they were supplanted by steel separators fitted with straw blowers.[3]

The third shaper of threshing culture on the plains was the agricultural economy, which from the late 1890s through World War I favored expansion of small-grain culture in that region. As wheat culture went, so went threshing, rising to a pinnacle of prosperity during World War I and suffering recession in the years immediately thereafter. Such economic conditions, combined with the environment of the plains and the level of technology, produced a complex of systems, roles, and traditions through which the task of small-grain threshing was accomplished.

Two basic questions defined the systems of threshing on the plains: Who owned the machinery? And who provided the labor? By and large, farmers

Unloading steam engines and bull threshers from flatcars in Moose Jaw, Sask., ca. 1906. (Glenbow Archives)

did not own the engines and separators they needed for threshing. The short period of use of such machinery on any one farm and its high initial cost made such investment prohibitive for the individual farmer. This situation created a need for threshermen, who purchased machinery, hired engineers and separator men, and provided threshing services on a custom basis. "The threshermen of my experience, and I worked for 3 different chaps, were entrepreneurs" was the characterization of a farm boy-turned-economics professor from Saskatchewan. "They owned the capital, hired the labor, and contracted with farmers." Thresher-men typically farmed a bit but were

willing to turn their hands to any task to make a dollar. They broke sod, did road work, sawed firewood, crushed stone, drilled wells, ground feed, or performed other custom work. The diary of a custom thresherman in Montana showed that in 1932, besides farming and threshing, he supplemented his income with plowing, woodcutting, fur trapping, and, oddly enough, selling teargas (probably for use against gophers or rats). Threshing, though, was the principal task and common joy of these steam engine men.[4]

If threshermen undoubtedly provided the necessary machinery, the answer to who provided the labor was not

Portable, straw-burning engine (probably a Buffalo-Pitts) run by the Allcock Threshing Syndicate, a cooperative threshing ring, at Eastview, Sask., 1902. (Saskatchewan Archives Board, Regina)

so simple. The threshing cooperative or ring was the system of labor that prevailed in the American midwestern states, spilled into the eastern portions of the plains, and was occasionally resorted to even on the western plains. The farmers of a locality agreed among themselves to exchange labor during threshing time and to contract together with a thresherman. At first the rings operated on informal, oral or customary agreements. The members kept rough recollections of who contributed what efforts of men and teams to the threshing of each farmer's grain, and after the conclusion of the threshing season—usually celebrated with an ice cream social—they arranged compensatory labor in other farm operations, such as working cattle, filling silo, and putting up hay. Each farmer paid

the thresherman the bill for his farm on the basis of the number of bushels threshed. Eventually, farmers, encouraged by the agricultural press and by professors in the agricultural colleges, made their ring arrangements more formal, written, and binding. They adopted constitutions and bylaws and settled balances of labor contributions in cash.[5]

In the western reaches of the plains, the threshing ring, like many other midwestern institutions, succumbed to the pressures of environment. It was one proposition for midwestern farmers to exchange a few days' labor to handle their oats and small patches of wheat, but quite another for farmers on the plains to exchange labor enough to handle far more expansive acreages of small grains. On the high plains, the

Threshing near Moose Jaw, Sask., ca. 1906. Farmers pooled labor, racks, and teams to bring sheaves from stooks to the custom man's threshing set. (The photographer snapped them from atop the straw stack.) (Glenbow Archives)

threshing season extended for two months or even longer. Moreover, there were fewer neighbors to help, farms being larger and farther apart than in the Midwest. Consequently, threshermen developed, and farmers availed themselves of, an alternative system for the provision of labor—pure custom threshing. In pure custom threshing the thresherman provided not only the machinery, the engineer, and the separator man but also the full crew of men required to do the threshing. The majority of men he hired were transient laborers who had come to the plains, worked the harvest for farmers, and then found long-term employment with the thresherman. In pure custom threshing the farmer was responsible only for hauling away the grain as it fell from the spout of the separator. The pure custom thresherman provided board for his crew, usually by maintaining a mobile cookshack and hiring a cook. As for lodging, the crew members found it as best they could, often sleeping in farm buildings.

Between the two extremes of ring threshing and pure custom threshing were a variety of hybrid arrangements. For instance, it might be agreed that instead of the thresherman providing a cookshack and meals, the farmer or, more accurately, his wife might board the threshing crew. Similarly, it might be agreed that the farmer would furnish the thresherman's coal. Agreement and tradition might also designate different practices in provision of field labor. In the threshing of headed grain from the stack, it was rare for there to be any other arrangement than the one in which the thresherman furnished all requisite labor. In the threshing of bound grain from the shock, however, a variety of stipulations prevailed. The farmers of a locality might combine to furnish the bundle wagons, drivers, and teams needed to transport the bundles from the field to the threshing set, with the thresherman providing field pitchers to load the racks and bundle pitchers to unload them at the separator. In another situation, the farmers might bring the racks, the drivers, the teams, and the field pitchers, with the thresherman furnishing only the bundle pitchers at the set. In such a case, the arrangements moved as far from pure custom threshing as was possible without becoming a pure ring.

The most organized, comprehensive explication of threshing practices in various parts of the American plains resulted from fieldwork done in 1921 by Don D. Lescohier, a researcher for the United States Department of Agriculture.[6] While investigating the conditions of harvest laborers, he and his assistants gathered information about threshing practices from 1,150 farmers in Oklahoma, Kansas, Nebraska, South Dakota, North Dakota, and Minnesota. Of these, 893 (or 77.7 percent) hired their threshing machinery, whereas only 257 (or 22.3 percent) owned all or a part of the machines that threshed their grain.

Those figures alone testified to the prevalence of custom threshing, but information broken down by state was even more revealing. In the winter wheatlands of Kansas and Oklahoma, nearly all farmers hired custom threshers with complete outfits and crews. Usually the farmer boarded the crew and hauled away the grain, but the thresherman did the rest. Only 12 percent of the farmers interviewed in Kansas owned any part of the machines that threshed their grain. On the other hand, in Minnesota and central Nebraska, where small farms and diversified cropping resembled midwestern conditions, few farmers hired complete custom outfits. Most engaged threshermen who provided only the machinery and certain skilled employees. A growing minority formed rings to own their own machines. In either case, the farmers traded work to fill out the crew with men and teams. In the Dakotas, both pure custom work and cooperative threshing were common. This did not necessarily mean that the two practices existed side-by-side in the same localities, however. More probably, cooperative methods prevailed in the eastern portions of the Dakotas, whereas farther west on the northern plains, pure custom threshing predominated. In the Dakotas, researchers found many instances of custom outfits providing their own cooks and cookshacks, an indication of self-sufficient custom practices beyond even those common in Kansas.

The findings of other researchers during the same era both confirmed and refined those of Lescohier. A study in Montana a few years earlier reported that "practically all" the thresh-ing was done with a "furnished crew." One in North Dakota at the same time said that farmers generally furnished no field labor except hauling away the threshed grain and that in some cases farmers boarded threshing crews, but in others threshermen provided cook cars.[7]

A survey in 1924 found farmers in Grand Forks County, North Dakota, and Spink County, South Dakota, em-ploying threshermen with full crews; however, those in Morton County, North Dakota—as well as those in three counties in Nebraska—were ex-changing labor. On the other hand, three counties in Kansas—McPherson, Pawnee, and Ford—showed more hy-brid arrangements, which reflected harvesting practices. Where wheat was headed, or was bound and later stacked, the custom men furnished all labor to thresh from the stack. Where bundles were hauled in and threshed from the shock, the farmers furnished the bundle haulers, and the thresher-men provided the pitchers to load bundles and feed the separator. The situation in Kansas was also scrutinized by the State Board of Agriculture in 1919. It did not record distinctions in labor arrangements, but it did find that of 1,113 farmers responding to a sur-vey, 877 employed threshermen; 168 owned their own threshing rigs, most of these being farmer-threshermen who did work for their neighbors; and 68 owned machines in cooperation with other farmers.[8]

Governments of the Canadian west were aware of the importance of cus-tom men in threshing operations. The Department of Agriculture of the Northwest Territories responded to shortages of threshing machines by ob-taining half-rates for threshermen shipping machinery on the Canadian Pacific Railway and cent-a-mile rates for crews accompanying such machin-ery—actions revealing that it was cus-tomary for threshermen to furnish la-bor. Subsequently, the Saskatchewan Department of Agriculture continued close relations with threshermen, even using questionnaires from thresher-men (not from farmers) as its chief source of data on crop production in the province. Then, during World War I, with machinery again in short sup-ply, the department arranged once more for half-rates for crews accompa-nying machinery on both the Canadian Pacific and the Canadian Northern Railways.[9]

The differences in threshing prac-tices between regions were evident even in the experiences of a single fam-ily. Ed Bever, a farmer in southeastern Kansas, bought a steam engine and a separator in 1892 and commenced threshing for farmers in the Walnut River Valley near Winfield. This area of eastern Kansas followed midwestern customs of threshing. Bever provided machinery for a ring of fellow farmers, but they provided the necessary teams and labor for threshing. In 1916 Bever bought another threshing outfit, in-cluding a twenty-five-horsepower en-gine and a thirty-six-inch separator. This heavy outfit was suitable for use on the plains. Bever did not even use it on his own farm but had it shipped di-

Ed Bever's outfit threshing on the Marriage Ranch near Greensburg, Kans., 1919. (Courtesy of Mr. and Mrs. Floyd Bever)

rectly to Greensburg, in Kiowa County, southwest Kansas. There he established himself as a professional custom man, furnishing farmers with both machinery and laborers.[10]

Similar was the case of A. O. Krueger, who threshed in partnership with his brother near Blue Hill, Nebraska—shock-threshing, pooled-labor country. Nevertheless, Krueger decided to go on his own in 1915, investing four thousand dollars in a gas traction engine and separator. Then the rains began, and the weeds grew, and there was no threshing in the locality. Acting on a tip from a relative, Krueger loaded his rig on a flatcar and shipped it out west to Chase County. There he threshed headed grain from August to January. In subsequent years he both threshed and plowed in western Nebraska and western Kansas.[11]

The accounts of other farmers and threshermen add to the portrait of threshing practices. Alexander Boan, who farmed and custom-threshed in Saskatchewan, said he furnished all labor—"the farmer contributed nothing"—and his son stated that he had never even heard of a threshing ring. At the other end of the plains, Texan

Ned McKinney recalled that his thresherman-father had also had a pure custom operation and had referred derisively to ring arrangements as "chicken and pie outfits." William Lies and George Hitz characterized the threshing of their experience in North Dakota as pure custom work, except that farmers might pool labor to save scant grain during drought years.[12]

The experiences of Richard Goering and Ernest Claassen in central Kansas indicated that such patterns were not static but evolved through time. Both said that in their earliest recollections, neighbors exchanged work, an arrangement that also extended to other seasonal tasks; when required, renting farmers were always willing to supply labor for pay. In Goering's experience, but not in Claassen's, pure custom work eventually supplanted this practice. The change was associated with the conversion from binding to heading for harvest. That report was akin to one from Oklahoma, where a newspaper reporter was delighted that the advent of furnished labor and cook cars had relieved farm wives of cooking for large crews. Even in Saskatchewan, where the Boans recalled only pure custom work, another writer said that early immigrants from eastern Canada threshed cooperatively with small portable engines ("pepperboxes") at which machinery-rich American settlers "snorted in derision."[13]

Custom threshermen of the plains required a forum wherein they might discuss such issues as labor arrangements with farmers. They found two such forums, named according to nationality but both patronized by threshermen on either side of the Forty-ninth Parallel: *American Thresherman* (subsequently *American Thresherman and Farm Power*) of Madison, Wisconsin, and *Canadian Thresherman* (subsequently *Canadian Thresherman and Farmer*) of Winnipeg, Manitoba. Hundreds of letters to the "Correspondence" section of the American magazine and to the "Men Who Make No. 1 Hard" section of the Canadian magazine told the threshermen's experiences in detail. Among their comments on furnishing labor to farmers were:

"Our crew consisted of five men and four teams. The farmer found the other two teams and men"—*Ernest Bierwirth,* Meridian, Saskatchewan, writing about threshing in 1894

"The farmer furnishes the crew excepting the men to run the machine"—*D. F. Miller,* Adams, Montana, 1908

"In some places here the farmer furnishes the bundle teams and the thresherman furnishes 4 pitchers and 1 bagger and carries a cook car.

. . . The thresherman in this locality would be well pleased to have the cook car done away with"—*H. G. Hewitt,* Brighton, Colorado, 1910

"The thresher furnishes the crew and the farmer boards them, that is, in shock threshing"—*George Klein,* Crystal Springs, North Dakota, 1911

"We do everything except taking away the grain and boarding the men and teams, which is done by the farmer"—*John A. McKenzie,* Cartwright, Manitoba, 1911

"The farmer furnishes all help excepting water boy, engineer and separator man"—*Lee Hinds,* Cleburne, Texas, 1913

"The farmers furnish the crew, board and water team"—*P. C. Rempel,* Winkler, Manitoba, 1913

What the threshermen made clear about labor matters was that they all shared the same concerns and that although they were aware of the broad regional patterns that researchers were recording, they also saw considerable local variation.[14]

Whatever the precise arrangements between them, the most important service supplied to farmers by custom threshermen, who were in their heyday from the turn of the century until the 1920s, was the provision of machinery. This allowed farmers to avoid a heavy investment in machinery useful for only part of the year. Equipment furnished by the custom man included the engine, the separator, a water wagon, sometimes a vehicle for quick transportation, perhaps a cookshack, and such minor tools as pitchforks and band-cutters. It was custom threshermen who bought the large separators, those with thirty-six-inch or forty-inch cylinders, and brought them into common use. Individual farmers could not afford to own such outfits. Custom threshing thus not only centralized capital in the hands of the thresherman but also implemented larger, more efficient units, thereby saving labor and resulting in a more capital-intensive agriculture.

The advantages of hiring custom men seemed obvious to most farmers, as indicated by their practices, but one, W. C. Netterfield, spoke for dissenters in an article for *Canadian Thresherman.* He advised farmers to buy their own small outfits of engine and separator because, although they would use them only a short time each year, they could expect them, with good maintenance, to last ten years. He said that they should consider the advantages of prompt threshing (thereby avoiding loss or discoloration of grain by weather) and careful threshing (thereby saving grain). Small outfits, too, required little hired labor.[15]

Farmers, nevertheless, turned to threshermen to supply at least some labor—a second important service of custom men. This was important because of the relative scarcity of resident labor and unfeasibility of cooperative efforts on the plains. The thresherman usually chose certain skilled employees, such as the engineer and the separator man, from among personal acquaintances in his own locality. If he then needed to provide a full crew rather than using farmer labor, he recruited the balance of his crewmen from among transient workers who had come to the plains to work the binder and header harvest.

The flow of migrant bindlestiffs with the harvest, a movement that began as soon as wheat was grown on the plains, swelled to its peak in the early twentieth century at the very time that custom threshing flourished. By the early 1920s more than one hundred thousand men made the harvest on the plains of the United States and Canada. Custom threshing made their situation more attractive. It created jobs for laborers who would work its long hours because custom threshing replaced traded work among farmers with hired labor by migrants. It also offered workers the possibility of more extended employment than could be found working the harvest for farmers, for threshing lasted from harvest well into the fall or winter. Most bindlestiffs sought first to work the harvest in a locality and then to hire on with a threshing crew for the remainder of the season.[16]

Finally, the thresherman lent the farmer expertise. Especially because of rapid technological change in threshing, farmers benefited from leaving the details of threshing to the custom man. The thresherman brought with him—in most cases even when he did not furnish the entire crew—an experienced engineer and separator man.

They were more knowledgeable in their specialties than most farmers could hope to be. The thresherman also shouldered the responsibility for managing the crew, thereby freeing the farmer for other tasks.

Within the framework of these various systems, the people who did the work of threshing fulfilled a number of distinct roles, the expectations of which were clear because within a few years they had become traditional. Few spoken instructions were necessary on a threshing outfit. Workers moved to their tasks customarily and knew what was expected of them.

"The men who own rigs do not always understand the operating of them," complained a writer from Billings, Montana, in 1908. "They depend on the engineer and separator man to get good results."[17] This situation was exceptional, however, for in most outfits the thresherman was his own engineer, unless he owned more than one outfit and so had to hire an engineer for each. "But I find that two rigs is just one more than one man can successfully run at one time," observed a custom man from central Kansas.[18] Owner or not, the engineer, with his technical knowledge of steam engine operation, was regarded as the aristocrat of the crew. This did not mean that he had little work to do. He was the first to awaken in the morning, and his whistle summoned the rest of the crew to work. Once he had backed his engine into the belt, his duties became more supervisory and technical than laborious; he could then eat breakfast.

He spent most of his time on the platform of the engine itself. His supervisory duties involved the overall coordination of the outfit rather than the minute monitoring of the crew members. He had to be closely concerned with the activities of those crew members who supplied him with fuel and water, because they contributed directly to his operation of the engine. Either the engineer or the separator man had the prerogative of stopping the machinery if necessary, and so the engineer watched for signals from the separator man.

Precocious youngsters claimed to have assumed engine duties at an early age. "I can run any engine, set up the slide valve if out of order, make the steam pump work and place my engine anywhere I desire," bragged seventeen-year-old Jacob F. Dyck of Lowe Farm, Manitoba. He was bested by George Vaughn, Jr., of Tulia, Texas: "I am thirteen years old and have been running the engine for two years. I weigh only ninety pounds, but I can handle it with ease and satisfaction to papa and his customers."[19]

Someone, owner or engineer, had to see to the maintenance of the engine during threshing days and the off-season. Certain tasks—cleaning the boiler flue tubes periodically with steam pressure, for instance—had to be done during threshing season to maintain efficiency and safety. Even more important to the longevity of the engine was storage and protection during the off-season. "I believe there is money in threshing if a fellow repairs his machine in the shed instead of in the field but there has got to be a system to make it go unless you are just threshing to have the name of a thresherman," cautioned a custom man from North Dakota in 1917. "I know of an engine here that is 35 years old and has been in the field 28 falls and is still running. Our engine is 14 years old and it is better today than the first year it ran."[20] Even without shedding, threshermen expected long life from their steamers. Thresherman Mc-Kinney of Texas stored his engine in the open but covered all exposed parts with cylinder oil, and his son insisted, "Steam engines gave less mechanical problems than today's tractors."[21]

Threshermen and engineers could learn the arts of steam engine operation by observation and informal apprenticeship in the field; they could take courses at agricultural colleges in the United States as well as in Canadian universities (Professor Evan A. Hardy of the University of Saskatchewan, for instance, was an acknowledged authority in this and other aspects of farm mechanics); and they could consult an abundance of written material, including periodicals, company manuals, and such excellent technical guides as *Science of Threshing*, by G. F. Connor. The sophistication of this practical manual was a tribute to the expertise of engineers. Connor began his engine section by defining "heat," moved on to a thorough explanation of the physical principles involved in running an engine, and concluded with

detailed information on such topics as firing the engine, setting valves, and lubrication. The last section contained a list of twenty-eight "don'ts"—"don't run an engine and separator out of line" and so on—that probably set the initiate's head spinning like a drive wheel.[22]

The second most elite job on the crew was that of the separator man, an individual recognizable by the tools protruding from the pockets of his overalls and by the quart-size oilcan in his hand. The separator man followed the engineer to the field to check belts, bearings, and boxings and to grease everything up. During the day he moved around the threshing machine, watching and listening for any irregularity in its operation. He supervised the pitchers feeding the machine because, should the pitchers "slug the machine"—that is, cause straw to clog the cylinder—the separator man was the one who had to clean it out. He often observed operations by standing atop the separator itself. During stops in the work, he made adjustments in chains and belts and oiled moving parts. Unavoidably, the separator man occasionally had to stop the work to replace a broken cylinder tooth or a fractured bearing.

Some experienced threshermen considered maintenance of the separator and engagement of a good separator man more important concerns than concerns of the engine. "His duties were many, and he was considered the most important man of the crew," said

Here is a Warranty That is Worth Something to You

We absolutely guarantee all cylinder and concave teeth used in our Niagara Second Threshers against breakage and will replace free of charge, any such broken teeth which are returned to Us, our Agents or Branch Houses

You Get More for Your Money in Buffalo Pitts Machinery

Get a Pitts Steel Frame Thresher and be Up-to-date

All Buffalo Pitts Cylinder and Concave Teeth are made from a specially high grade steel, made expressly for us. *Our faith in our new teeth is proven by the warranty*

A frequent job for the separator man was to replace broken or nicked cylinder teeth. This advertisement appeared in American Thresherman. *(From* American Thresherman)

Ned McKinney. Wrote a custom man from central Kansas, "In this part of the country we can't get a good man to take care of a separator, and it takes a better man for that than to run the engine. Some may say he doesn't have to work as many hours as an engineer, but he has more to look after and more to contend with."[23] This position was commonly filled through partnership, often within a family. "My brother runs the engine and I run the separator," said a custom man from Mona, North Dakota.[24] William Bachman of Nashville, Kansas, described how he covered his separator with a tarpaulin every night in the field and shedded it in the off-season. "I have learned from experience," he said, "that a man had better not buy an outfit until he can afford a shed to house it in when not in use." As for operation of the separator, he wrote, "it is better to hire a good separator man than an engineer for if you don't you will surely have wheat in the straw pile."[25]

It did not pay, however, for the separator man, despite his importance, to put on airs. Some people recalled that "as soon as they were going good, the engineer and separator man would set down by the engine and eat their breakfast." Others even claimed to have known separator men who dozed off during a run. This caused resentment, for even if he had nothing in particular to do, the separator man was supposed to get on top of the machine, "keep his eyes open, and tend strictly to business." It was not unknown for hands to wake up an idle separator man by pitching some bundles in sideways to slug the cylinder.[26]

Although efficiency in operating the separator was always a concern—more to the farmer than to the custom man, according to some—it became a preoccupation during and just after World War I. In periodical articles and advertisements, more so in the United States than in Canada, off-season maintenance was patriotically transformed into "preparedness," with threshermen urged to "clear the decks and get into fighting trim for the coming season," when they would be expected to "do their bit" for their country by saving grain. The United States Department of Agriculture issued in 1918 Farmers' Bulletin 991, *The Efficient Operation of Threshing Machines*. The department also worked through agricultural colleges on the plains to organize crash courses in separator operation, teaching separator men their "three R's"—running, repairing, and readjustment.[27]

The militaristic hoopla only emphasized what the periodicals and manuals had codified. Connor's *Science of Threshing* gave the same meticulous attention to the separator that it did to the engine; company manuals gave specifications for individual models; and periodical articles both advised and exhorted. As one writer noted, the separator had "five fundamental functions," each of which required attention:

1. To properly feed the grain to the cylinder.
2. To properly thresh the grain from the head.
3. To properly separate the grain from the straw.
4. To properly clean the grain and deliver it to the weigher.
5. To properly deliver the straw and chaff to the stack.[28]

Any of these parts might give trouble, but certainly the separator man's greatest concern was the threshing cylinder. He had to renew or replace worn or bent teeth; tap all the teeth with a hammer to see that they were tight; and if they were not, tighten them with the special wrench provided by the manufacturer. He had to check the keys and especially the bearings of the cylinder shaft to see that they were sound. He had to file off any corrugations of the cylinder shaft. Most important, he had to adjust and balance the cylinder. Cylinder and concave teeth must not nick one another, and there must be no vibration. Whenever any teeth were replaced, the balance was disrupted, and the separator man had to take out the cylinder, rest it on sawhorses, and balance it by adding teeth or slugs of lead.[29]

Engineer and separator man were the only two threshing-crew jobs considered so skilled that they might be advertised as specialized trades. Engineers and separator men often sought positions through advertisements in such publications as *American Thresherman,* and the wording of their an-

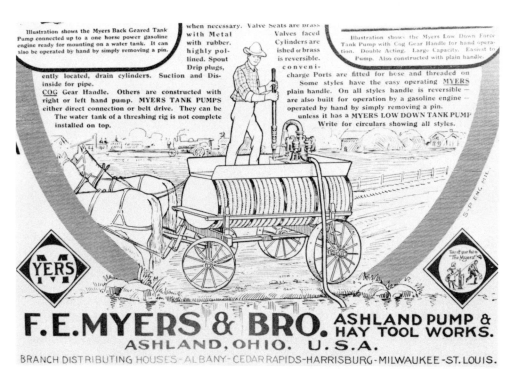

Illustration shows the Myers Back Geared Tank Pump connected up to a one horse power gasoline engine ready for mounting on a water tank. It can also be operated by hand by simply removing a pin.

ently located, drain cylinders. Suction and Discharge inside for pipe.

COG Gear Handle. Others are constructed with right or left hand pump. MYERS TANK PUMPS either direct connection or belt drive. They can be installed on top.

The water tank of a threshing rig is not complete

when necessary. Valve Seats are brass with Metal with rubber. Valves faced Cylinders are highly polished or brass lined. Spout is reversible. Drip plugs, conveni-charge Ports are fitted for hose and threaded on Some styles have the easy operating MYERS plain handle. On all styles handle is reversible — are also built for operation by a gasoline engine — operated by hand by simply removing a pin.

unless it has a MYERS LOW DOWN TANK PUMP. Write for circulars showing all styles.

Illustration shows the Myers Low Down Force Tank Pump with Cog Gear Handle for hand operation. Double Acting. Large Capacity. Easiest to Pump. Also constructed with plain handle.

F.E.MYERS & BRO. ASHLAND PUMP & HAY TOOL WORKS.
ASHLAND, OHIO. U.S.A.
BRANCH DISTRIBUTING HOUSES – ALBANY – CEDAR RAPIDS – HARRISBURG – MILWAUKEE – ST. LOUIS.

The tank man drew water with a pump from the nearest convenient windmill, stream, or pothole. This advertisement appeared in American Thresherman. (*From* American Thresherman)

nouncements showed that threshermen valued experience and clean living in their skilled employees. "WANTED—Position as traction engineer for the coming season; have license; no boozer or cigarette fiend" was the notice placed by Hugh Haskin of Winfred, South Dakota, in July 1910. A Minnesotan named G. A. Drews advertised in the same month for a "position as separator tender on a good rig; fifteen years' experience; western Minnesota or South Dakota preferred." Other ads specified the type of engine or separator that individuals preferred to operate.

The person who supplied the engineer with water might be a grown man, in which case he was referred to as the tank man, or he might be a boy and be called the water monkey. Hauling water was a considerable challenge for a boy. He drove the tank and team to the source of water, perhaps a windmill and stock tank or perhaps a slough; dipped or hand-pumped the tank wagon full; hauled it to the engine; drained the water from the tank into the engine reservoir; and endured the verbal abuse of the engineer. If the water was getting low and the engineer noticed the steam in the steam gauge

Hauling water back to fill the reservoir (here with an extra front-mounted tank, optional on Minneapolis engines) on the engine, the tank man might also bring some for the hands, such as these on the R. Doris crew, Lane County, Kans. (Lane County Historical Museum, Dighton, Kans.)

turning blue, the water boy got an earful. "Our father gave us jobs according to our size," recalled Guy Bretz. "When I was 12 years old, I had the job of hauling water. By the time I was 14 years old, I graduated to a *pich fork*." Not that water hauling was that easy— Bretz obtained the water by bucket-dipping from stock tanks. He carried a two-by-six board on the wagon, laid it on top of the stock tank, and dipped to the tank wagon. A farm wife timed him one day as he dipped from a tank in her yard; it took ten minutes to fill the wagon.[30]

In areas where water had to be hauled long distances, such as southern Saskatchewan, some outfits needed two tank wagons and two tank men. Hal Lewis of Gray, Saskatchewan, remem-bered that a tank man hauling to his father's farm from a slough tired of hand-dipping up to the tank and thought dipping would be easier if he backed the wagon right into the slough. Unfortunately, his mules refused to pull the loaded tank out of the slough. The second tank man arrived with another team of mules, but the men had only a piece of binder twine with which to attach the second team to the doubletree of the bogged wagon. The men tied the second team on with the twine and held the new team back so as not to break the strand. The first team, thinking it had help, promptly pulled the tank wagon out and headed back for the outfit.[31]

If an outfit burned coal (or, in a few cases, wood), then either the farmer or

The Holden brothers outfit of Indian Head, Sask., had no self-feeder in 1903, and so a band cutter and feeders fed the thresher. The engine was a straw burner; hence the pile of straw behind the engineer. (Saskatchewan Archives Board, Regina)

a designated fireman had to haul it, depending on who had agreed to supply the fuel. Outfits that burned straw rather than coal required the services of a straw monkey, who, as the name indicated, was also usually a boy. The straw monkey had a team hitched to a straw buck or rick. Using the crank adjustment on the straw blower, or using lines tied to the blower, he directed straw to fill his rick and pulled it around to the engineer. "This was no big job, but for a little fellow it was a big deal," said William Lies, who started work as a straw monkey when he was about ten years old. Straw was free fuel, of course, but less convenient than coal and somewhat more dangerous on windy days.[32]

Unlike wheat farmers in the Mid-west, those on the Great Plains had little use for grain straw except as fuel. A few wanted a straw stack built in the pasture as food and shelter for their animals; this sometimes meant that bundles had to be hauled to an inconvenient threshing site. The Bretz family of Kansas was one that made such use of the straw: "When we were too small to run the water wagon we tromped around on the stacks, shoved it here and there, making as nice a stack as we could," recalled Guy Bretz. "That was our cattle and horse feed for the winter. The stock would use it for shelter; to eat and also a good bed."

As for the other male members of the threshing outfit, their roles depended on whether the outfit was threshing bundles from the shock or

The rack drivers brought their loads in and awaited turns at the separator. The James and John Mc-Ewen outfit threshing on the George Kidd farm near Lumsden, Sask., ca. 1910. (Saskatchewan Archives Board, Regina)

threshing bundles or headed grain from the stack. Threshing from the shock required from four to eight bundle wagons or racks, each with a team and driver. There was a set order in which they should be filled and return to the separator, and it was a disgrace to lag behind. The driver piloted his rack alongside the shocks or stooks standing in the field, tied his reins to the frame, and directed his horses largely by voice while he and the field pitchers, using three-tined bundle forks, loaded the rack. He then drove it back to the separator. When his turn to unload came, he pulled alongside the feeder at just the proper distance— too close and the drive belt rubbed on the bundle rack; too far and it was difficult to throw bundles onto the feeder.

The field pitchers stayed in the field, moving from shock to shock with their bundle forks, methodically filling racks. The first bundles could be pitched on helter-skelter, but as the rack filled, the field pitchers were supposed to build up the sides carefully, laying the bundles butts out. Boys were boys, however, as Ernest Claassen recalled: "We boys sort of had baseball on our minds. [When we] would throw one bundle on the rack at a time, that was merely a single; we'd try to get a two-bagger or a three-bagger and possibly go to the extra trouble and try to get a home run and throw four at once." The wagons always departed for the set with full loads. "There was a kind of unspoken code at work: it would not be manly to leave the field with less

Three-tine forks for handling bundled grain were standard on the Archie Baker outfit near Castle-wooden, S. Dak., 1913. Only one older fellow carried a four-tine fork. (South Dakota State Historical Society, Pierre)

sheaves than some magic minimum," one Canadian thresherman confessed.[33]

At the set were additional bundle pitchers to help the driver unload. One rack was situated on each side of the feeder, and from two to four men pitched from each rack onto the feeder. They coordinated their pitching so that each bundle they tossed headfirst onto the feeder overlapped the previous one but did not pile upon it. "That's one thing a good separator operator would see, that the bundles be pitched in the right way," a veteran custom man observed.[34] Another counseled his crew to "be sure they went in headfirst, and one at a time. Too many at once would plug the machine and make the separator man awful mad."[35] Sloppy pitching made the farmer "awful mad," too, for it meant grain was lost through the blower. "Many people

think that the farmer who kicks because the pitchers working on a thresher do not pitch all the bundles straight and heads first, is an old fogy, or a crab," observed J. H. Hohaus of Brown County, South Dakota. "He may be both, but, at that, he is certainly justified in kicking under such circumstances."[36] Most of all, advised another thresherman, "hang onto that pitchfork. They were hard on concave teeth, and the separator didn't digest them too well."[37] Because half of the crew always had to pitch over the belt onto the feeder, and because the ever-present wind always favored one side over the other, the bundle pitchers exchanged sides at regular intervals.

Until the invention of the self-feeder, there was another laborious step involved in threshing bundles. A man or men (sometimes boys) called bandcutters had to cut the twine of each

A bundle wagon driver was expected to carry a full load from field to set. Shown is George Hitz, on crew in North Dakota, 1925. (Courtesy of George Hitz)

A self-feeder cut the bands on bundles and fed them into the separator. This advertisement appeared in the January 1914 issue of American Thresherman. *(From* American Thresherman)

bundle, and a man or men called feeders had to stand on a platform and hand-feed each bundle into the cylinder. Professor P. S. Rose of the University of South Dakota described this craft:

In the best hand-feeding the straw was all fed lengthwise, all the bands were cut and the straw was spread as evenly as possible the entire length of the cylinder. The butts of the bundles were elevated and the cylinder teeth were allowed to comb the top straws off from the bundle first. Where necessary, the feeder retarded the under side of the bundles with his hands. He endeavored also

to maintain an even, steady stream of straw to the cylinder at all times.[38]

The self-feeder brought the bundles into the separator via a raddle; a revolving knife cut the twines; and a revolving rake combed the bundles apart from the top, feeding the straw lengthwise in an even flow into the cylinder. David C. Ruth of Halstead, Kansas, patented the first workable self-feeder in 1894. This one and a competitor rapidly went into licensed commercial production, and by the first years of the twentieth century, new separators had this device and old ones were adapted to it. A Canadian journalist in 1903 observed that "the sacred feeder

Two feeders and a band cutter are in place here to feed the bundled grain from the stack. Shown is the C. R. Voth outfit, Harvey County, Kans., ca. 1900. (Courtesy of Moses Voth)

Pitching headed grain from both sides onto the feeder. Shown is the Ed Bever crew near Greensburg, Kans., 1919. (Courtesy of Leona Bever)

Wing feeder, extending to either side of the separator. Shown is the Charles Barrows crew near Belpre, Kans., ca. 1914. (Santa Fe Trail Center, Larned, Kans.)

is bound to be hurled from his pedestal ere long by the baleful inventor." Few others mourned, however. "The self-feeder is the device that pleases me most," wrote a South Dakota custom man in 1910. "I love to watch it cuff the bundles in without sweating as I used to. Then I say God bless the man who had brains enough to invent the self-feeder." [39]

Whether there were bundles to cut or just headed grain, threshing from the stack was somewhat different. Sometimes bound grain was stacked, but most grain in the stack was headed grain. Because stacks of headed grain were erected in yards at harvest time and were grouped so that a separator could be drawn between them, the only laborers required were the spike pitchers, who pitched from two stacks on opposite sides of the feeder. Eight spike pitchers, four on each side of the extension feeder (usually about fourteen feet long but sometimes as long as twenty), constituted a full crew. They exchanged sides at intervals. They maintained an even flow of spikes, the feeder always filled as it entered the cylinder. Spike pitchers used a four-tined pitchfork. In bad grasshopper years, they stuck the forks handle first into the stack during breaks "so as to keep the hoppers from roughing up the handles, so you would blister your hands," Bretz remembered.

Besides caring for blisters, pitchers in any scheme of threshing had to be

The farmer was responsible for hauling away his grain. Louis Bever's outfit threshes kaffir in western Kansas, ca. 1920. (Courtesy of Flava Bever)

aware of the special properties of different grains. Oats threshed easily, so they could pitch fast; wheat was harder to thresh; and rye, with its tough straw, pulled down the cylinder. The worst grain for pitchers, though, Ned McKinney recalled, was barley: It was so itchy, "you could hardly wait to find a horse tank."

Because headed grain was stacked in long stacks, hands often had to pitch a good distance to reach the feeder. In Montana, where labor was not so plentiful as in many other parts of the plains, local inventors made derrick tables for threshing. A derrick table was a wooden platform, some twelve-by-eighteen feet, built of two-inch lumber and set on the running gear of a wagon. At the corners of the platform were fixed the four legs of the derrick, from the apex of which was suspended

a pulley. The derrick table was parked between two stacks of grain. Using the derrick, a rope, a team, and a heavy hayfork (a Jackson made for dragging), two men and a team could pull parts of one stack, then the other, onto the platform. Two other men stood on or next to the platform and raked the grain onto the feeder using four-tined forks with the tines bent ninety degrees to make rakes.[40]

The farmer was responsible for hauling the threshed grain to the granary or elevator. Hardly any grain on the plains was bagged; rather, it was handled in bulk. A measuring device on the separator weighed thirty-pound units (considered half bushels) and was closely watched by both the farmer and the separator man. One man might handle the hauling work with two wagons (commonly a fifty-two bushel size),

Most grain was handled in bulk, but in some localities it was bagged. The bagger on this outfit in the Qu'Appelle District, Sask., ca. 1905, kept a supply of strings on the separator for sewing bags together. (Saskatchewan Archives Board, Regina)

When storage was tight, farmers near Dighton, Kans., piled the wheat on the ground, ca. 1919. (Lane County Historical Museum, Dighton, Kans.)

driving one to unload while the other was being filled from the separator. Good threshing often required two men to keep up with the unloading.

This also depended on where the grain was being hauled—that is, the distance to the elevator or bins—and the unloading facilities available. Elevators

Elevators and granaries were far away; this outfit in South Dakota, ca. 1910, kept running by dumping the grain into a temporary granary at the set. (Courtesy of Ted Worrall)

generally had hoists; at the bins, however, the wagon man had to scoop.

In any arrangement of labor, the support role of feeding the crew was almost always performed by women. "We like to see the threshers come," went a saying among rural women, "and still more we like to see them go."[41] In a situation where local farmers supplied most of the labor, feeding the crew was quite a social occasion. Farmers commonly ate breakfast and supper at home, but morning lunch, dinner (the noon meal), and afternoon lunch came from the kitchen of the woman on whose farm the crew was working. She was up early—bread to rise, chickens to be killed, roast to be

put on, potatoes to be peeled, ready for boiling in a big canning kettle. The wives and daughters of the other members of the ring came to her house in midmorning, often bringing pies or slaw and other side dishes. Before the men came in, the women set out soap, towels, and pans of water for washing up. The host farmer and his wife supplied the bulk of the food. The most common staple was fried chicken. (Farm women reckoned on threshers when they decided how many chicks to buy or raise in the spring; threshers made jokes about how their behavior became more and more avian from daily consumption of chicken.)

Camaraderie among the cooks eased

Cook and cook car of the R. Doris crew, Lane County, Kans.; water and towels are set out for the men to wash up, ca. 1925. (Lane County Historical Museum, Dighton, Kans.)

demands but also set the stage for womanly competition. "Each farm wife tried to outdo her neighbor in putting up a good meal," said one from Saskatchewan.[42] So F. M. Redpath of Kansas reported that his mother was more dismayed than gratified to hear from threshing hand Lew Pate about the fare put on by a neighbor woman: "My mother asked him what Mrs. Zimmerman had for dinner. He replied that she had so much that he could not eat it all."[43] Quality in food was desirable, but quantity was imperative. "At harvest time we all take a pardonable pleasure in setting a good table," noted an extension home economist from Kansas in 1917. "Threshers are working hard and need a heavy diet, so there

should be plenty of potatoes and bread and foods containing starch and sugars to furnish the necessary energy for their work."[44]

The cooks for most pure custom outfits were generally also women, often with girls to assist them. Some outfits had male cooks, and a few had man and wife teams. These individuals presided over the cook car, rising early to bake in their wood or coal stoves, setting out pans and towels for the crewmen to wash up with, and putting substantial fare on the table or passing it out the serving window. "The menu was very simple, but lots of it," Guy Bretz wrote. "Home-made bread, roast pork or fried potatoes, stewed tomatoes, slaw, stewed turnips, peas, corn

Cooks, cook car, and bunkhouse traveled with this outfit in Alberta, 1928. (Glenbow Archives)

and gravy, and bushels of BEANS. For fruit it was dried apples or stewed prunes and dried peaches. At least once a day we had pie or cake. My father believed in feeding his men good." The cook's day extended through cleanup after the evening meal. "How they managed to get by with so little time to sleep I don't understand," wondered George Hitz.

Anna May Handley, a hired girl on a cook car in Saskatchewan in 1928, recalled how food preparation and serving filled the entire day. "Breakfast consisted of bacon, eggs, hash brown potatoes, and a gallon of coffee," she began. "For dinner at 11:00 A.M. we cooked a fifteen pound roast, two types

of vegetables and what seemed to me to be a half bushel of potatoes. (I had to peel them.) All the men liked pie for dessert, so we baked three pies every day. At 3 P.M. we took lunch out to the field. This was another gallon of coffee, sandwiches, and cookies. For supper we had cold meats, potatoes, salads, and cake for dessert." Not even this routine dulled Handley's appreciation of the threshing life, however. "The highlight of our day was when we took lunch out to the threshing crew," she recalled. "We waited until the men had finished eating so we could bring the plates home. I enjoyed the ride home on those beautiful autumn days, when there wasn't a breath of wind and a haze hung over the landscape. It felt good to be alive." [45]

Cookshacks—or cook cars, as they were known in most areas—were large, for besides accommodating the stove and storage cabinets, most also had a long table in the center that seated up to eighteen men. George Hitz recalled that his outfit's cook car seemed as big as a boxcar but was probably some eighteen feet long, built with light lumber, and set on wheels salvaged from a separator. All cook cars were on steel wheels of some kind, and many were more than twenty feet long. Some were designed to feed the men outside as they stood at wing tables that folded down from the long windows. [46]

"The morale of a threshing crew depended on a good cook," averred a Saskatchewan farm woman. She remembered that her thresherman-father had the same woman cook year after year until she became too old to manage and he had to hire a new cook. "The next one the men didn't like"—not her roast beef or even her apple pie—and one dinnertime her father looked up to see "all the men parading down to see the boss. It looked as if they meant business too." The thresherman stood down the food strike in this instance, but he quickly hired "another famous cook" who came back for many years thereafter. [47]

The most oppressive manner of boarding occurred when the farmer and the thresherman agreed that the farm wife would board the crew of the thresherman. In such situations, the farm wife could count on little help from neighbors because their men were not involved in the threshing operation. With the help of daughters or a hired girl, the farm wife had to turn out all the meals consumed by the thresherman's crew. Unfortunately, she did not relish social contact with these individuals. (Farm wives were notable advocates for the adoption of the combine during the 1920s.) Lorena Hickok, subsequently known for her service to President Franklin Roosevelt's New Deal, penned an account of her experience as a hired girl on a farm that was boarding a Dakota threshing crew:

I was shown the stove and supplies and cooking utensils, and the old lady, who had hardly spoken to me all day, handed me an alarm clock set for 3 A.M. I was to get out the next morning and have breakfast ready for the crew by 5. One of the men laid a fire in the stove. In the morning darkness I staggered sleepily out, poured some kerosene into the stove, as I had been told to do, and tried to start a fire. . . . I was still trying when one of the men appeared at daybreak and took over. I finally got them fed, but not at 5 o'clock. During the next three days I never did catch up. I was a squirrel in a sweltering cage, running frantically round and round in a wheel, never getting anywhere. Dripping perspiration, in clouds of steam and smoke and soot that caked on my skin and smarted in my eyes and nostrils, I struggled along, losing

When the cook (with apron) gets back into the car, the John Zook outfit in Pawnee County, Kans., will be ready to move to a new set, ca. 1915. (Santa Fe Trail Center, Larned, Kans.)

ground all the time, through an agonizing routine of boiling, baking, frying, through bushels of grimy potato peelings, through sliding avalanches of greasy dishes, with never enough soap or hot water, shoving hunk after endless hunk of filthy soft coal in that stove that never got enough. My mistress did not berate me. She only growled and, when I got too far behind, grudgingly gave me a hand.[48]

However severe the demands on isolated women and however hard the physical labor of men, because every participant understood his or her role, operations usually proceeded with amazing smoothness, barring breakdowns of machinery. Workers took their positions at the threshing site and did their jobs without audible commands. More remarkable yet was the

easy, natural fashion in which a crew accomplished a move of the outfit. Upon completion of threshing at a particular farm site or stack yard, the engineer pulled the engine forward to loosen the belt while the separator man gathered his gear. Men from the crew shouldered the belt off the engine and stashed it inside the separator. The engineer wheeled his machine around and backed up to hitch it to the separator. If there was a cookshack, the men hitched it behind. They then climbed aboard the separator or the bundle wagons to ride to the next site or yard.

Arriving there, they efficiently accomplished the process known as "making a set" or "lining up." The engineer drove into the stack yard or where the farmer wanted the straw stack. Hands leaped to earth, unhitched the separator, and commenced leveling it, taking a spade of earth from here and there beneath the wheels; the final judgment on whether the separator was level enough was made by the separator man. If the outfit was not stack threshing and thus had discretion in placing the separator, the separator man would test the wind with a handful of straw before positioning the separator with the feeder facing the wind. Meanwhile, the engineer pulled the engine around in a circle to face the separator, lining it up with the separator by "eyeballing." ("An engineer took pride in 'lining up' on first trial, and after some experience he usually did the job on the first try," William Lies remarked.) At this point, the hands were already stretching the belt out from the separator drive pulley. The engineer crept closer; a hand, wearing gloves, shoved the belt onto the engine; the engineer backed into the belt; it slipped, then tightened; a hand blocked an engine wheel; and the outfit was ready to thresh again, the pitchers taking up their forks.[49]

Moving and making a set, ordinarily routine tasks, were not always so. Areas with sandy ground, especially sand hills, posed problems in moving heavy engines, as did rivers and creeks, for many rural bridges were inadequate to hold the engines. Watercourses therefore defined the limits of many threshing runs. From near Almeria, Nebraska, a thresherman reported, "The sand hills bother some unless well grassed over. We don't try to follow the road. We can get the engine any place but sometimes we have to go back to horse flesh to get the separator

through." Another custom man from the Nebraska sand hills informed his fellows of how he used chains and ropes to move stuck outfits, but one from northwestern Oklahoma said that he had lost part of his run because he could not pull through the sandy ground to reach it. As for river crossings, some operators avoided shaky bridges by waiting for low water and then fording it; this was common on the upper Arkansas River, for instance. In 1926, however, an engineer drowned while trying to ford the Missouri River at Fort Benton, Montana.[50]

The worst source of trouble in making a set was the belt. Its length of some forty or fifty feet made for good alignment on pulleys and distanced the engine, with its sparks, from stacks. Belts were of either leather, cotton canvas, or rubber. The best leather belts were of hide taken from the backs of steers and glued into a belt. Leather, however, was the most expensive and the most difficult to maintain during bad weather; it also set off a debate as to whether the hair side or the flesh side should go on the wheel (most authorities voted for the hair side). Canvas, on the other hand, was relatively inexpensive and in good supply and gave good service. Rubber came into common use only late in the era of custom threshing. A variety of belt dressings—neat's-foot oil, caster oil, tallow, and linseed oil, among them—were used as preservatives. The most sensitive point was the lacing: The operator punched an intricate series of holes in the ends of the belt and either single-

The long belt sets the engine at a distance from the stacks. An outfit near Belpre, Kans., ca. 1910. (Santa Fe Trail Center, Larned, Kans.)

or double-laced them together. Late in the custom threshing era, metallic fasteners simplified this craft. In the field, the separator man stashed the belt in the separator during the night to protect it from dew. Despite all precautions, however, belts would continually stretch, come off pulleys, come unlaced, and just wear out.[51]

Discussion of the broad systems and even the individual roles involved in threshing does not highlight many of the more subtle traditions that ornamented the fabric of its folk life. Detailed interviewing and photographic study reveal elements of the culture: the crockery water jug (often with a spoonful of oatmeal added to combat the diarrhetic effects of alkali) wrapped in burlap and stashed beneath the

separator; the pitchforks stacked like stands of arms, handles to earth, tines entwined; graniteware cups in the field and thresher's china on the table.

One of the common indications of the distinctiveness of threshing was its vocabulary. Threshers spoke of "making a set," "slugging the cylinder," and "making a good day's run." One of their most notable traits of speech was their habit of making a person the object of the verb "thresh." If they were threshing on the farm of someone named Swenson, they would not thresh Swenson's wheat, they would "thresh Swenson," or, worse yet, "thresh out Swenson." That usage brings to mind one Texas thresherman's habit of saying to his farmer-customer at the end of the day, "Well, you may not feel or look like it, but you sure got a threshing today."[52]

Such lingo spoke no more articulately than the nonverbal communication of the steam whistle. "How I still remember how the steam whistle sounded," recalled one resident of Lane County, Kansas. "You could hear it for a mile on still days. One to stop—two to start—three for water, and four for wheat wagons."[53] As this fellow indicated, steam threshing outfits had definite steam-whistle codes given by the engineer. Collections of whistle signals from various individuals and regions differ somewhat.

According to a North Dakotan, in his neighborhood if the engineer wanted the pitchers to stop pitching, he gave one short peep. Two short ones meant to start pitching again. If he was running low on water, he gave three long blasts. If the grain wagon was getting full, he signaled with two long blasts for the haulers to hurry with another wagon. Three short toots told the bundle wagon drivers to hustle in from the field with more bundles. One long blast meant quitting time. "Then there was the one that used to send a tingle down my back," he recalled. "That was when we heard four long blasts, which meant the boss was wanted for some reason or another."[54]

A fellow North Dakotan recalled one long blast as the signal given at one-half hour before starting work, at noon, at one, at quitting time, and, just for self-satisfaction, on finishing a set. Two short toots meant the engine or belt was to be put in motion; three

meant a call for bundle teams, which was repeated as needed; two long blasts with a short toot between them told the water monkey to hurry; a series of many short toots meant some problem, such as a plugged straw blower or a detached belt; and five long blasts meant fire or injury.[55]

Some recollections of whistle signals were purely personal. Ned McKinney remembered the long morning wake-up blast: It "seems as tho [it lasted] five minutes but probably [was] ten seconds." George Hitz got in some horseplay with the whistle: "We young fellows got a hand on it, too, pulling the whistle string when they pulled the outfit in from field to yard when they had finished the run till the pressure in the boiler diminished to the point that it wasn't interesting anymore."

It was not often that the engineer gave the emergency signal for an accident, but when he did, it was memorable. There were four types of accidents dreaded by threshers, the foremost being entanglement in machinery. "Safety First" columns of *American Thresherman* warned workers not to reach between belts, which could easily take an arm. Guy Bretz recalled a thresherman of his acquaintance who leaned in to oil a boxing on the spinning cylinder, got his coat caught in the cylinder shaft, and was spun around time after time, crushing his head and shoulders on the front wheel. Said Bretz, "It was a terrible tragedy that shocked the entire area and for years it was the foremost topic in the county."

The second, most spectacular type of

accident was a boiler explosion. Press accounts of these were gory and always told the position—engineer, owner, or water monkey—of the pitiful casualties. A writer from Schuyler, Nebraska, in 1911 reported that while the crew was eating lunch, the Hradec brothers' engine blew up, flew through the air, and came to rest ninety feet away. The Hradec running the engine flew only half this distance and escaped with just a broken toe, but the new water man, who had just delivered his first tank, flew the whole distance with the engine and was scalded to death. With similar dispassion a recorder from Douglas, Oklahoma, said of an explosion there: "The man who owned the outfit was standing on top of the separator. Something hit him and his head was torn completely away and landed back of the straw pile. The engineer was picked up about 60 or 70 steps from the engine." [56]

A third type of accident was fire, often caused by explosive combustion of the dust from smutty wheat. Guy Bretz recalled that although his thresherman-father emphasized safety, once, while threshing some smut-infested wheat, "you could see the black dust coming from the separator for a mile." The farmer insisted that the outfit continue work; sure enough, "the fog smut ignited . . . [and] exploded in a ball of fire," and the separator and stack were destroyed. Such smut explosions were studied extensively by scientists from the United States Department of Agriculture, who recommended, among other precautions, that threshers be grounded to remove static electricity from them.[57]

A final, often theatrical accident was the bridge breakthrough. Accounts of engines breaking through bridges were full of wondrous escapes by men who jumped clear, grisly details about those who did not, and outrage at authorities who failed to maintain good bridges. A South Dakotan wrote of an accident at Canton: "Mr. Lund, the owner, was crushed between the steering wheel and tender, suffering a crushed hip and internal injuries, and died four hours later. The little boy riding on the tender was caught between the cab and coal tender and suffered a broken neck and died instantly." An angry witness who photographed a similar incident near Mayetta, Kansas, demanded, "Will any man with a thimble full of brains claim that a bridge, wrecked as it is shown in the illustration, would have been made secure by simply stringing a couple of planks along for the engine to pass over? The time has long since gone by for Kansas threshermen to submit further to those legalized murders."[58]

Such perils were merely a caution, not a deterrence, to threshermen, who, as entrepreneurs, sought return on their capital and labor. Judging by their writings, the greatest concern of threshermen was not the occasional loss of life but rather the continual question of rates. From time to time, government researchers collected data on rates for threshing wheat. A bulletin of the United States Department of Agriculture summarized its findings on

Table 3.1. Threshing Rates in North Dakota, 1913 (in cents per bushel)

Method	Wheat	Oats	Barley	Flax
From shock	10.4	6.4	6.6	25.7
From stack	6.1	3.8	4.0	11.4

Source: Adapted from C. M. Hennis and Rex E. Willard, *Farm Practices in Grain Farming in North Dakota,* U.S. Department of Agriculture Bulletin 757 (Washington, D.C.: GPO, 1919), p. 13.

rates in North Dakota in 1913 with a table (see Table 3.1). The table revealed certain facts, such as the disparity in rates between shock threshing and stack threshing, and gave a rough indication of the cost of threshing. The problem with this summary was that it took no account of the varied terms of the agreements between farmers and threshermen—who would provide what labor, who would furnish fuel, who would board the crew, and so on.[59]

Subsequently, compilers of a multi-state study of the winter wheat region attempted to correlate such terms with the rates they had recorded during 1920. This produced a much more complicated summary (see Table 3.2). This sophisticated presentation indicated rather high costs overall, but the range of rates and terms—from 10 cents to 31 cents—was so great that it demanded more explanation than the bulletin provided. Obviously, not only unknown terms of agreement but also local circumstances such as weather, grain yield, and unusual short-term demand must have been at work.[60]

Threshermen showed their intense interest in rates, including those charged in distant localities of the plains, by continually exchanging data on them through letters to *American Thresherman* and *Canadian Thresherman.* Usually they attempted to make their reports comparable by detailing the

Table 3.2. Threshing Practices and Rates, 1920 (in cents per bushel)

County/State	Threshing from	Crew Furnished by		Rate
		Thresherman	Farmer	
Gage/Nebr.	Shock		All	10
Clay/Nebr.	Shock		All	14
Clay/Nebr.	Stack (bundles)	All		14
Cheyenne/Nebr.	Shock	Field pitchers	Bundle pitchers	12
Cheyenne/Nebr.	Shock		All	11
Thomas/Kans.	Stack (headed)	All		15
McPherson/Kans.	Shock	Field pitchers	Bundle haulers	19
McPherson/Kans.	Stack (bundles)	All		17
McPherson/Kans.	Stack (headed)	All		18
Pawnee/Kans.	Stack (headed)	All		17
Garfield/Okla.	Shock	All		31
Garfield/Okla.	Shock	Field pitchers	Bundle haulers	16
Woodward/Okla.	Stack (headed)	All		22

Source: M. R. Cooper and R. S. Washburn, *Cost of Producing Wheat on 481 Farms in the States of North and South Dakota, Minnesota, Kansas, Nebraska, and Missouri,* U.S. Department of Agriculture Bulletin 943 (Washington, D.C.: GPO, 1921), p. 16.

terms they had with farmers. A report from North Dakota in 1911 was typical: "We got five cents for wheat, three cents for oats, barley and speltz, and ten cents for flax. The machine man furnishes four pitchers."[61]

General trends were evident and rough estimates were possible from the threshermen's letters. First, the lead rate was clearly that for wheat. The cash grain set the scale, followed by other, less valuable feed or oil grains. The second most often quoted rate was that for oats, which typically was a bit more than half the rate for wheat—wheat at six cents, oats at three and a half, for instance. Second, shortages of machinery occurred often in isolated, developing localities, causing high rates in the short term. This soon eased as opportunistic threshermen either shipped rigs into the area or moved there themselves and as farmers bought rigs and became threshermen themselves. Third, the rate structure for wheat was basically divided between the rate for headed grain (stacked) and that for bound grain (usually threshed from the shock). Other terms of threshing agreements refined the rates within these basic divisions. Fourth, threshing rates moved from a period of stability during the first decade and a half of the twentieth century to a profitable pinnacle during and just after World War I; they then plunged in 1921 to a lower level. As could be expected, rates roughly rose and fell with the price of wheat.

To generalize (and thereby obscure a multitude of varying terms), the early stable rates for threshing hovered at five to seven cents for threshing headed grain and eight to ten cents for threshing bound grain. Regardless of exchange rates, threshing prices ran a cent or two lower in the Canadian provinces than in the states. During the years 1918 to 1920, rates became both higher and unstable, with prices varying within a season; but the direction was always up until threshing of even headed grain brought from fifteen to twenty-five cents per bushel. In 1921 these prices crumbled, with many threshermen back to ten cents for headed wheat and a few cents more for bound grain. Over the next several years, threshers' rates recovered only a few pennies.

Although these rates indicated the rough cost of threshing to farmers, they did not reflect the profitability of the threshing business. Testimony on this point was conflicting, full of both success stories and woeful tales. Successful threshermen frequently wrote immodest accounts for periodicals. A splendid example was M. T. Austin, who became a thresherman in southwestern South Dakota after beginning work as a tank man on a crew.[62] He bought his rig—a secondhand, twenty-horsepower Minneapolis engine and a thirty-six-inch separator, along with tank and other equipment—for $1,841.25 in 1902. With this outfit he reported his expenses and earnings from 1902 through 1905. In 1906 Austin bought a second rig—a new twenty-two-horsepower Minneapolis engine and thirty-six-inch separator with simi-

Table 3.3. M. T. Austin's Earnings and Expenses, 1902–1905 and 1906–1909 (in U.S. dollars)

	1902	1903	1904	1905	1906	1907	1908	1909
Earnings	3,304.00	2,637.53	3,766.80	2,871.92	2,069.42	2,280.46	2,765.60	1,607.97
Labor	1,504.00	1,337.75	1,833.00	1,534.65	1,335.00	1,336.87	1,318.85	836.25
Coal	440.72	408.20	490.88	365.12	315.59	299.55	290.00	178.25
Repairs	124.00	263.78	163.40	248.50	27.43	122.04	133.00	50.75
Oil and grease	41.50	38.58	41.05	31.15	26.40	22.00	32.00	24.25
Interest	22.00	25.25			20.00	161.10	232.80	56.13
Net earned	1,171.78	563.97	1,238.47	692.50	345.00	338.00	758.90	432.34

	1902–1905	1906–1909
Net earnings	3,666.72	1,875.14
Less cost of rig	1,841.25	2,345.00
Add sale of used rig	1,000.00	—
Add value of used rig	—	1,500.00
Add value of shed	175.00	—
Total profits	3,000.47	1,030.14

lar equipment—and threshed four years with it, again keeping records (see Table 3.3).

Austin failed to figure interest into his costs, but there was no question he had made good money in threshing. Others did, too. E. Dobson of Kenton, Manitoba, said that he made "[$]1,150 over all expenses" in 1910; J. N. Dibble of Marquis, Saskatchewan, reported earnings of $800 plus the cost of his machinery; W. G. McGill of Boissevain, Manitoba, retired in 1914, before he was thirty-five, rich from threshing— and all this was in western Canada, where rates ran low, and before the wartime boom.[63]

Systematic analysts of the threshing business cautioned that these were not typical cases. In 1909 Professor P. S. Rose, in a series of articles for *American Thresherman*, itemized all expenses and income for a hypothetical outfit in North Dakota. He figured an initial debt of $4,000 for the rig, to be paid over four years. During those four years, Rose said, the thresherman would pay off his rig, but the only money he would make would be the $6 per day he would pay himself as engineer. The rig would be good for another three years of work, however, and during that time he would make $990 per year—after which he would sell the rig for scrap at $150. Rose sketched threshing to aspirants as a promising business but not one in which to make a quick fortune. He urged them to keep careful books.[64]

Other students of threshing also continually urged threshermen to be more

businesslike. Threshermen were told to keep better books; to be firm in setting their rates; to be prompt and persistent about collecting from farmers; to compute their expenses more carefully; and, in general, to be better capitalists. Threshing was strictly a business, the commentators said, and if it did not pay out, it should be dropped.[65]

Regardless of whether threshermen were this hardheaded, a notable flaw in such analyses of the economics and business practices of threshermen was that they focused on only the threshing. Threshermen were threshermen only part of the year. The rest of the time they were farmers, plowmen, well drillers, and practitioners of all manner of crafts that not only occupied their time but also gave additional use to their machinery or at least to their power units. Threshermen often adopted businesslike rhetoric, and they developed pride in their common endeavor; but threshing was only part of their economic and personal life.

As guides for their efforts, threshermen favored commonsense principles more than cold figures. Ira W. Surritte, of Cummings, Kansas, offered advice on customer relations: "I say, give them all the same kind of job, charge them all the same price and be honest in your dealings and never make a promise that you can not fulfill."[66] As for business economics, they were simple, according to twenty-five-year veteran thresherman W. G. Garnett, of Marquette, Nebraska: "Any man who will pay $3,000 for a threshing rig, buy on time and pay seven per cent interest

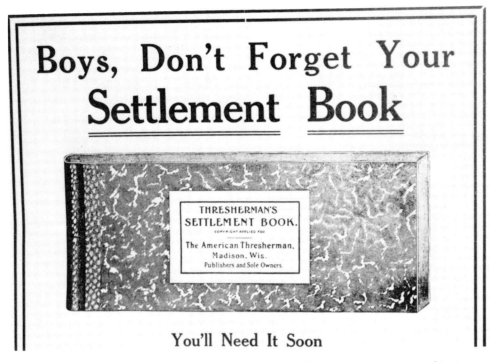

For businesslike operations, threshermen used settlement books. This advertisement appeared in American Thresherman. *(From* American Thresherman*)*

and then go out and cut prices has either got a soft place in his head or else he is a poor thresherman and doesn't stand well in his community."[67]

Many threshermen also found it difficult to be exacting with farmers and neighbors. "Each thresherman is a farmer first and a thresherman second," observed a North Dakota custom man, "so each man sees for himself from both points of view, consequently prices are satisfactory to all concerned. . . . I think it is unfair for threshermen to figure the investment in the power plant, also depreciation on same to the cost of threshing, as the power plant

should be used for other purposes also."[68] Other custom men set rates whereby they shared in the risks of farming: For example, some took every twelfth bushel as payment, and others took 10 percent of the price of wheat.[69]

Besides rates, there were other details in customer relations for the thresherman to work out. A perennial question was, Who was to be threshed out first? Within a ring of farmers, or among a collection of neighbors that constituted a run, there was a logical order based on convenience. The idea was to move deliberately from one job to the next adjoining so that as little time as possible was wasted in moving. This could not be done the same way every year, however, for then the same farmer would always be first and the same always last. So, as Ernest Claassen put it, "whoever was threshed first this year was last next year." There were exceptions to the best practices, however. The thresherman generally threshed his own grain first, of course. In a close neighborhood, he might also try to do a bit of work for each farmer before coming around for the remainder so that everyone could get started plowing early. Unfortunately, sometimes a large customer, or perhaps a relative, would try to pull rank within the order, and this caused hard feelings. After the run the thresherman used care and delicacy to avoid hard feelings in collection of accounts. He kept clear records of work done, recording it either in a simple notebook or in a form account book published and continually advertised by the threshing periodicals. Before he came collecting, he gave everyone time to sell a little wheat.[70]

The management abilities and personal accomplishments of threshermen varied, and threshermen were not averse to boasting about good runs. Bragging was circumstantial and seasonal, for the lengths and times of runs varied with the weather and with the machines available. Threshing continued until the job was done or until the weather destroyed the grain; a long rainy spell in the southern plains might make it sprout in the head, or the onset of winter in the northern plains might freeze it to worthlessness.

Some runs reported to *American*

Thresherman include E. C. Van Wald, Alberta, 1909—twenty-three days, 60,000 bushels ("Threshing was good although most of the wheat was frozen"); Lorne J. McRitchie, Zealandia, Saskatchewan, 1913—twelve days ("Threshing in this country has not been very good the last two years"); Garnet McDonald, Lewiston, Montana, 1907—eighty days, 90,000 bushels; F. J. Bignall, Sanborn, North Dakota, over several years to 1908—twenty to twenty-five days; R. C. Schroeder, Wagner, South Dakota, 1907—eighty-four days; George Pasco, Huerly, South Dakota, 1907—sixty-two and a half days; J. R. Huffman, Orman, South Dakota, over several years to 1914—thirty days; James Houfek, Malmo, Nebraska, 1913—fifty-five and a half days, 41,163 bushels of oats, 24,973 bushels of wheat, and dabs of other grains; Wildeman brothers, Phillipsburg, Kansas, 1916—fifty-three days, 57,000 bushels.[71]

In 1926 a thresherman gave a secondhand report of an old-timer who had shipped a ten-horsepower engine and a thirty-inch separator into Paul's Valley, Oklahoma Territory, and threshed 225,000 bushels in ninety days, but that may have been a windy story. Guy Bretz recalled that his father's outfit one year threshed 100,000 bushels of wheat, including 25,000 of his own. Experienced and conservative custom men discounted much of what they heard. "I notice some threshermen claim to thresh 5 months out of the year," noted one from Colorado, "but I think they are talking through their hats."[72]

This South Dakota outfit just completed a good run. (South Dakota State Historical Society, Pierre)

To thresh two thousand bushels of wheat per day was considered excellent threshing. This varied with the amount of straw to be run through, but, nevertheless, bragging rights ran much higher. Earl W. Hays of Tappen, North Dakota, claimed to have threshed four thousand bushels in twelve hours of shock threshing in 1915, making three sets during the day. The grains were barley and oats, however, not wheat; he had never threshed more than eighteen hundred bushels of wheat in a day. In 1908 F. J. Bignall said that his best day in North Dakota was fifteen hundred bushels of wheat. George Pasco of Huerly, South Dakota, summed up the veteran's attitude: "I don't believe in record-breaking runs.

Thresh steady, do good work, and you will win out." [73]

A strong plurality of threshermen were not so confident that they could succeed merely by attending strictly to personal business. "We have a threshing outfit, I am sorry to say," complained a North Dakotan in 1911. "Why? Because it is the very poorest business in which a man can engage to make money." [74] The initial cost of machinery was so high and its useful life so brief that as soon as one rig was paid for, it was time to buy another. In 1930 another North Dakotan put the blame for his business woes on farmers. "There is no money in threshing here, only lots of hard work and a man has to take lots of dirt," he said. "I don't mind the dirt that comes from the machine, but I do object to the way some farmers mistreat us. They think they have license to abuse a man, but things will change when the threshermen hold their heads up and feel they are as good as other human beings and charge a fair price for good work and have gumption enough to put the rig in the shed if they cannot get a living price." [75]

The greatest complaint of threshermen year after year, though, was excessive competition. "I did not make much money threshing this year with my three rigs," recounted a custom man in South Dakota after the 1908 season. "Grain was poor and prices were still worse and there were too many machines around here to make money at any price." [76] Competition was especially resented when it was not local: "This is a great community for having strangers come in and thresh," said a man from Rossville, Kansas, in 1917.[77] To custom men, "price cutter" became a hostile epithet. "I would like to see the subject continually discussed in your paper," wrote a Kansas custom man to *American Thresherman* in 1909, "as to how we shall exterminate the price cutter. He is a curse to his brother threshermen, himself and even the farmer." [78]

Many brother threshermen said patience and firmness could solve the problem. "The price cutter has never hurt me any," averred a South Dakotan in 1908. "I simply ignore his existence. I aim to do the square thing for the farmer and myself." [79] "A good outfit can claim the good jobs year in and

year out," agreed the Holland brothers of Liberal, Kansas. "By good jobs we mean the large ones and the ones that pay well. . . . This country is infested with 'tramp' machines [but] farmers are getting wise to the fact that they must patronize their home machines or have no end of trouble getting a machine when they really need one." [80]

Throughout the plains, threshermen rejected such conservative counsel and took direct action to uphold rates. They organized threshing brotherhoods, generally on a county (or, in Canada, municipality) level. These organizations had some social purposes, and members also were concerned about such local political questions as the maintenance of bridges; but their reason for existence was to hold the line on rates and, to a lesser degree, on wages. They were not secretive but rather openly avowed their purpose and presented a public image of solidarity.

"Everybody has an organization but the threshermen," declared one from Faxon, Oklahoma, in 1910. "Wake up, men, and look around and pull for the good of the trade, instead of knocking." [81] The threshing periodicals encouraged such organization, gave it an open forum, and published model bylaws for a local brotherhood.[82] Some brotherhoods adopted bylaws, whereas others just met informally, divided up territory, and set rates. At least one brotherhood had rate cards printed for all members to post on their separators. There was a certain irony in such farmer-threshermen organizations, as an editor in Stillwater, Oklahoma Territory, noted in 1898: "A good many of these threshers are populists and of course they would abhor the idea of going into a trust . . . but will go into an 'association' to get all for threshing that they possibly can."[83] In words often echoed by threshermen and farmers alike, the same editor found that however tight their organization, the power of the threshermen was not absolute: "Now the wheat growers have retaliated and threatened to get their own machines unless the rate is put at not over seven cents. These trusts don't always have their own way about business matters."[84] Exorbitantly priced threshermen found themselves displaced by others coming into the area or by farmer-organized rings.[85]

For greater effect in political matters at the state or provincial level and for the encouragement of social contact among threshermen, local organizations federated into regional and state or provincial brotherhoods. The Threshers Association of the Southwest, comprising threshermen mostly from Kansas but also from Oklahoma, was said to be the oldest threshers' association on a broad regional or state level. It was founded in 1901 and held annual meetings thereafter, generally in Wichita, occasionally in Hutchinson or another city. Attendance at meetings was good: 505 registered in 1909 (in which year one speaker estimated the number of threshermen in Kansas at 16,000), 850 in 1912. Several meetings were marred by dissension, such as accusations that machinery companies were attempting to sabotage the organization or the splintering of an orga-

nization into rival factions. Competitive organizations, formed for uncertain reasons, included at various times the Interstate Association of Threshermen (mainly Oklahomans), the Oklahoma Threshers Association (formed from the Interstate Association), and the Northwestern Kansas Brotherhood (including some Nebraskans). Annual meetings usually fell into a congenial routine, however, including entertainment, speeches by representatives of machinery companies and state agencies, greetings from the threshing periodicals, passing of resolutions, strolling through exhibits (Thresher Row, Machinery Row), and surreptitious drinking.[86]

Other state or regional brotherhoods in the plains included the Nebraska Brotherhood of Threshermen, the South Dakota Brotherhood of Threshermen, the Montana-Wyoming Brotherhood of Threshermen, the Saskatchewan Threshers' Association, the Canadian Threshermen's Association, and, no doubt, others not so well covered by the press. The activities of these groups were similar except for their responses to state legislation and for the South Dakotan brotherhood's plunge into the insurance business. All these state and regional associations were affiliated at various times with the National Brotherhood of Threshermen, which included representatives from the midwestern and Pacific northwestern states.[87]

When brotherhoods assembled, the leading legislative topic was the thresher's lien—a source of redress by which a thresherman could be ensured payment for his services. "Threshers' liens, as everyone knows, are indispensable to the thresherman where he has to extend credit for threshing mortgaged crops," observed the *American Thresherman* in 1924, following a discussion of the issue in Montana. "Without them he has no protection without going to law under a mechanic's lien."[88] At that time Montana had a threshing lien law but had amended its mortgage law to give crop mortgages priority over threshers' liens. Threshermen argued that threshers' liens had to precede all others; otherwise, who would thresh the grain to pay the others? Threshermen seldom resorted to liens to collect accounts, but they believed that because the lien laws were on the books, their use was unnecessary.

Threshing lien laws varied from state to state and from province to province, but the main difference was the one between the states as a group and the provinces as a group. That of Kansas was typical of the states. Passed in 1886 and amended in 1923, it provided that the thresher had a lien on the crop threshed to pay the threshing bill. To enforce such a lien, the thresher was to file it with the county register of deeds within fifteen days after completing the work. This lien had priority over any other encumbrance (at least in theory; in practice this was sometimes weakened by courts). For a farmer to dispose of grain in disregard of a thresher's lien was a misdemeanor.[89]

How such a lien law worked for a thresherman was described by a South Dakota custom man in 1922. R. P.

Bargmann threshed out a tenant farmer, then noticed that the fellow had left town; so he filed a lien. Next he found that the first farmer had sold the grain to a second, who not only declared he would not pay on the lien but also sold the grain to an elevator. Bargmann finally took a certified copy of the lien to the elevator operator, who paid it off without question.[90]

A custom man in Montana showed by his diary that use of the lien was a last resort. This fellow collected his bills casually but persistently throughout the year. He was flexible enough to take payment in the form of grain, half a hog, or credit at a farm sale. In 1932 a customer named Helfrich remained recalcitrant. The thresherman's diary recorded that on October 14 he drove into the town of Columbus and "seeing Helfrich . . . filed lien on Helfrich's grain."[91]

In the Canadian west, with its separate legal tradition and more on-farm storage of grain, provincial lien laws provided for the taking of grain by threshermen in a physical, not just a legal, sense. The law in Manitoba said that the thresher could "retain"—that is, physically seize—enough threshed grain to pay the bill. The law in Saskatchewan specifically said that the thresher could "take" grain—that is, go to the farmer's granary and haul it off. Perhaps Canadian threshermen needed this right, for, unlike Americans, they did not have the power to pursue future grain purchasers for payment. Although some Canadian custom men thought their laws were inadequate, one of them wrote in 1914 that "the thresherman in Canada does not have much trouble in collecting debts, being protected by a lien law, which allows him to seize enough grain to pay his bill."[92]

The second most important political concern was road and bridge law, insomuch as it affected the transportation of engines. Local authorities maintaining roads were reluctant to improve bridges so that they would support heavy engines. Instead they prevailed upon legislative bodies to pass planking laws requiring engineers to lay heavy boards across bridges before crossing. Kansas in 1911 was said to have "one of the most obnoxious bridge planking laws," but it was unclear whether the law was more severe or the threshers of Kansas were just noisier about it. The law provided that before crossing a bridge (except an earth-covered stone, brick, or concrete bridge) with an engine of five tons or more, the operator had to plank the bridge with boards three inches thick, one foot wide, and the length of the bridge. The intent of the law obviously was more to remove liability for breakthroughs from local authorities than to safeguard bridges. Threshermen often disregarded the law. They likewise ignored the law that on encountering an animal-drawn conveyance, the engineer was to bear off to the right one hundred yards, shut off the steam, and wait until the team was one hundred yards past. Threshermen probably benefited from the general movement for good roads and for progressive reform because they were suc-

cessful in state after state in obtaining better standards for bridge construction and inspection and better rights to use of roads. State engineers such as W. S. Gearhart of Kansas were on the threshermen's side. In 1911, although his speech was reported to have been "rather long and technical," the Threshermen's Association of the Southwest warmly received Gearhart's allegations that the bridge laws of Oklahoma, Kansas, and Nebraska had been written by grafters seeking to sell inferior "tin bridges."[93]

Several less controversial matters also claimed the attention of organized threshermen. Custom men had little quarrel with the noxious-weeds statutes of the various states and provinces, for instance. These laws required them to clean their machines to prevent the spread of weed seeds, and one, that of Saskatchewan, required posting the noxious-weed law on the separator. The Canadian provinces in general had more regulations applying to threshing operations—laws requiring the licensing of engineers, for instance, and for fire prevention. Threshermen usually were not liable for fires in the same manner as were railroads. A case in the Supreme Court of Nebraska in 1915 said that the thresherman must "exercise a degree of care and prudence commensurate with the danger to which farm property is exposed by him in the lawful conduct of his business"—he must not take unusual or unnecessary risks, in other words.[94]

Extensive and important as were the activities of plains threshermen, only a

Table 3.4. Threshing Records of Haselwood and Son, various years, 1917–1926
(in Canadian dollars)

Year	Accounts	Wheat		Oats		Barley		Receipts
		bu.	¢/bu.	bu.	¢/bu.	bu.	¢/bu.	
1917	10	639	4.0, 4.5	8,081	3.5	1,732	3.5	398.96
1919	8	1,957	7.0, 7.5, 8.0	5,477	4.0, 4.5	1,678	5.0, 5.5	455.52
1921	7	1,467	7.0	1,136	4.0	363	5.0	173.78
1926	6	3,636	6.5	1,602	4.0	522	5.0	326.49

few, in scattered points, left behind systematic documentation by which the business details of their operations might be reconstructed. One of these was the threshing firm of (Ernest W.) Haselwood and Son, Bittern Lake, Alberta. Their intermittent ledger entries, spanning the late 1910s to the mid-1920s, were those of a small-scale custom operation that depended on farmers to provide labor and teams. Their rates were moderate—just four to four and a half cents for wheat and three and a half for oats and barley until late in World War I (see Table 3.4). Their returns, too, were modest. Obviously, the Haselwoods were small-time farmers who owned a small rig perhaps just a portable gas engine—and picked up a little extra income threshing for six to ten neighbors; but they duly registered their rig with the provincial minister of agriculture.[95]

Malcolm Robson of Bawlf, Alberta, was a bit more entrepreneurial when he did custom work during the 1930s. Besides threshing and farming, he did road work with his tractor (not a steamer—it ran on distillate) and took stallions around on stud service. In threshing he relied on farmers to provide men and teams; but when they had finished his and their work, they threshed out other neighbors, too. Those who provided men and teams received either credit on their threshing bills or wages. Robson kept the records and saw that all settled up afterward (see Table 3.5). He was not meticulous about recording expenses, and when he did, they were only out-of-pocket expenses during harvest—mostly for fuel. This operation was a pure ring except that the engine was individually, not cooperatively, owned.[96]

An example of a pure ring arrangement was the Spruce Home (Saskatchewan) Threshing Syndicate. On September 13, 1921, six men—three more had been expected but had failed to show—met in the Hanna schoolhouse and organized this company. In good parliamentary order, they elected officers (president and secretary-treasurer); voted to buy a Rumely 16-30 oil-pull tractor and an Advance-Rumely 28-44 separator; and chose the name for the ring. The members of the Spruce Home Threshing Syndicate were M. Brandon, Olaf (Oly) Engebregtson, T. Larson, C. G. Nelson, W. H. Randall, and Eric Ueland.[97]

Table 3.5. Threshing Records of Malcolm Robson, 1930–1937 (in Canadian dollars)

Year	Workers	Accounts	Days	Bushels	Man & Team (per day)	Total Expenses
1930	6	7	28	19,533	1.80	—
1931	7	5	28	23,640	—	267.79
1932	—	—	—	—	1.80	72.41
1933	8	6	23	25,353	2.00	40.95
1934	7	5	22	24,516	—	—
1935	8	—	15	16,704	2.00	—
1936	8	4	11	10,722	—	—
1937	10	4	11	—	2.00	—

The membership remained intact until 1931, with the six stalwarts routinely taking care of their own threshing needs (see Table 3.6). They also threshed for nonmembers, who had to supply their own men and teams. The secretary-treasurer documented all their business with a double-entry ledger and a minutes book; members audited the ledger and approved the minutes. Nelson acted as separator man (except for a few years when perhaps he was ill) and Brandon as engineer, each receiving $7.50 a day for their services. The syndicate each year also established a pay rate for the services of a man and team (four to six such units were needed), with a lesser payment for a man without a team; set the rates to be charged for threshing the various grains (see Table 3.7); decided the order in which farms were to be threshed; borrowed the funds needed for operating expenses (see Table 3.8); balanced or paid the costs of threshing bills and labor; and covered all obligations, keeping only a small balance between threshing seasons.

The syndicate usually met twice a year to transact regular business and to deal with special situations. The members once got together to build a shed for the machinery and periodically thereafter to inspect or repair the machinery. On several occasions they sent

Table 3.6. Threshing Records of the Spruce Home Threshing Syndicate, 1921–1929 (in bushels)

Year	Accounts	Days	Wheat	Barley	Oats	Rye
1921	24	15	7,848	4,391	19,601	—
1922	24	15	9,279	2,685	6,542	210
1923	28	22	15,425	2,599	12,258	240
1924	15	6	3,445	125	2,134	—
1925	21	16	15,970	135	10,930	48
1926	17	14	11,091	105	6,784	100
1927	16	12	4,480	235	7,015	—
1928	7	5	5,585	118	2,038	—
1929	8	8	9,819	765	6,058	—

Table 3.7. Rates for the Spruce Home Threshing Syndicate, 1921–1930 (in Canadian dollars), per day, per bushel

Year	Rate for Threshing (per bushel)			Rate for Services (per day)			
	Wheat	Oats	Barley	Sep. Man	Engineer	Man & Team	Man
1921	.10	.08	.06	7.50	7.50	—	—
1922	.09	.08	.06	7.50	7.50	—	—
1923	.10	.08	.06	7.50	7.50	—	—
1924	.11	.09	.07	7.50	7.50	5.00	3.00
1925	.10	.08	.06	7.50	7.50	5.00	—
1926	.11	.08	.06	7.50	7.50	5.00	—
1927	.11	.08	.06	7.50	7.50	5.00	—
1928	.11	.08	.06	7.50	7.50	6.00	—
1929	.11	.08	.06	7.50	7.50	—	—
1930	.10	.08	.06	7.50	7.50	5.50	—

delegations to take grain from a non-member farmer who had failed to pay his threshing bill. Thus the Spruce Home Threshing Syndicate was a success. It paid for its rig in four years and ceased borrowing for operating expenses after five. (The interest entered on its ledger was interest on bank notes; interest paid the Rumely company was lumped with the principal payment.) It operated without evident dissension until 1929.

A meeting in July of that year marked the beginning of instability within the syndicate. The members voted to advertise the outfit for sale at $1,000 cash or $1,200 on time in a Prince Albert newspaper. No sale took place, but two years later the membership began to turn over after Randall and Brandon were bought out by the other four members. More changes ensued, and record keeping became sloppy, although the syndicate remained in operation at least until 1947.

During the same period Lowell Ay-ers was custom threshing near Oberlin, in northwestern Kansas, and keeping a journal of his work (in which he also recorded such miscellaneous information as the serial number of a shotgun he bought in 1930). By 1929 combines were doing most of the harvesting and threshing in western Kansas. Ayers's journal is the record of a remnant: He threshed for those who for some reason had not bought combines and who probably further deferred such purchase because of the onset of the Great Depression. He powered his threshing with an Avery 2550 tractor until 1936, when he bought an Oliver 2844. Farmers fed the crew, and the men slept in barns or on the ground. Rates varied according to whether Ayers or the farmer furnished the pitchers. For the smallest customers Ayers levied a flat set charge of three dollars (see Table 3.9). His records also highlighted the impact of drought during the mid-1930s; for several years, the amount threshed was minuscule. The large

Table 3.8. Income and Expenses of the Spruce Home Threshing Syndicate, 1921–1929 (in Canadian dollars)

	1921	1922	1923	1924	1925	1926	1927	1928	1929
Loans	650.00	747.92	1,128.30	2,385.62	1,000.00	—	—	—	—
Threshing	2,312.14	1,461.33	2,359.98	535.89	2,235.75	1,644.35	1,263.00	754.72	1,418.93
Other	—	383.67	56.36	39.62	74.76	38.25	14.77	59.41	79.38
Income	2,962.14	2,592.92	3,544.64	2,961.13	3,310.51	1,682.60	1,277.77	814.13	1,498.31
Machine	1,120.00	1,220.00	1,200.00	1,200.00	—	—	—	—	—
Notes	650.00	555.95	920.67	817.15	1,968.47	364.00	181.40	48.00	648.00
Fuel	299.19	330.51	326.33	97.37	302.53	282.40	254.03	134.24	184.96
Wages	427.50	348.37	770.50	311.25	805.49	875.24	775.00	465.00	621.00
Interest	24.70	131.03	260.18	368.47	173.13	—	—	—	—
Other	295.34	134.51	36.85	79.40	61.30	175.85	117.85	145.90	94.61
Expenses	2,816.73	2,720.37	3,514.53	2,873.64	3,310.92	1,697.49	1,328.28	793.14	1,548.57
Balance	145.41	17.96	10.51	87.49	87.08	72.19	21.68	42.67	2.41

46

Thieves See

gas tor $\frac{1}{8}$

Threshing 1937

		Bu	@	Total	
W	Alexander, Jess	550	6	33	00
W	Lake	498	6	29	88
B	Bob	450	4	18	00
O	Alexander, Glen	96	4	3	84
W	" "	640	6	38	40
W	E chart, Eldon	406	6	24	36
W	Pool	340	6	20	40
W	Hicks Lee	410	6	24	60
W	Gilquist, Willey	490	6	29	40
W	Seabough	565	6	33	90
W	Kist, Jack	604	6	36	24
W	Rails Harry	603			
	½ of 90 =	45	6	38	10
W	Beichel,	135	6	8	10
W	Shoe	475	6	28	50
	½ of 90 =	45	6	2	70
B	Butler,	274	4	10	96
W	"	135	6	8	10
W	"	787	6	47	22
	Total			6 6	28
O	Fifflerton, Hiram	84	4	3	36
W	" "	190	6	11	40
W	Brown, Bob	255	6	15	30

A page from the account book of thresherman Lowell Ayers records the type of grain (wheat, oats, or barley), the customer, the number of bushels, and the charges for 1937. (Courtesy of Lowell Ayers)

Table 3.9. Threshing Records of Lowell Ayers, 1929–1941 (in U.S. currency)

Year	Accounts	Bushels (all grains)	Rates (in cents)
1929	15	24,208	7.0, 9.0
1930	15	24,522	6.0, 7.0
1931	17	16,333	4.0, 5.0
1932	31	28,050	2.5, 3.0, 3.5, 4.0, 5.0
1933	30	10,057	3.0, 4.0, 5.0
1934	27	3,732	4.0, 5.0, 5.5, 6.0
1935	11	3,337	—
1936	17	13,335	4.0, 6.0, 8.0
1937	56	16,757	4.0, 6.0, 7.0, 9.0
1938	29	26,344	—
1939	26	6,970	5.0, 6.0, 7.0
1940	34	16,537	—
1941	27	—	4.0, 5.0

number of accounts in 1937 (56) also may have been a function of drought. Perhaps instead of combining, farmers stacked loose heads from a short crop and had Ayers thresh the stacks. On the other hand, perhaps he temporarily took over someone else's run.[98]

Most of the surviving business records of threshing operations documented outfits atypical of the heart of the plains, where large custom outfits predominated. The outfits of Haselwood and Son, Robson, and the Spruce Home Threshing Syndicate were in the parklands of western Canada, peripheral to the true plains. Ayers's surviving ledger documented only his operations well past the heyday of custom threshing. Fortunately, a body of records documenting one substantial threshing operation on the central plains during the era of custom threshing did survive: the account books of thresherman C. R. Voth, which were preserved by

his son, Moses H. Voth of North Newton, Kansas. The records document the years from 1902 through 1930, during each of which Voth had up to four rigs in the field. During the latter part of this period, Moses Voth was in charge of one of the rigs. The records are not complete—books for some rigs have been lost—but enough remain to give a good picture of a major threshing operation. Each account book documents the transactions of one rig during one year.[99]

The threshing culture associated with C. R. Voth's operation was a technological overlay on German-Russian Mennonite agricultural society in central Kansas. Voth's family was among the Alexanderwohl colonists; he himself had been born in the Crimea, and his antecedents occasionally showed in his account books through entries such as "Juli" instead of "July." The names of the customers listed in the books were also of obvious German-Russian Mennonite derivation, but the account books themselves were a symbol of the mechanization penetrating their culture. Most of them were forms published by *American Thresherman;* some came from machinery companies such as Reeves, probably as gifts from the dealership; and one came from the Sterling Refining Company of Cleveland, Ohio, "manufacturers of high grade lubricating oils, greases, belt dressings, boiler compounds, paints, etc." The operations documented in the books were those of Geiser Peerless steam engines (eventually succeeded by

C. R. Voth (left), the thresherman, ca. 1910. (Courtesy of Moses Voth)

Steam outfit and crew of pitchers for C. R. Voth, ca. 1910. (Courtesy of Moses Voth)

In his account books, Voth kept a record of the days his crewmen worked. (Courtesy of Moses Voth)

Rumely oil-pull engines) powering a variety of separators—Reeves, Peerless, Frick, Avery, Minneapolis, Rumely, Case—mostly of the thirty-six-inch size.

Into this cultural-technological pattern, C. R. Voth early inducted his son, as Moses later recalled. One day he was playing in the yard of the farm where the family lived in traditional fashion with the grandparents, near Goessel, Kansas. His father said to him, "This is it now. You're coming out to the shop and help." Moses was seven or eight years old then, but thereafter he was a part of the threshing business.

The organization of threshing among the farmers in this locality took on a peculiar arrangement. Although headers had been used in the nineteenth century, by the early twentieth century the winter wheat in the area was all bundled. To do their threshing, the Mennonite farmers organized themselves into "shock gangs"—groups of about six farmers who collectively

had some twelve hundred acres of grain to thresh out. The farmers within a shock gang banded together to provide men, teams, and racks for shock threshing and to negotiate with the thresherman, C. R. Voth. Voth usually assigned three shock gangs to be threshed out in succession by one threshing rig. "I still remember them keeping Dad up until three o'clock in the morning, trying to argue out which one would be first," recalled Moses Voth.

When it came time for threshing, the shock gang had to provide six men with teams and racks to haul bundles to the separator. Voth provided the threshing machinery, the separator man, the engineer, the water man, four field pitchers, and one hired boss to oversee the entire outfit. Farmers who were not a part of any shock gang had to stack their bundles and wait for the outfit to finish with the shock gangs. Voth would then take on their work,

Table 3.10. Threshing Records of Outfits Owned by C. R. Voth, various years, 1902–1930 (in U.S. dollars)

Year & Outfit	Accounts	Wheat bu.	Wheat ¢/bu.	Oats bu.	Oats ¢/bu.	Receipts
1902A	43	21,862	6.0	28,700	3.0	2,491.72
B	50	31,472	6.0	28,596	3.0	2,777.81
1903A	47	31,211	6.5	9,996	3.5	2,533.20
B	42	27,065	6.5	10,430	3.5	2,252.44
1905A	38	35,643	6.5	11,789	3.5	2,809.62
B	48	41,037	6.5	16,077	3.5	3,230.11
1908	53	56,609	6.25	531	3.0	3,576.97
1909A	50	55,760	7.0	20,124	3.5	4,665.68
B	48	60,062	7.0	20,964	3.5	4,922.68
1910A	29	697	6.0	30,761	3.5	1,129.09
B	43	363	6.0	59,060	3.5	2,077.10
1911	44	57,072	6.0, 6.75	12,261	3.5	4,114.85
1912A	50	42,794	6.0, 7.0	28,606	3.0, 3.5	3,861.61
B	49	43,822	6.0, 7.0	34,585	3.0	3,994.74
1913A	44	38,666	7.5, 7.25	8,868	3.5	3,125.61
B	35	25,205	7.5	8,151	3.5	2,852.76
1914A	40	56,753	6.5, 6.0	19,642	3.0, 3.25	4,040.62
B	50	72,111	6.0, 6.5, 7.0	22,430	3.0, 3.25, 6.0	5,215.42
C	35	57,917	6.0, 6.5, 7.25, 7.5	15,716	3.0, 3.25, 3.62	4,199.85
1915A	28	28,075	7.0	10,228	3.5	2,455.70
B	34	26,485	7.0	14,452	3.5	2,338.51
C	47	30,281	7.0	15,412	3.5	2,702.02
1916A	28	21,437	7.0	14,405	3.5	1,834.32
B	25	17,933	7.0	12,658	3.5	1,697.21
C	34	27,332	7.0	15,585	3.5	3,942.96
1917A	34	24,051	8.5	26,414	4.5	3,207.76
B	26	26,891	8.5	15,555	4.25	2,946.82
C	27	22,041	8.5	24,141	4.5	2,988.09
1918A	28	26,417	12.0	15,223	6.0	4,053.66
B	42	39,009	12.0	20,572	6.0	5,960.98
C	42	48,365	12.0	19,338	6.0	7,294.85
D	30	36,368	12.0, 16.0	16,020	6.0, 8.0	5,553.33
1919A	49	31,338	16.0	10,055	8.0	5,856.52
B	48	32,945	16.0	13,412	8.0	6,344.16
1920A	21	16,839	16.0	13,795	8.0	3,797.84
B	38	27,146	16.0	26,838	8.0	6,490.40
C	42	31,110	16.0	27,180	8.0	7,152.00
1921A	33	33,291	10.0	9,748	5.0	3,816.50
B	34	39,822	10.0	12,318	5.0	4,598.10
1922A	27	42,301	8.0, 9.0, 10.0	4,444	4.0, 4.5, 5.0	4,100.85
B	23	46,140	9.0, 10.0, 12.0	2,510	4.5, 5.0, 6.0	4,414.67
C	34	41,825	9.0, 10.0	7,063	4.5, 5.0	4,388.22
1923A	27	18,919	10.0, 12.0	11,554	5.0, 6.0	2,707.73
B	34	18,412	12.0	12,767	6.0	2,975.46
C	30	20,436	10.0, 12.0	13,800	5.0, 6.0	3,016.59
1924A	58	62,690	8.0, 9.0, 10.0	26,062	4.0, 5.0, 8.0	6,843.10
B	35	32,313	8.0, 9.0	12,966	4.0, 5.0	3,566.11
1925A	36	36,591	8.0	15,865	4.0	3,459.58
B	35	26,058	8.0	10,801	4.0	2,563.72
C	30	38,346	9.0	12,975	4.5	3,044.23

Table 3.10, *continued*

Year & Outfit	Accounts	Wheat		Oats		Receipts
		bu.	¢/bu.	bu.	¢/bu.	
1926A	34	41,179	10.0	12,888	5.0	4,762.30
B	26	35,839	10.0	5,982	5.0	3,883.00
C	42	57,704	8.0	13,093	4.0	5,140.04
1927	—	32,368	10.0	5,482	5.0	3,510.90
1928A	28	23,193	8.0, 10.0	9,762	5.0	2,807.40
1928B	27	31,022	6.0, 8.0, 10.0	9,279	3.0, 4.0, 5.0	2,610.39
1929	30	29,129	10.0	15,522	5.0	3,466.01
1930	22	25,115	7.0, 9.0	11,779	3.5, 4.5	4,136.37

threshing from the stack. Such arrangements provided Voth with a fifty- to sixty-day run for each outfit.

The rates charged by Voth (see Table 3.10) reflected both general trends evident throughout the plains and local conditions and customs. The only two grains threshed in quantity by Voth were wheat and oats, and the rate for wheat was about twice that for oats. (The threshing of small amounts of barley, rye, kaffir, and other grains never contributed significantly to Voth's income.) As was the case throughout the plains, the years from the turn of the century through 1916 were a time of overall stability in threshing rates. The rate for wheat ranged from six cents to seven and a half cents per bushel; the rate for oats ranged from three cents to three and five-eighths cents per bushel. An upswing in these rates came with American entry into World War I, or, as the local people called it, the Kaiser's War. Rates rose incrementally in the next few years, until by 1920 the going rate was sixteen cents for wheat and eight cents for oats. Rates plummeted in 1921, how-

ever, and remained at lower levels throughout the succeeding decade.

During this time, too, competition became more intense as gasoline tractors as well as combines proliferated in the area. In addition to the cents-per-bushel figure, there were other arrangements reflecting the new competitiveness. The account books registered that certain large customers received a 5 percent discount for paying cash within thirty days. Voth also competed with other threshermen by adjusting the weight used as the basis for calculating the bushels threshed. Sixty pounds per bushel had been the standard weight, but if the number of pounds considered to constitute a bushel was increased, then the threshing rate would be effectively reduced. The account books intermittently recorded a gradual rise in the number of pounds figured for a bushel: The basis for wheat rose to sixty-two pounds, then sixty-five, then sixty-seven, and finally, for some customers, seventy pounds; that for oats rose to thirty-six pounds, then forty.

The provision of fuel and meals

A threshing statement for Peter P. Unruh, 1902, took account of expenses for coal and meals. (Courtesy of Moses Voth)

pay the cash expense for fuel consumed on his place, but when his threshing bill was figured, the coal expense was deducted. Thus, under these arrangements, the figures on the threshing bill of one customer, H. R. Schmidt, in 1902 were:

Wheat 691 bu. × 6¢/bu. =	$41.46
Oats 990 bu. × 3¢/bu. =	29.70
Total charges for threshing	71.16
Less payments for coal	10.79
Less cost of meals	11.50
Cash due	$48.87

What Voth accomplished by these arrangements was a reduction of his capital outlay during the threshing season, in effect obtaining an advance on threshing charges to meet operational expenses. Voth bought his first Rumely oil-pull engine in 1914 and had converted entirely to Rumely oil-pulls by 1916; thereafter he furnished his own fuel.

Records of bushels threshed and receipts for threshing showed a combination of long-term trends and short-term volatility. Overall, the years up until World War I showed steady, probably prosperous operations for Voth. The year 1910 must have been one of wheat crop failure: Winter kill, disease, or some sort of infestation reduced the amount of wheat threshed to insignificance. Whatever afflicted the wheat must have been evident early in the spring, however, for the amount of oats threshed indicated that farmers compensated for the loss of the wheat by

were matters closely related to rates in the economics of threshing. As Moses Voth recalled the arrangements, it was the obligation of the farmers to board not only the shock gang but also the full crew of the threshing outfit. The women of the farms composing the shock gang gathered at the home of the farm being threshed to provide meals for the group. The men received breakfast, morning lunch, dinner, afternoon lunch, and supper.

According to the account books, however, the arrangements for the earliest years of the twentieth century must have been somewhat different. Evidently, the farmers at that time were expected to board the crew, but the expense of such boarding could be translated into credit on the threshing bill, which meant that in fact the threshermen was boarding the crew. A similar arrangement applied to the provision of coal. The farmer was expected to

Lunch for a South Dakota crew is taken to the field, ca. 1920. Tillage has already commenced around the stacks. (South Dakota State Historical Society, Pierre)

seeding additional spring oats. The lower rate for threshing oats only partially eased the loss of revenue to Voth. The years of high threshing rates were generally profitable for Voth, although the wheat crops during this time were not outstanding. Through the 1920s, a period of lower rates, good crops kept Voth's revenue up; but toward the end of the decade the bushels of wheat threshed were tailing off. This no doubt was due to the advent of gasoline tractors and combines. That Voth in the late 1920s was still threshing significant amounts of oats showed that he was threshing for those farmers who were still relying heavily on horsepower, a dwindling minority by this time.

Although C. R. Voth kept records of

hands employed on his crew in the back of his threshing account books, his surviving records are obscure and intermittent. They are sufficient, however, to show that he relied little on transient labor. Most of the names of crewmen are immediately recognizable as German, and many are surely German Mennonite—Schmidt, Wedel, Woelk, Hiebert, Unruh, Schultz, Lehman, Wiebe. Voth obviously hired local men and boys to fill out his crew.

According to Moses Voth, not all the Germans hired were Mennonites. He particularly remembered that for several years the Voths employed German-Russian Lutherans, Volga Deutsch from the nearby community of Lehigh. These fellows made it a rite of young manhood to work as bundle pitchers, and their habitual employment with the Voth outfits gave them not just an economic but also an emotional commitment to this operation. "They not only worked for their own interests," said Moses Voth, "they also worked for my dad's interests. They wanted to see that he was successful." They recruited hands among their own people for the Voth operation and hired out to Voth as a group; when one of their number failed to measure up, they expelled him from the crew without Voth's having to fire him. Voth had an American flag that he used as a symbol of competition among his several outfits. The outfit that threshed the most bushels on any particular day had the flag run up over it the next, and the several crews competed for the honor.

"These were real husky men," said Moses Voth of the Lehigh boys, and they were the best hands he could remember. On beginning a threshing run, each of the Lehigh men selected a pitchfork from among those provided by the Voths. The Voths bought four-tined forks rather than the three-tined ones commonly used for bundle pitching elsewhere. The pitchers from Lehigh seized the tines of these broader forks and spread them with their hands still further. They then paired off to begin filling racks in the field.

As a rack pulled up to a shock, two Lehigh men would approach the shock from opposite directions and spear it together with their splayed forks. They would then attempt to throw the entire shock into the rack at once, usually dropping a bundle or two but quickly tossing these up into the rack also. The man in the rack trying to arrange the bundles for the ride to the threshing set frequently was overwhelmed by these whole shocks thrown in upon him, which was quite a joke to the Lehigh boys. They thus loaded the rack quickly and sent it back toward the set. While they waited for more racks to come to the field, each man speared a bundle with his fork, sat against a shock, and held the bundle overhead to shade him from the sun.

The Voth threshing operation and its Lehigh hands became locally notorious. Someone in the neighborhood made up a long poem about C. R. Voth, the thresherman, although Moses Voth could not recall the words. The coming and going of the Lehigh boys also was of note in the community. There was an old book peddler who made the Voth farm the headquarters for his calls in the area and kept a few horses there. Because it was a Mennonite area, C. R. Voth generally did not thresh on Sunday, and so the Lehigh boys went home for the day. For transportation they took the book peddler's horses out of the pasture and hitched them to a spring wagon. They would drive back to Voth's on Sunday evening, after having evidently spent the day in good German fashion, for as they rode, they boisterously sang old folk songs. Sober Mennonites and their families came onto their driveways to watch them pass and to hear their songs.

The Lehigh boys sang traditional songs from the Old Country even though they worked in the mechanized

Threshing near Belpre, Kans., ca. 1910, was late enough that weeds were growing up in the stubble. (Santa Fe Trail Center, Larned, Kans.)

agricultural world of twentieth-century Kansas. They were a part of that web of ways, that grand system that grew up within a generation and annually accomplished the threshing of small grains, that became the stock in trade of traveling photographers. Steam whistles, aspiring entrepreneurs, stolid workers, hearty meals—this collection of images and sounds may seem too idyllic, but they are there, not only in the photographs but also in the recollections, the ledgers, and other documents. Also present, of course, are the evidences of bone-wearying and dirty work, of bosses and customers and comrades who did not always deal honorably, and of countless unfortunate personal experiences—but the theme of common endeavor, and even of romance, is much stronger. The severity

of life with a threshing outfit was not so great or the rewards so slight as to discourage the development of a threshing culture on the plains, even where wage labor was a part of the system. Within this culture, traditional expectations and common knowledge governed behavior. Its members were moved by the spectacle of wheat-raising on the plains, by the wonders of steam technology, by a consciousness of their place in the geography of the region and in the economic order, by personal obligation to fellow laborers, and by the satisfaction of hard work done—bundles and spikes disintegrating, grain pouring from the spout, straw stacks looming. This lost culture of the plains deserves fuller explication than the mute language of albumen prints.

CHAPTER FOUR.
HANDS

No one ever accused Carey McWilliams of looking at the world through rose-colored glasses. His book, *Ill Fares the Land: Migrants and Migratory Labor in the United States,* was a bitter indictment of a nation that callously exploited its small farmers and migrant agricultural laborers. Surely much of the sensation that the book provoked derived from public familiarity with John Steinbeck's novel *The Grapes of Wrath,* a connection that McWilliams consciously utilized. But his indictment was not limited to the type of people or geographical area represented by Steinbeck's Joad family. He chronicled oppression from coast to coast.

That was exactly what made Chapter 5 of *Ill Fares the Land,* "Blackbirds and Scissorbills," so peculiar. This chapter dealt with migrant agricultural labor—"bundlestiffs" or "bindlestiffs," as the workers were called—in the small-grain region of the Great Plains. Here McWilliams found a pattern of agricultural labor that was an exception to the overall picture on the continent. "The wheat migrant was not despised," he observed. "His services were eagerly sought after and his working conditions were tolerable." Unfortunately, this relatively benevolent system of agricultural labor broke down at about the time of World War I, and McWilliams mourned its passing. The decline of opportunities for work in the small-grain harvest on the Great Plains contributed to the worsening picture that he drew for farmers and laborers in the mid-twentieth century.[1]

During the early years of the twentieth century, there evolved a system of harvest labor that not only met the needs of small-grain farmers on the North American plains but also offered desirable opportunities to farmers and working folk from other regions of the continent. This system of labor was well adapted to the agriculture of the plains in terms of both their geographic conditions and the technology of the time. Transient labor within this system was not an evil; it was an answer. Only after certain special interests intervened to define transient labor as a problem did it become so, thereby disrupting the system irreparably. Thus ended a remarkable encounter between bindlestiffs and the North American plains, a meeting of migratory laborers with the region, its agriculture, and its people.

Several circumstances made migratory labor in the wheat belt a more complicated proposition than migratory labor in most other agricultural regions. The first was that harvest labor was not purely harvest labor: It was harvest and threshing labor. These two related but distinct processes brought laborers into contact with two related but distinct sets of employers—farmers and threshermen. A second circumstance was that small-grain harvest labor was both seasonal and geographically progressive. The harvest in any one locality of the plains lasted only a couple of weeks, with threshing stretching from a few weeks to several months; the harvest for the plains overall, however, in a progression from Texas to Alberta, lasted from May to October. The possibilities for movement and employment of laborers within the wheat belt were prodigious and complex. To many observers in the early twentieth century—a time when progressive reformers (using this term more in the American than in the Canadian sense) advocated the rationalization and systematization of both society and the economy—the situation seemed to demand the intervention of managers. These managers, especially representatives of government employment agencies, constituted the third special circumstance shaping the development of harvest labor on the plains. The fourth circumstance was that during the harvest transient labor entered into a judicious mix with resident labor. Unlike in other agricultural regions where farmers represented purely capitalistic interests and contractors delivered outside labor to them, capitalists on the plains—both farmers and threshermen—worked alongside their employees. Transient workers not only mixed with their employers, they also mixed with local resident laborers. Indeed, as the Voth operations (see Chapter 3) showed, local employees might predominate.

Just as railroads had been the key to the agricultural settlement of the North American plains, so also they were the key to the transportation of transient labor into the wheat country for harvest. Until the advent of the automobile in the 1920s, railroads were the arteries for harvest labor. Nowhere did the arteries surge with such a heavy pulse as they did in Canada, where railroad companies were the architects of a system for the recruitment and transportation of harvest labor. This was directly in the interest of the railroads, inasmuch as labor shortages resulted in losses of grain and traffic. Moreover, at the close of the nineteenth century and the beginning of the twentieth, the railroads were engaged in campaigns to recruit settlers for western Canada, the "Last Best

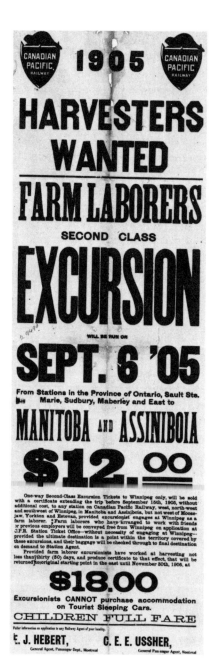

The Canadian Pacific Railway advertised for harvesters to go to the Canadian
west. (Public Archives of Canada, Ottawa, Ontario)

West." Railroad officials hoped that many who came west for the harvest might either stay or return, after having seen the region, to settle down. Added to this was Canada's harvest labor situation—it differed from that of the United States in at least one respect: Whereas the harvest within the United States was a protracted affair stretching from Texas to Montana and North Dakota, the harvest within Canada, although not simultaneous everywhere, did take place in three prairie provinces of the same latitude and therefore was of relatively short but intense duration.

So during the 1890s the railroads of western Canada initiated efforts to recruit and transport harvest labor into the western provinces, mainly from eastern Canada. The Canadian Pacific Railroad began in a small way in 1890 by offering a few seats on its homeseeker excursion cars (used to recruit prospective settlers) to men who wished to make the harvest from eastern Canada to Manitoba. Within a few years, at least by 1896, the Canadian Pacific was setting aside excursion trains specifically for harvesters, and other railroads—the Soo Line, Canadian Northern, Grand Trunk Pacific, and Canadian National—ultimately adopted similar systems.[2]

The most concrete aid given to harvest excursionists by the railroads was reduced rates for excursion tickets. This arrangement allowed the harvester to travel from a point in eastern Canada to a destination in the wheat belt and back at a much reduced rate, commonly less than one-half the regular passenger rate. During the 1890s the fare in some years was as low as ten dollars, but in both the first year of the harvest excursions (1891) and during several years in the 1920s, the rate was as high as fifteen dollars. Tickets on such excursions until 1912 were good to some designated western point beyond which little labor was expected to be needed, or to any point in the wheat belt short of there. After 1912 a harvest excursionist's ticket was good only to Winnipeg; then the harvester had to decide where he wished to go farther west and buy a ticket at one-half cent per mile for that destination. Early excursionists, upon making the trip west, received certificates from the railroads that had to be signed by farmers testifying that the excursionists had indeed worked in the harvest. The excursionists could then buy the second half of their tickets back east. Later, special harvest excursion ticket stubs signed by farmers performed the same function. The railroads continued practices along these lines through 1929, when the advent first of depression and then of prolonged drought reduced demand by farmers for outside labor. During and immediately after World War II, the railroads again offered excursion fares subsidized by federal and provincial governments. By this time, however, the advent of the combined harvester made the revival of harvesting excursions merely a brief anachronism.[3]

The organization of harvest excursions required that parties at the western end generate some estimate of the number of men that would be re-

As this advertisement shows, the Canadian Pacific Railway continued harvest excursions to western Canada through the 1920s. (Glenbow Archives)

quired. At first railroad station agents in the west canvassed farmers and made estimates of local needs. This was unreliable, however, so territorial or provincial departments of agriculture soon intervened to provide information to the railroads. Already in 1901 the Department of Agriculture of the Northwest Territories noted that there had been considerable confusion about the number of men required for harvest that year and suggested that the department, which was developing its statistical functions, should supply estimates. Territorial and provincial departments did so thereafter. The departments annually surveyed local governmental officials on the number of men that would be required, the railway stations where they ought to be delivered, and the date when the harvest was expected to begin. This information was provided by departments of agriculture until the individual provinces created bureaus of labor that took over such functions; Saskatchewan did this in 1911, Manitoba in 1915, and Alberta in 1919. Even after the creation of such bureaus, the respective departments of agriculture remained active in assisting the bureaus of labor in estimating harvest labor needs.[4]

In 1920 the Canadian federal government began coordinating estimates of harvest labor requirements through the provinces and imposed a more theoretical structure on the process. It gathered data on crop acreage and growing conditions, which served as a basis for estimates of labor needs. It next considered what labor was available locally and also figured in a small number of casual laborers who were expected to show up unbidden, riding the rails. The employment service then had an estimate of the laborers required, which it passed along to the railroads in meetings. Such was the procedure from 1920 to 1929.[5]

However reliable or haphazard the methods of estimating harvest labor, someone had to recruit the laborers

Table 4.1. Number of Harvest Excursionists in Western Canada, 1890–1919

Year	Number	Year	Number
1890	292	1910	14,387
1891	3,000	1911	33,115
1892	2,000	1912	26,500
1893	1,489	1913	18,120
1894	1,555	1914	11,501
1895	5,000	1915	29,253
1896	2,350	1916	35,334
1897	6,000	1917	42,690
1898	4,520	1918	9,384
1899	11,004	1919	6,452
1900	2,175	1920	28,228
1901	18,375	1921	32,426
1902	13,000	1922	39,740
1903	18,000	1923	50,451
1904	14,000	1924	26,483
1905	16,858	1925	54,850
1906	23,657	1926	34,202
1907	21,000	1927	32,250
1908	27,500	1928	52,225
1909	23,000	1929	3,592

and see that they boarded excursions for the wheat belt. This was initially handled by the railroad companies, operating largely through their immigration agents, who issued public statements and posters advertising the need for laborers and the excursion fares available. If necessary, western provincial officials such as W. R. Motherwell of Saskatchewan could be counted upon to issue appeals to workers to come west. Once the federal government got involved in harvest labor in 1920, its employment offices also assisted in recruiting harvest excursionists.[6] Laborers by the scores of thousands took to the prairies as harvest excursionists (see Table 4.1). From meager beginnings in the early 1890s, the number of working men crept upward throughout most of the first few decades of the twentieth century. Poor

Canadian railroads and public authorities solicited harvest laborers from the United States for only a few years. The Soo Line placed this advertisement in 1911. (Public Archives of Canada, Ottawa, Ontario)

crops in certain years curtailed the movement, but harvest labor shortages during the early years of the Great War augmented it. After a wartime and postwar disruption in 1918 and 1919, the number of men involved climbed above fifty thousand during the mid-1920s, dwindling finally in 1929, after which the excursions ceased.[7]

As for the regional and social origins of the hands, the records left by participants were impressionistic, not comprehensive. It was clear that the majority came from Ontario, Quebec, and the Maritime Provinces, with the proportion probably in that order. They were a mixture of small or young farmers seeking seasonal employment to supplement income at home and in-

dustrial laborers without firm ties back east. The farm men making the excursions were partially inspired by the desire to look over prospects for resettlement in the west. Joining the eastern Canadians on the excursions were substantial numbers of European immigrants. Many of these were also exploring opportunities for homesteads in the west, but harvest wages were attractive to them whether they sought to acquire farms or planned to return east. Sporadically, the Canadian railroads sought to fill excursions with workers from Britain, the United States, and British Columbia. With the exception of British Columbia, which supplied significant numbers of bindlestiffs through the 1920s, these other sources were not of long-term consequence to the general movement. British excursionists as organized groups were a feature during only three harvests. American excursionists were organized for only five harvests and never numbered more than five thousand a year.[8]

To many observers the origins of harvest hands who worked on the American side of the border seemed even more obscure than those on the Canadian side. A correspondent in Dakota Territory in 1887, although he described the men as "Americans, Scandinavians, and Irishmen," was befuddled about their more immediate origins, which were "unknown to man."[9] A later writer in Kansas City called the movements of harvest hands "as mysterious to the people hereabouts as the migration of the birds," and still another reporter surrendered, "They come from nowhere, cut the grain, then vanish mysteriously."[10]

Still, many other contemporaries were more willing and able to describe and categorize the American bindlestiffs. These observers' first impression was diversity: They came from "every class," a writer in 1902 noted, including tramps, clerks wanting outdoor exercise, and businessmen and college students seeking novelty. The same writer was more to the point when he spoke of "the majority who are hard workers from the cities and farming sections not demanding their prowess."[11] As later analysts would make clear, the dilettantes were but decorations in a movement composed largely of men from the industrial and agricultural working classes.

The Kansas State Board of Agriculture began classifying these individuals in 1920. A professor of farm management from Kansas Agricultural College, E. L. Rhoades, informed the board that although hands came to Kansas from every state in the union, they fell into certain regional and occupational categories. The first "class of help" was composed of farmers and farmhands from eastern Kansas, southern Missouri, and Arkansas, who "are generally considered the best help." The second class consisted of "itinerant laborers," who were "intelligent, widely travelled," and gave "an honest day's work for their pay." These were genuine migrant laborers, not farmers making a brief working tour of the harvest fields. A third class comprised urban laborers taking a "vacation" to work briefly in the harvest; many had done this regularly for a period of years. Fourth were "homesteaders from Colorado" who made the harvest to raise a bit of hard cash while trying to prove up their claims. The fifth group was "a sprinkling of 'drifters' with no definite program and little ambition"—tramps, in other words, who had "given the 'harvest hand' a much worse reputation than the average one deserves." Finally, the smallest class consisted of college students, whom the professor would not even have mentioned "were it not for the popular impression that there are great numbers of them," which, he insisted, there were not. Farmers, he conceded, did consider the students "willing workers" and "able to learn quickly."[12]

Rhoades's categorization was astute,

but shortly afterward the work of another scholar authoritatively expanded and refined the profile of the bindlestiff. This scholar was Don D. Lescohier, a former superintendent of the Public Employment Office in Minneapolis, who during 1920 and 1921 collaborated with the United States Department of Agriculture and received the cooperation of employment offices of the United States Department of Labor to conduct a massive study of the harvest labor question in the wheat belt. Lescohier not only gathered copious data but also presented it well—in a popular vein with two fascinating articles for *The Survey* magazine, and in scholarly fashion through three magisterial bulletins of the United States Department of Agriculture.[13] Lescohier and a corps of assistants from the department visited more than 1,300 farms of all sizes and 115 threshing crews, collecting the personal experiences of 3,600 hands. These interviews were done in depth and were supplemented with information taken from other parties involved in the harvest—county agricultural agents, employment service officials, chambers of commerce, businesspeople, and, of course, farmers. In addition, Lescohier obtained basic information on some 29,000 hands through offices of the United States Employment Service. In 1921 he returned to the field to collect additional information on other harvest hands along more specialized lines.

Lescohier, although he was most interested in laborers who traveled with the harvest, recognized that a mixture of resident and transient labor made

Table 4.2. Labor Employed in Wheat Harvest, 1921 (in percentages)

State	Family Labor	Hands Hired by Month or Year	Hands Hired by Day
Oklahoma	32.4	3.4	64.2
Kansas	39.8	5.5	54.7
Nebraska	62.0	17.2	20.8
South Dakota	40.9	21.6	37.6
North Dakota	35.2	24.2	40.6
Minnesota	47.4	13.0	39.6
Total	40.6	15.0	44.4

Source: Adapted from Don D. Lescohier, *Conditions Affecting the Demand for Harvest Labor in the Wheat Belt*, U.S. Department of Agriculture Bulletin 1230 (Washington, D.C.: GPO, 1924), p. 17.

up the harvest labor force each year. Through extensive survey work in selected counties of six states in 1921, he determined that family farm labor contributed more than 40 percent of the effort in accomplishing the harvest (see Table 4.2). An additional 15 percent of the work was done by hands hired by the month or by the year. Transient laborers stepped in to do 44.4 percent of the work. The proportions varied from state to state and area to area, but Lescohier concluded that "on the average, for each field hand resident in the wheat farms when the harvest begins, whether a member of the farmer's family or a man hired by the year or month, approximately one extra hand [transient] had to be hired."[14]

It was surprising to find that transient labor played a smaller part than resident labor in the harvest, and Lescohier attempted to explain. He found that generally the smaller farms were the ones that got along without hiring much transient labor; of those that did not use transients at all, most had fewer than three hundred twenty acres. Moreover, small farmers who harvested with binders rather than headers were those most likely to get by without any transient labor. This was because binders commenced cutting earlier than headers, making a longer harvest season possible. When money was tight, the farmer was even more inclined to cut down on hiring shockers. The binder driver might first bind a patch, then go back and shock it. Or the farmer might hire just one shocker to follow two binders, or two shockers to follow three binders. He had to leave bundles lying on the stubble for a while; but if the weather cooperated, he got by. With headers it was more difficult to do away with hiring transient labor; a few farmers could manage it, however, either because they had large enough families or because they traded work with neighbors.[15]

How many bindlestiffs did work the harvest, then? The number, Lescohier admitted, "never has been and probably never can be counted."[16] It was, however, "not nearly as many as most people think." Publications from the Kansas Agricultural College estimated that one man's labor was required for every fifty acres of crop. Lescohier discovered that the proportion was nearer to one man for every one hundred acres. Virtually no labor from outside the state came to the wheat fields of Texas, and little came to Oklahoma—probably never as many as ten thousand bindlestiffs in one year. Transient labor on an interstate basis became important only as the harvest progressed

into Kansas, where the western reaches of the state annually required twenty thousand to thirty thousand transient laborers. At the time of peak demand, perhaps thirty-five thousand laborers were at work in the winter wheat regions of the southern plains. Considering that the harvest then continued into the spring wheat regions and also that numerous bindlestiffs were continually leaving the harvest to be replaced by new ones entering it, Lescohier concluded that "probably, first and last, more than 100,000 individuals [transients] find work in the harvest."[17] He stuck by this estimate of more than one hundred thousand bindlestiffs in official reports of his research.[18]

Most bindlestiffs came from an area not far from the wheat belt—the adjacent valley of the Mississippi River and its western tributaries. Of this labor force, Lescohier summarized, "the supply that counts is the supply that comes from the Mississippi Valley. The stragglers from the outside add more to the picturesqueness of the harvest than to its economic efficiency."[19] More specifically, Lescohier and his collaborators gathered data on state residence from thousands of harvesters during both 1920 and 1921 (see Table 4.3). The order of precedence among states supplying harvest labor varied between the two samples; but in both cases Missouri led all states, and in both cases the predominance of the Mississippi River Valley was clear, although small numbers of hands came from every state of the United States as well as Canada (see Figure 4.1). Eighty percent of the tran-

Table 4.3. Place of Residence (Top 12 States) of Transient Harvest Hands, 1920 and 1921

1920			
Missouri	421	Oklahoma	80
Illinois	251	Arkansas	79
Ohio	173	Wisconsin	73
Iowa	180	New York	66
Kansas	143	Pennsylvania	66
Indiana	129	Texas	64

1921			
Missouri	2,821	Texas	494
Illinois	1,257	Ohio	414
Kansas	903	Wisconsin	357
Minnesota	773	Michigan	338
Oklahoma	682	Tennessee	332
Iowa	655	Arkansas	325

Source: Adapted from Don D. Lescohier, *Sources of Supply and Conditions of Employment of Harvest Labor in the Wheat Belt,* U.S. Department of Agriculture Bulletin 1211 (Washington, D.C.: GPO, 1924), p. 2; and idem, *Harvest Labor Problems in the Wheat Belt,* U.S. Department of Agriculture Bulletin 1020 (Washington, D.C.: GPO, 1920), p. 16.

sient laborers, Lescohier concluded in 1921, came from states in the wheat belt or one tier to the east; "in other words, the Mississippi Valley furnishes more than three-fourths of the transient harvest hands."[20] It was worth noting, too, that a small element of the bindlestiffs could give no state residence, for they "had none," the researcher reported, "which was literally true."[21]

Some general traits of harvest hands were evident from Lescohier's observations, the foremost being that they were predominantly white Americans. Blacks as a class figured not at all in Lescohier's observations, and Mexican immigrants rated only the briefest mention. This was partly because Lescohier did no fieldwork in Texas and only limited work in Oklahoma, where those racial minorities might have been more important. For the plains overall, however, Lescohier's findings are confirmed by the numerous photographs of harvest and threshing crews: Nonwhite laborers were scarce. Lescohier, too, reproduced in one of his articles a poster headed "Harvest Hands Wanted!" from Greensburg, Kansas, including the legend "Cannot use colored."[22] Among the white laborers, the American-born were the majority. "One seldom meets a harvest hand with a marked foreign accent," Lescohier observed. "The southern harvest, particularly, is handled by Americans."[23] In the Dakotas greater numbers of foreign-born, especially Scandinavian and German, showed up among the laborers, but most were longtime residents of the United States. Lescohier found overall that 11 percent of the hands interviewed in 1920 were foreign-born. In 1921, 110 of the 995 hands interviewed were foreign-born, and 88 of these came from non-English-speaking countries.[24]

The bindlestiffs were young and generally unmarried. Data on 919 laborers in 1920 revealed that 51 percent were in their twenties, with 31 percent at the lower end of the scale, twenty to twenty-four. Only 10 percent were under age twenty, 22 percent were in their thirties, 11 percent in their forties, and 6 percent in their fifties. Overall, less than 18 percent of the harvest hands in 1921 were married.[25]

The education of harvest hands, as a class, was neither uncommonly good

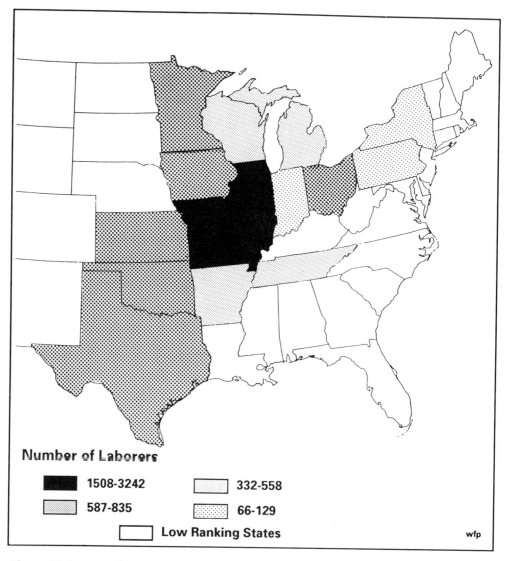

Figure 4.1 Sources of Harvest Labor in 1920 and 1921. *Source:* U.S. Department of Agriculture.

nor particularly poor. Educational information gathered on 153 hands in 1920 found that 67 percent had completed an education through the fifth, sixth, seventh, or eighth grade, and only 8 percent had less than a fifth-grade education. More extensive data on 1,016 hands in 1921 showed that al-

Black laborers on threshing crews were few; this crew on the John P. Linscheid farm, Reno County, Kans., ca. 1915, was integrated. Linscheid, the farmer, holds a pitchfork with a black laborer. (Mennonite Library and Archives, Bethel College, North Newton, Kans.)

most 42 percent had completed the eighth grade, about 18 percent had completed the fifth, sixth, or seventh grade, and only 14 percent had less than a fifth-grade education. More than 20 percent had attended some high school, and about 5 percent had completed high school. Considering that bindlestiffs represented laboring, humble classes, their education was rather respectable.[26]

If the year 1921, and the 14,168 hands on which data were taken, were at all typical, then the harvest brought together a mixture of neophyte hands and experienced stiffs. That year 30.6 percent of the hands were making their first harvest, 19.4 percent their

second, 12.0 percent their third, and 38.0 percent their fourth or more. The new blood kept the transient stream flowing, but it was the old hands who passed along the customs and lore that created the culture of harvest and threshing on the plains.[27]

In his categorization of bindlestiffs, Lescohier admitted to the same mystifying diversity as had other commentators, but he met the problem more bravely. In the first place, he discerned that certain hands, by geography or by experience, had the best chance of landing jobs with farmers. These he classified as "local and contract hands." The local hands, men from towns in the wheat belt, composed "a large frac-tion" of the harvest labor force of the wheat belt. Although they were on the spot and in good position to get jobs through reference or acquaintance, few moved along to other localities on the harvest circuit. The contract hands came from points distant to the place of work, but their job destinations had been arranged in advance, usually either because they were contacted by a farmer for whom they had previously worked or because they linked up with someone who had. The other broad class, with less chance of getting good jobs, was the "transient hands." Lescohier also divided this class into two groups according to whether they had other, regular jobs or subsisted entirely on seasonal labor. The first group in this class was composed of farmers, mechanics, and other laborers who worked the harvest for a brief period and then went back to their regular jobs. The seasonal laborers, however, moved from the harvest on to some other seasonal work; they were the true transients. Transients overall were "short time help" to be employed by farmers mainly during the "peak load" of the harvest.[28]

Probing the background of the hands further, Lescohier was surprised at their urban cast. In a sample of about one thousand hands in 1921, just over 55 percent said that they had been raised on farms, but almost 45 percent said that they had been raised in cities. Considering that many of those raised on farms had later moved to cities, it appeared that the transient labor force was more urban than rural.[29]

The clearest profile of the bindle-stiffs emerged from data gathered on the "customary occupations" of thirty-two thousand hands in 1920. Through prose description and a pie graph, Lescohier divided these subjects into rough thirds under the headings Farm Workers, Skilled City Men, and Laborers.[30] The Farm Workers comprised both small farmers and farmhands from areas or states not far distant. These were good hands, Lescohier thought, because "the farmers and farm hands from these neighboring states were the backbone of the Kansas harvest, so far as transient labor is concerned." He continued, "Skilled, hardened, ambitious to learn, and with a farmer's point of view toward harvest work, they are eagerly sought by the Kansans."[31]

The esteem in which Lescohier held these hands was evident as he recounted an instance when he stood on Main Street in Hutchinson, Kansas, with Harry Allen, a representative of the United States Employment Service, watching the laborers arrive in town. "They're not hobos, either, Harry. Look at their stride," Lescohier quoted himself. The hands had come into Wichita on the Rock Island Railroad and taken the Wichita Interurban out to Hutchinson; they were hiking across town to the Santa Fe Railroad station to catch trains for western Kansas. "And fine boys they were, straight, strong and bronzed; with a spring in their stride and a laugh on their lips. Clad in clean overalls, some carrying bundles or suitcases, but hundreds with only

WHEN THE HARVESTER IS NOT A-HARVESTING

This chart shows the "customary" occupations of 32,000 wheat harvesters: one-third of them gave farm work as their regular job, one-third were laborers, and one-third skilled workers from cities. The percentages are not absolutely accurate, for the relative proportion of harvesters of the several types varies from season to season. Data collected in 1919, 1920 and 1921 indicates that the distribution as given in this chart is substantially correct

Lescohier's pie graph detailing "customary occupations" of bindlestiffs. (From Survey magazine)

their working clothes on their backs, the boys of the Southwest were coming to the harvest."[32]

The Skilled City Men, which constituted another third of the bindlestiffs, included, along with a few high school and college students, a large number of "mechanics and factory workers" as well as many skilled laborers (for example, carpenters, electricians, painters, and plumbers). Farmers prized these hands, because of their regular habits, their mechanical abilities, and their quickness in learning tasks. Contrary to stereotypes of effete and soft-handed students, college men seemed to acquit themselves well in the field and were appreciated as able-bodied and quick-minded hands by farmers. Their numbers were significant only in certain localities, however. In western Oklahoma, for instance, some eight hundred college men were employed in 1920, with three hundred in the Woodward area alone.[33]

Less reliable but still essential were the men in the Laborers category. This third of the labor pool was further divided by Lescohier into two groups, the first of which was simply urban, unskilled laborers who had turned to the harvest not as a routine but rather because of unemployment or some other special circumstance. True migratory laborers (in the classic sense) composed the second group. These were the "flitters" or "drifters" who seemed to move from job to job and locality to locality as chance forces compelled them. Further delving into the biographies of these drifters, however, showed that

only a few truly "drifted." Many of them had a "definite cycle of seasonal occupations from which they seldom depart[ed]."[34] Such "seasonal occupations" included certain endeavors common throughout the midsection of the country—railroad maintenance, road construction, building construction—but also comprised a number of local occupations peculiar to particular places in or adjacent to the wheat belt. In Texas and Oklahoma, for instance, bindlestiffs might combine harvest work with roughnecking or teamstering in oil fields, picking cotton, or working on cattle ranches. The traditional combination of seasonal labor for those who worked the grain harvest of the northern plains was winter work as lumberjacks. Ice cutting, too, was a common recourse but did not furnish the length of employment that lumber work did.[35]

Despite their diversity, bindlestiffs were motivated to work the harvest because of common concerns. Lescohier observed three in particular: "(1) lack of other employment; (2) the hope of making 'big money'; and (3) the desire for adventure and experience."[36] These motives, although they applied as truly to the bright-eyed college boys as they did to the seasoned transients, were not all equally benign. "The hope of large earnings and the lure of adventure attract men to the harvest," Lescohier qualified; however, "*unemployment drives them.*"[37]

To comprehend the movement of all these bindlestiffs within the sprawling landscape and extended duration of the wheat harvest required some understanding of the agricultural geography of the North American plains. Variations in such things as the type of implement used in the harvest (binder or header) and the organization of threshing (custom or cooperative) had myriad effects on the needs of particular localities for harvest labor, but the greatest division across the wheat belt was that between the winter wheat country of the southern plains and the spring wheat country of the northern plains. As Lescohier put it: "The harvest consists of two distinct but connected episodes."[38] The harvesting of winter wheat commenced around June 1 in northern Texas and southwestern Oklahoma and reached its crest in early to mid-July in Kansas. Shortly afterward, in late July, the harvest of spring wheat began in South Dakota and reached its crest during mid-August in North Dakota. Frequently, an interval of a week or so separated the period when most winter wheat harvesting was done and the period when significant spring wheat harvesting commenced. Whatever the length of time between the two harvests, there was always considerable geographic distance between them, because the winter and spring wheat areas were divided by the eastern corn belt and western sand hills of Nebraska. The separation was complicated further in that the major railroad lines ran east and west instead of north and south.

So the harvest of the winter wheat area had to be considered almost as a unit unto itself. Hands who worked only in harvesting operations and did not land jobs with threshing crews could expect to work only a week or two on a job before they had to, as they said, "catch up with the harvest" by quickly traveling one hundred miles or more northward. Lescohier commented, "Most of the men make the mistake of not jumping far enough."[39] Once the winter wheat harvest was done, the majority of the harvesters declined to go north into spring wheat country. Instead, they sought jobs threshing winter wheat; went home; moved to corn farms or other diversified farms that might offer employment; or went to cities. Therefore, Lescohier said, "most of the men in the Dakota harvest are men who did not work in Kansas."[40]

Where did the men who worked in the spring wheat area come from, then? They were composed of "three distinct elements," according to Lescohier. These three elements corresponded roughly to the general divisions of transient laborers that he had outlined, but the geographic origins of these workers differed from those on the southern plains. Again there came an influx of farmers and farmhands from adjacent states, but this time the adjacent states were not Missouri and Arkansas. Rather, they were more likely to be such states of the Old Northwest as Indiana, Illinois, Iowa, Wisconsin, and Minnesota. Industrial laborers from the cities of the same belt also came. Cities such as Chicago, Minneapolis, Milwaukee, and Duluth were likely places for the hands to hail from.

Then there were the migratory laborers—some were working cycles of seasonal labor, including lumber work and
other occupations in the northern area;
others were coming up from the winter
wheat harvest in the south.[41]

Even after mechanization had reduced transient labor in the winter
wheat regions, it still continued in the
spring wheat regions, where the binder
remained in use and the combine in
abeyance. In 1938 researchers from
the United States Bureau of Agricultural Economics studied the situation
in North Dakota. They found that only
25 percent of the wheat was harvested
by combines and that the state still employed twenty-five thousand transient
laborers for the harvest. This body of
men, which the researchers termed "a
convenience rather than absolute necessity," still came from much the same
sources as it had during the heyday of
the harvest bindlestiffs on the plains.
The great majority came from Minnesota, Wisconsin, Iowa, and Illinois.
Even more than in the day of Lescohier
the stiffs were American born, and
they were young, with half of them
twenty-five years of age or younger.
The education level of the hands had
improved a bit, with 40 percent having
completed the eighth grade and only
20 percent not having gone that far in
school; this was probably more a function of stricter attendance legislation
for schools and the proliferation of
high schools than it was of a change in
the social status of the hands. Again, as
in the day of Lescohier, the researchers
found large numbers of skilled labor-

ers among the harvest hands. The writers in 1938 attributed this to
depression-era unemployment, although the earlier research of Lescohier would have indicated that it was
nothing new. Overall, the harvest
hands' profile in 1938 was remarkably
similar to that a half-generation earlier.[42]

Likewise, the general motives of the
hands remained similar, although by
1938 they were heavily tempered by
years of depression and fewer hands
believed they were going to find big
money or grand adventure in the
wheat belt. These men were much
more directly reminiscent of Lescohier's comment that unemployment
drove them. "Of these transients, about
half said plainly that they had no other
jobs," wrote the researchers of 1938,
"and what most of the others said was
to the same effect. . . . [T]hose who
made it for a lark or vacation jaunt
were only a scattered fringe to the
ranks of those impelled by the necessity
of earning a scanty living."[43] A number
of workers had given up hope of ad-
vancing themselves, prompting one
surveyor to say that elements of them,
"usually older men, do not care very
much if they get work or not, they will
probably always be floaters. They are
here because this town happens to be
on the main railroad line."[44] Among
them were many colorful types with
their own stories explaining their circumstances—the fellow whose mother
burned his homestead papers, preventing him from making a new start in
Canada; or the fellow who was a vet-

eran of the imperial Russian army, had made a fortune in the United States, but then had lost it in an unfortunate divorce; and so on through many personal tales of woe. Still, most of the stiffs were young men struggling hard to make a stake.

Although to an observer at any one point in the plains the movement of harvest hands might appear as mysterious, spontaneous, and autonomous as that of wild geese or a chinook, there arose throughout the plains region individuals and networks committed to— or at least claiming to be committed to—the "management" of the harvest labor supply. David W. Blaine, a farmer and implement dealer from Pratt County, Kansas, right in the middle of winter-wheat header country, was a case study in the movement for management of harvest labor. He became concerned with the question at least as early as 1899, and during that year and the one following he took it upon himself to canvass Pratt County's farmers and assess their needs for harvest labor. Once this information was gathered, it was not easy to disseminate, for Kansas had as yet no public employment bureau. Blaine sent the information to Missouri's public employment bureau office in Kansas City and also obtained the cooperation of newspaper editors and businessmen in issuing calls for laborers to come to Pratt County and to the wheat belt in general.[45]

In 1901 Kansas established a free employment bureau. Blaine meanwhile had stepped up his efforts for recruitment of harvest labor. He not only got

wheat farmers in his own county to meet at their district schools and compile information on their needs, but he also sent a call to all county assessors across the state, asking them to tell him how many hands their communities would need. Blaine then commenced the usual publicity effort to recruit laborers, this time advising them that they should answer the call by reporting to the Kansas Free Employment Bureau in Kansas City. A conflict quickly developed, however, between Blaine and the free employment bureau, or more particularly its director, T. B. Gerow, who was backed by Governor W. E. Stanley. Blaine, by this time styled in newspaper reports as the father of harvest labor recruitment in the wheat belt, estimated that western Kansas would require from ten to fifteen thousand hands from outside the state. State authorities, responding to pressures on the governor connected with labor issues unrelated to the wheat harvest, opposed recruitment of labor from outside the state. Eventually, state authorities gave way to the pressure exerted by Blaine and his supporters and recruited labor from outside the state. Even so, as the harvest developed, there were, at least as farmers saw it, severe shortages of labor in certain areas, forcing up wages and bringing about a one-day strike of harvesters in the Salina vicinity.[46]

Blaine's prestige reached its peak in 1902, when he made his effort to assess needs more comprehensive and structured. On March 1 he sent a circular to the assessor of every township in Kansas, asking for data on acres of wheat sown by farmers, their labor needs the previous year, and prospects for the current year. He then tabulated the information and reported it to the employment bureau. Again Blaine struggled with state authorities over the need to recruit outside the state, and again he prevailed.[47]

Blaine's struggle was vocal and important enough that it attracted feature coverage from the New York magazine *American Monthly Review of Reviews*. The author in that journal, William R. Draper, presented Blaine as representative of a new age. "The policy of the farmer of to-day is expansion," Draper announced. "The farming west is a country gone to wheat." This development was not entirely smooth, however, for "importing labor into the wheat belt during the period of harvesting has caused a new and serious problem to the grower,—that of obtaining the extra workers at the right time and at reasonable prices." The key word here was "problem": Blaine, Draper, and the many who agreed with them considered the movement of harvest labor not a phenomenon to be observed but a problem to be solved in progressive fashion. Neither was it a problem only of farmers, for "abundant crops infuse the towns as well as the country with prosperity and bustling life"; thus businessmen and the entire commonwealth should join in the effort. Underlying the journalistic approval of Blaine's ideas, however, lay a tension that plagued any effort to solve the harvest labor "problem." Blaine, as portrayed

by Draper, was assessing the needs for labor carefully and striving to match precisely the recruitment of labor to the need. Regardless of whether this was possible, which was dubious, it was even more dubious that it was politically feasible within the wheat belt. People who supported Blaine and what he stood for cited the labor shortage of 1901 and similar events in other years as the reason management of labor was needed. However efficiently and honestly managers might attempt to match supply with demand, there always would be pressure from producers to increase supply regardless of the welfare of the laborers.[48]

Blaine stood right in the middle of the process whereby harvest labor was transformed from a local, private matter into a broad, public problem. On the local level, the recruitment of harvest labor was always a matter of public comment even before Blaine and similar individuals stepped forward. Already in 1892, for instance, an attorney in Miner County, South Dakota, systematically assessed local needs for harvest labor and publicized them; in Brown County a local real estate promoter did the same. A committee of farmers was doing similar work in Rush County, Kansas, and by the time Blaine got to work in Pratt, real estate promoters in Kingman, just to the east, were also doing some assessment and recruitment. A few years later a banker from Larned, just to the north, rode the Santa Fe branch line through central Kansas, circularizing harvesters on it and bringing them into his own Pawnee County. These were mere examples of the general trend of business interests allied locally with farmers in concern over harvest labor. Local booster editors supported them by publicizing their efforts.[49]

A weakness in all these efforts was that although they might identify needs, the organizers had no connections at points of supply of harvest labor. Some big farmers procured laborers through private employment bureaus in midwestern cities, but as a general solution, this was hardly satisfactory. Jobs in harvesting were of such short duration that it did not pay for agencies to handle them or for laborers to seek them through agencies. Among private interests, there was only one that could coordinate assessment of needs with recruitment of laborers and that had connections at both ends of the transaction: the railroads. The interest of the railroads along these lines was first evident in that brakemen and detectives of railroads serving the wheat belt were at least intermittently obliging to bindlestiffs who hopped freights into the region. Individual railroad bulls occasionally took it upon themselves to shake down the transient laborers for a dollar apiece, and when railroad officials judged that there was a labor surplus, there might be a more systematic attempt to discourage free passage on the freights. But in ordinary years they recognized that the harvest was essential to their own prosperity, and they let the laborers ride.[50]

The next step was for American railroad companies to follow the example of those in Canada—that is, to establish special fares for harvesters. This occurred as an isolated incidence during 1892, when both the winter and spring wheat areas were short on help. Serving the winter wheat area, the Sante Fe and Rock Island railroads stipulated that harvesters who paid full fare into the wheat belt could return east to cities along the Missouri River for one-sixth fare. Only groups of ten or more men were eligible for this fare, and it was not low enough to attract large numbers of men. During the same season more northerly railroads—the Great Northern, the Chicago, Milwaukee and St. Paul, and the Chicago and Northwestern—offered a special five-dollar fare for bindlestiffs traveling from certain cities in Minnesota or Wisconsin into the spring wheat area. This fare applied only to groups of five or more laborers and was not nearly so liberal as many farmers desired. Besides establishing these fares, the railroads publicized labor needs and actively recruited hands to go to the wheat belt. For some twenty-five years thereafter, American railroads offered a variety of special fares for harvesters, tinkering with the formula year by year, attempting to match supply of labor to demand, but never getting so organized or putting in so much effort as did the two western Canadian lines. Public officials in the United States subsequently would review the efforts of the American railroads and judge them wanting in comparison with Canadian ones. Many farmers, too, were dissatisfied. In 1919, after the railroads had discontinued harvester fares, thousands of farmers in Kansas and elsewhere, faced with another labor shortage, themselves prepaid the fares of hands, personally or through representatives sent to cities back east. A few farmers had prepaid fares for hands in other years, too, especially for ones whom they had employed before and knew to be reliable and capable.[51]

Because of the multiplicity of railroads involved and each line's concern with crops mainly in its own area and because of the lack of any disinterested parties to direct the flow of labor, state authorities stepped in. Well before World War I, three states in the winter wheat belt established free employment bureaus largely concerned with the distribution of farm labor: Nebraska acted in 1897, Kansas in 1901, and Oklahoma in 1907. (Other states subsequently established their own bureaus.) These offices were a manifestation of good progressive doctrine. They were to be neutral brokers of employers and laborers, serving the broad public interest rather than either class. Unfortunately, the early histories of these first three agencies proved them to be rather feeble. The handling of harvest labor required not only a state office but also local offices in numerous localities throughout the state. This was inordinately expensive. Authorities in Kansas attempted to avert the expense by requiring the clerk of each county to act as a harvest labor representative, but this was a spotty solution at best, for the clerks neglected this duty and could not be compelled to fulfill it. The

Kansas bureau, too, was continually involved in embarrassing public disputes with David Blaine, who insisted on pointing out its shortcomings. The problem with such agencies' handling transient labor, however, was more basic. They might gather information within the harvesting states and publicize it as best they could, but they had no formal connections with points to the east where laborers were recruited.[52]

State employment officials also sensed a need for interstate cooperation, which was the impetus behind a meeting in Kansas City, Missouri, early in 1904. There, representatives of the employment bureaus of Nebraska, Iowa, Missouri, Kansas, Minnesota, South Dakota, and Oklahoma agreed to cooperate and pool their estimates of harvest labor needs. They agreed to report through the employment bureau office in Kansas City, which they designated the center for distribution of hands throughout the wheat belt because of its strategic geographic location. This meeting came to naught, however, for the constituent state bureaus were too feeble to form a viable consortium.[53]

Not until 1918, with the creation of the United States Employment Service, did there exist even on paper any entity that not only could pull together from various states estimates of harvest labor needs but also could recruit laborers from outside the wheat belt. Lescohier was a part of this work in Minneapolis and subsequently studied the process in his research throughout the wheat belt. He was a firm believer in cooperative, centralized management of labor. As he said, "It is more than a local venture; it is a national enterprise."[54]

Still, Lescohier knew that the direction harvest labor was receiving was almost a farce. Newspapers published reports of wildly variable reliability drawn on all manner of unauthorized sources; railroads put out publicity about labor needs along their own lines; handbills from private parties circulated freely. A strange contradiction had taken shape. As Lescohier noted, the United States Employment Service, setting up a central office in Kansas City, seemed to have "marked success" in coordinating among the states. The states, in turn, were opening the welter of local offices required to do the job. But people were not paying attention to them. "Year by year this service has been obtaining a higher degree of efficiency," maintained Lescohier; but he found that the great majority of laborers he interviewed had no contact with employment offices.[55] Perhaps they recognized, as Lescohier himself admitted, that "up to the present time the forecasts in most states have been hardly more than guesses."[56] Few farmers placed orders for laborers through employment bureau officials, and few laborers applied to the officials. Farmers continued "picking up men," and laborers still sought to "pick up a job." The state bureaus often quoted impressive statistics about their work, but these proved suspect on closer examination. The Kansas bureau

in 1921 reported 30,572 hands "directed"—but did not say that they were "placed." A publication of the state extension service, which generally supported placement efforts, admitted that "no public labor bureau can guarantee employment to men applying, but can go only so far as to tell the prospective harvest hands that a certain man in a certain county or at a certain town has advised that so many harvest hands were needed."[57]

With the employment services floundering, newly organized agricultural extension services in the respective states, especially in Kansas, attempted to assist. County agents were on the scene and vitally interested in agricultural matters. During the Great War the extension service of Kansas ostensibly cooperated with the employment service and the state council of defense, but in fact the extension service took over the harvest labor work. County farm bureau chapters assisted by calling meetings of farmers to discuss the question. By 1921, when the Kansas State Extension Service published its *Kansas Handbook of Harvest Labor,* county agents were obviously carrying the ball in the matter. The bulletin devoted its first few pages to a list of all extension officials and county agents in the state, and it asserted, "County agents are in general the most responsible local labor agents, and give the most accurate information."[58] Meanwhile, George E. Piper of Kansas State Agricultural College had developed a mathematical formula designed to assist county agents in their estimates.

Expressed in prose, the formula stated, "Where there is a normal shortage of help, every additional 50 acres will require one additional man."[59] This seemed a little imprecise, and so Piper also expressed it as a formula:

$$\frac{\text{Total acreage of wheat to be harvested}}{50 \ (\text{average acres per man})} - \frac{\text{Number of laborers already in county}}{} = \frac{\text{Number of men to be imported}}{}$$

This was commonly known as the Kansas Formula. Lescohier subsequently tested and refined the formula and expressed it thus:

$$\frac{A}{50} - (mf + mt) = mo$$

where A = number of acres of wheat within county

mf = manpower on the farms (number of farms × 1.3)

mt = manpower available from towns within the county

mo = number of men needed from the outside

This formula no doubt made county agents feel better about their duty, but given the varying crop conditions year to year and the varying technology and methods in different localities, it was not too relevant.[60]

The machinery for management was cumbersome, the theory was doubtful, and it was even uncertain whether the purpose was sound. Lescohier, to be sure, had a solid understanding of the question and couched it in good progressive terms:

The outstanding labor problem of the wheat harvest is the mobilization of an adequate but not excessive supply, followed by a proper direction of the workers over the harvest areas, not only once, but again and again. This problem consists, on the one hand, of dividing the available force in an equitable manner so that each wheat farmer may have the number of men that he needs, and, on the other hand, of helping each harvester to work as steadily as possible with a minimum expense of travel and board.[61]

These sentiments would have been the more laudable had they been those of an effective entity rather than of the ineffective employment services. Perhaps the task was just too difficult; but farmers became disgusted, and their extension services accused the labor agencies of continually "passing the buck." This disaffection led farmers to attempt to take matters into their own hands. During 1918, 1919, and 1920, under the influence of the extension service and the farm bureau, farmers held local meetings and attempted to set standard wages for harvest labor across the state at levels that would attract sufficient laborers but also cap payments. They found that they simply could not control wages. In 1919 the standard wage was supposed to be fifty cents an hour, but as shortages of labor developed in the western parts of the state, farmers did not hesitate to raise the wage to seventy cents and even to prepay railroad fares for hands. A standard wage set at seventy cents pur-portedly worked better in 1920, but this was largely because the wage acci-dentally corresponded to what the going wage would have been anyway. What all this meant was that despite rhetoric, no one was in command of the harvest labor situation—a welter of voices put out conflicting information and attempts to coordinate matters often did more harm than good.[62]

Although public agencies could not control harvest labor, they did report steadily on the flow of men and the wages they earned. Such data was com-prehensive for the prairie provinces of Canada, where the harvest excursion scheme, the central roles of the two principal railroads, and the involve-ment of provincial agencies produced good records. A table of average wages for harvest laborers (weighted between highest and lowest wages paid and among the three prairie provinces) re-veals the trends in wages over the first three decades of the twentieth century (see Table 4.4). The averages, of course, are averages only, means de-rived from round figures that consti-tuted the "going wage" in countless lo-calities and at different times. Wages varied year to year, but they varied at certain plateaus, which from 1901 to 1909 stood at two dollars. In all likeli-hood, for this decade or so, two dollars per day would have been the most common going wage. Inasmuch as threshing usually paid a little more than stooking or other harvest labor, two dollars probably would have been at the lower end of going wages for

Table 4.4. Estimated Average Daily Wages of Harvesters in Western Canada, 1901–1929 (in Canadian dollars)

Year	Wage	Year	Wage
1901	1.88	1916	2.75
1902	2.75	1917	4.00
1903	2.00	1918	4.55
1904	2.00	1919	4.69
1905	2.25	1920	5.73
1906	2.57	1921	3.88
1907	2.00	1922	3.55
1908	2.05	1923	3.75
1909	2.00	1924	3.38
1910	2.13	1925	4.10
1911	2.88	1926	3.40
1912	3.13	1927	4.50
1913	3.13	1928	3.90
1914	2.55	1929	3.48
1915	2.60		

Source: Adapted from John Herd Thompson, "Bringing in the Sheaves: The Harvest Excur-sionists, 1890–1929," Canadian Historical Review 59 (1978): 482.

threshing and at the upper end for harvesting. From 1910 to 1916 the pla-teau was around three dollars, and during the period 1917 to 1920, the wartime and immediate postwar booms took the level almost to six dollars, only to fall back to around four dollars through the 1920s. The retrenchment after 1920 showed that harvest wages had a rough, if not consistent, corre-spondence to the price of wheat.

Generally speaking, supply and de-mand determined wages in the wheat belt. On a few occasions farmers mounted organized attempts to set wages arbitrarily low—for instance, in 1902 through farmers' meetings in Manitoba and in 1920 through the United Farmers of Alberta—but such attempts had only brief success if any. The organization could not hold farmers in line when labor was at all scarce. Laborers seemed to have good bargaining power in that their wages, considered on a daily basis, were excellent compared with wages for other sorts of manual labor. This was deceiving, however, because the bindlestiffs spent so much of their time in travel to and from work and in idleness between jobs or during spells of bad weather. So it was a fortunate and diligent laborer indeed who returned east with any tidy sum, and fewer still were those who made enough to make a new start in the west.[63]

Unfortunately, some bindlestiffs found themselves cheated even of such wages as they earned. Farmers wished to hold their crews through to the end of the harvest, or threshing as the case may be. To do this they declined or made excuses not to pay their laborers until the work was completed. This practice was understandable and not onerous except that it was easily abused. Dishonorable or financially embarrassed farmers might remain unwilling or unable to pay after the work was done, and other creditors might have precedence over laborers in claims on the farmers' sale of grain. Bindlestiffs needing to get down the road to the next job were in a poor position to seek legal redress. The greatest influence preventing this sort of situation from being common was that farmers needed dependable harvest labor and often sought to have the same fellows return to the place year after year. Laborers who worked for threshermen did obtain legal safeguards of

their right to be paid their due wages. Saskatchewan in 1909 passed "An Act for the Protection of Wages to Threshing Machine Employees," which gave laborers on threshing outfits a prior claim on all earnings of the thresherman. Alberta passed substantially the same law in 1913.[64]

Reporting of data on harvest labor was not as centralized in the United States, but a variety of sources did provide a picture of the scheme of wages. In 1909 Professor Rose of North Dakota Agricultural College, in his writings for threshermen, outlined the costs of labor to a threshing outfit: engineer, $5.00; fireman, $3.00; separator man, $5.00; water boy with team, $5.00; bundle team with driver, $5.00; spike pitcher, $2.50; field pitcher, $2.50; cook, $4.00; manager, $6.00. Rose's figures made several points clear. First, skilled employees such as engineers, separator men, and managers (who would be needed if the engine owner was not a manager) received wages about double those for unskilled employees. Second, in the spring wheat country of bundle threshing from the shock, most of the human labor was paired with teams and racks and therefore had to be provided by local laborers, either through ring or wage arrangements; these jobs could not be won by transients. Third, those positions that might be open to transients, such as pitching in the field or at the separator, were the lowest paying, at just $2.50 a day. These wages were comparable, however, with those reported for harvest excursionists at

Western Canadian threshing crew, ca. 1907. The engineer and the separator man, perched above the other crewmen, drew superior wages. (Saskatchewan Archives Board, Regina)

about the same time in western Canada.[65]

Wages on the American side of the border evidently rose, as did those on the Canadian side, in succeeding years. A map in a publication of the Kansas State Board of Agriculture depicted harvest wages paid in 1919 (making no distinction between wages for harvesting and wages for threshing). It showed a progression in wages from east to west, with $5.00 prevailing in the east, $6.00 prevailing in bands of the west-central part of the state, and $7.00 (or more) prevailing in much of the western part of the state. Supply and demand were at work: The western reaches of the state were more remote and received fewer laborers but had a heavy demand for labor. An-

other map recording conditions in 1920 gave the prevailing wage in eastern Kansas as $5.00 to $6.00, in western Kansas $7.00. Bindlestiffs in the winter wheat region, then, were drawing wages well above those in the weighted averages of the prairie provinces of Canada. Farmers repeatedly failed to organize and set wages. Authorities in the Kansas State Extension Service believed that although wages for harvest labor bore some relation to the price of wheat, they were more directly tied to industrial wages and employment opportunities in the east, for farmers were forced to offer wages high enough to attract men west.[66]

Lescohier gathered extensive data on harvest wages, and what distinguished his compilation from others was that he was concerned not only with what farmers had to pay but also with what workers might net after covering their own expenses. Lescohier believed it would be desirable to have fair standard wages set at the state or local level, but this was "impossible." Bindlestiffs and farmers bargained locally and, indeed, individually, to continually reestablish wages. The wages were generally higher than those for urban industrial labor, but laborers could not understand, and neither could farmers, why there had to be such great variation even between localities. Lescohier's maps for 1919, 1920, and 1921 showed amazing variation, even between adjacent counties, but also certain broad trends (see Figure 4.2). The western reaches of the winter wheat belt, in general, paid the best wages. Wages in the spring wheat belt averaged somewhat lower. Notably, although Lescohier understood the technological and social arrangements required for harvesting and threshing, he did not segregate his data according to harvesting, threshing, and the skilled tasks within each. The variations of tasks and of wages from place to place and time to time almost defied summary.[67]

With such a wage situation and with the known problems of finding employment and reemployment and of travel between jobs, how much could a bindlestiff make harvesting and threshing? Lescohier sought to determine this in 1921 by asking bindlestiffs in the field about their earnings in 1919 and 1920. He asked 703 hands about 1919.

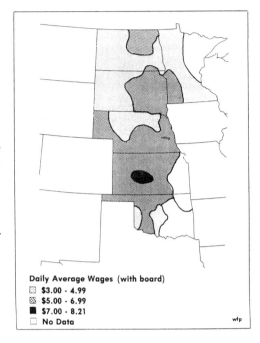

Daily Average Wages (with board)
- $3.00 - 4.99
- $5.00 - 6.99
- $7.00 - 8.21
- No Data

wfp

Figure 4.2 Average Wages for Wheat Belt Labor in 1919. *Source:* Data from Don D. Lescohier, *Sources of Supply and Conditions of Employment of Harvest Labor in the Wheat Belt,* U.S. Department of Agriculture Bulletin 1211 (Washington, D.C.: GPO, 1924).

A substantial number, 201, reported that they had made between $100 and $250. A smaller number made either more or less than these amounts; but perhaps the most significant figure was the number of bindlestiffs—260—who reported that they did not know what their earnings for that year might have been. Similar results came in for earnings during 1920: Of 696 bindlestiffs, 226 reported earnings in the $100 to $250 bracket, but a nearly comparable number, 179, said they did not know what they had made. Bindlestiffs were poor accountants. This might render all the data suspect, but Lescohier went on to interview 83 harvesters in the 1921 season who at the time of interviewing had made $100 or more. From these he gathered data on both earnings and expenses. The main expenses were subsistence during idle times and travel between jobs. The average earnings of these men at the time of interview was $146.54; they had made this money on an average of 2.2 jobs apiece. Their average expenses were $49.44. Thus at the time of interview they had netted an average of $97.10. These men showed the potential for profitability in making the harvest, but they represented only the relatively successful among the bindlestiffs. Thus the researcher could not conclude that harvesters came to the wheat belt and took home tidy nest eggs.[68]

If it was difficult to make a stake in the harvest of Lescohier's time, how much more difficult it must have been by the 1930s, when opportunities for harvesting had been depleted by mechanization in the winter wheat belt and depression lay heavily on the spring wheat belt. Researchers in North Dakota in 1938, as would be expected, found wages depressed: An average of $2.44 was paid for shockers, $2.58 for field pitchers in threshing, and $2.71 for separator men. The lessening of the gap between the wage for skilled labor (separator men) and unskilled showed that under such depressed conditions, no laborer enjoyed strength in bargaining.[69]

If bindlestiffs were poor accountants,

threshermen often were better ones, and their vital concern about the expense of wages resulted in good documentation of the wages paid to threshing crews (see Table 4.5). Wages reported in letters to threshermen's periodicals were not inconsistent with those of published researchers, but the threshermen's reports better reflected the variance in pay according to the job held. A key point again was that the higher-paying jobs—those of the machine men (engineer and separator man), bundle haulers with teams, and tank men—were ones likely to be filled by local men, and those positions that paid the lowest—spike pitchers, bundle pitchers, field pitchers—were the only ones frequently open to transients.[70]

For at least a generation the daily wage, whatever it was, was an institution in the harvesting and threshing of small grains on the plains. Only occasionally, mainly late in the history of stationary threshing, did bindlestiffs draw their pay on some other terms than the daily wage. During World War I and the immediate postwar years, there was a movement toward paying by the hour instead of by day. In most places this was short-lived, but a report from North Dakota in 1925 indicated that hourly wages were being paid by some there, with laborers drawing fifty to sixty cents per hour. Hourly wages protected the thresherman from paying full daily wages on the many occasions when weather prevented working a full day. On the other hand, many threshermen who had worked as laborers themselves devised, whether in a

Table 4.5. Reports of Wages by Threshermen Writing to *American Thresherman* and *Canadian Thresherman*, various years, 1902–1915

						Wages Paid[a]					
Year	Locality	State/Province	Engineer	Separator Man	Spike or Bundle Pitcher	Field Pitcher	Bundleman and Team	Tank Man	Fireman	Cook
1902	(southwest)	South Dakota	4.00	4.00	2.00	—	—	3.00	—	—
1909	(southwest)	South Dakota	5.00	5.00	2.00	—	—	3.00	—	—
1909	Nashville	Kansas	3.50–4.00	3.00–3.50	2.00	—	—	—	—	—
1909	Honeyford	Kansas	6.00–7.00	2.75–3.00	—	—	—	—	—	—
1910	Cartwright	Manitoba	—	—	2.50	—	5.00	—	—	—
1910	Rokeby	Saskatchewan	6.00	—	2.50	2.50	4.00	5.00	2.75	—
1911	Kirwin	Kansas	4.00	3.00	2.50	—	—	—	—	—
1911	Ruth	Manitoba	6.00–8.00	6.00–8.00	2.50–3.00	—	4.00–5.00	—	—	—
1912	Winkler	Manitoba	—	2.50	—	—	—	—	3.00	—
1913	Harlan	Kansas	—	—	2.00–2.50	—	—	—	—	—
1913	Newton	Kansas	4.00	4.00	2.25	—	—	—	—	—
1914	Zealandia	Saskatchewan	—	9.00	3.00–3.50	—	6.00	—	4.00	—
1915	Newark	South Dakota	—	—	4.00	3.00	—	—	—	3.00

Source: Compiled from letters in the following issues of *American Thresherman*: 13 (July 1910): 14, 2 (March 1909): 39–40, 13 (June 1910): 56, 14 (October 1911): 40, 15 (March 1912): 73–74, 16 (August 1913): 84–85, 16 (October 1913): 59, 17 (June 1914): 64, 18 (September 1915): 27, 19 (June 1916): 67; and *Canadian Thresherman*: 16 (May 1911): 38, 16 (June 1911): 40.

[a]Reports from the United States are in U.S. dollars, and reports from Canada are in Canadian dollars.

A job on a threshing outfit with a good run—such as that of George Bretz in western Kansas—paid the best wages, ca. 1915. (Courtesy of Guy Bretz)

spirit of cooperation or in the hope that they could inspire the men to work harder, arrangements of profit-sharing. A thresherman in Saskatchewan in 1915 complained that "wages have certainly not increased in the same proportion as the thresherman's rates"; but a colleague in northwestern Kansas had an answer. He decided to pay his pitchers twenty-five cents per one hundred bushels threshed. "I think this is a good way to hire help as they all pull together," the Kansas thresherman concluded. "The same crew pulled in with us that went out, which I think is holding up pretty well."[71] Likewise Guy Bretz recalled the wage arrangement of his thresherman-father in western Kansas: "His plan was to take out a fair wage for himself and the machine, which was agreed by all. Then divide the balance equally among the men. This worked real good. The more the

pitchers put through the machine, the more money they made."

Before he could draw any wages, the harvest hand had to get to his job; thus travel, not just work, was a constant. Geography and the harvest excursion system accounted for basic differences in travel for bindlestiffs on the two sides of the Forty-ninth Parallel. The Canadian hands had a common experience in travel: Nearly all of them were excursionists. They all went through a railroad journey of several days, and they made it on the colonist cars of the two great Canadian railroads. A colonist car commonly seated fifty-six men in groups of four. The seats unfolded flat to sleep two of the four, and a rack overhead pulled down to sleep two more. Each car contained a cook stove, but the excursionists usually carried supplies of cold food in their suitcases. The accommodations were far from luxurious, but they were adequate and predictable.[72]

The traveling experiences of American bindlestiffs during the railroad era varied much more. A minority availed themselves of harvesters' rates on the railroads and probably had somewhat better accommodations than did the Canadian excursionists. The great majority, however, went blind baggage on freight trains, if necessary slipping a dollar to the railroad bull to stay on board. This was a poor arrangement for distributing harvest labor because the men tended to go where they could get a ride instead of where they were known to be needed; but the bindlestiffs regarded the harvester fares of the American railroads as too steep, considering what they could expect to make in the fields. Lescohier in 1921 found that almost 60 percent of the harvest hands he interviewed rode freights to the harvest; only 36 percent paid fares. However they traveled, the men went with little luggage and dressed in working clothes. Experienced hands believed not only that this was convenient for travel but also that farmers were more disposed to hire a man who looked the part of the harvest hand—dressed in overalls and jacket, carrying only a small roll of clothing.[73]

Traveling by freight train was, as Lescohier put it, "one of the most objectionable aspects of the harvest."[74] Blind baggage travel endangered the hands in two ways: Freight train wrecks were more frequent than passenger train wrecks, and a criminal element shared the ride with legitimate harvest hands. Most crime associated with the harvest occurred on trains and in freight yards, where the men were particularly vulnerable to hijackers and gamblers seeking to lift their hard-earned wages. The ways of conductors and detectives, too, were capricious. As Milo Mathews recalled, "Those days you got kicked out a lot of times before you got out of town, because I wasn't too smart a traveler on those railroads. If some of those guys who had traveled for years would take to you a little bit, they'd show you the ropes—but I wasn't much of a railroad traveler."[75]

By the 1920s an alternative was available for the traveling hand: the automobile, which ushered in the era of what one journalist termed the Honk Honk Hobo. In 1921 Lescohier found less than 4 percent of the hands traveling by automobile, but this percentage was destined to grow. Milo Mathews was a part of this trend, first taking up hitchhiking with his pack, then traveling by Model T with a group of hands pooling resources. The transition to automobile transport proceeded rapidly during the 1920s. By 1926 United States Department of Labor officials estimated that 65 percent of the harvest laborers in Kansas traveled in their own cars, and in northwestern Kansas, which was poorly served by railroads, 90 percent went by car. It was much easier, too, for hands from the southern plains to proceed north to the spring wheat region by automobile. Two thousand cars were counted crossing the Missouri River bridge at Yankton, South Dakota, during three days

The honk-honk hobo. Shown are Lowell Ayers, one of his hands from Iowa, and the Starr automobile. (Courtesy of Mr. and Mrs. Lowell Ayers)

in midsummer. A journalist subsequently reported the streets of Aberdeen, South Dakota, filled with cars of harvest hands tagged in states all over the country. Most of the cars were Fords. Farmers approved of this development, for they believed that a good class of hands came by automobile, and they were relieved of having to transport them to and from town. The experience of the laborers themselves took on aspects of a vacation, as they camped out, fished in streams they crossed, cooked on the ground, decorated their vehicles with smart-aleck signs, and generally enjoyed the feeling of independence. However, independence ceased and work started when

they ran out of gas. These carefree experiences soured somewhat by the Great Depression. By 1938, according to researchers' reports, about half the hands in North Dakota were riding the rails again, and hitchhiking and commercial buses transported a large proportion of the remainder. The number of independent motorists had declined.[76]

On arriving in an area where the harvest was getting under way, bindlestiffs congregated in certain traditional areas. In some towns a pool hall or similar establishment was a place for making connections with farmers; more often, however, areas such as a park, where the hands might camp out, or well-traveled streets were where the hands congregated and where farmers drove in to seek them. A common ritual was for a farmer to pull up to a congregation of men obviously looking for jobs and ask with a straight face, "Anyone here looking for work?" The farmer and the stiffs sized one another up for a while, sometimes negotiating wages but other times not even mentioning the subject. A key consideration often was that a farmer required a particular number of laborers, and the bindlestiffs traveled in groups. A farmer might announce that he needed four men, and the job was most readily filled if four men who had been traveling together stepped forward in unison. This whole ritual was obviated, of course, in such cases where farmers and particular hands had ongoing arrangements year to year.[77]

On the job, the foremost concern of the laborers was good food and plenty of it. On threshing crews where the thresherman provided a cook car and board, the hands could count on abundant fare that was adequately prepared. Boarding with farmers, the hands found the food better or worse, but more often better. Complaints about food only rarely derived from incompetence or niggardliness on the part of farmers or cooks; more commonly there was a reasonable explanation. During the pioneer era in any part of the plains and again during the Great Depression, farmers themselves were doing so poorly that they could hardly make the board groan. Those who failed to provide the best they

could bore a stigma, however; people talked, and not just among the hands. A journalist summarized the general attitude toward feeding harvest and threshing hands: "Let them have the best of what you have (and see, too, that the quantity is sufficient for the demand)."[78] Sometimes the best fare of the country seemed a little strange to the hands. Ontario boys working among the Ukrainians and other eastern Europeans of western Canada, or midwestern Americans working among the Volga-Deutsch and other immigrants on the southern plains, occasionally complained when they encountered the starchy, meat-poor food of those peoples. No complaints were heard, however, when they went into areas where local ethnic culture dictated that in addition to the three main meals, midmorning and midafternoon lunches should be taken to the field. Only one thing stifled the pleasure of hands in such a situation—the occasional problem with drinking water. Well and surface waters of the plains often are alkaline, and digestive problems made it hard to enjoy the fare.[79]

Given the loose talk that frequently circulated about drunkenness among harvest hands, complaints about drinking on the job were surprisingly few. The hours and intensity of labor prevented such abuse. Conduct between jobs was a different story, however, and was talked about to the point of legend. A newspaper in central Kansas delighted in 1913 to report in mock-tragic tone the mishap of a harvest hand: As a train containing harvesters

Exposure could be severe for hands on the northern plains in late season. Shown is an outfit on the J. R. Brown farm, Qu'Appelle District, Sask., in January 1890. (Saskatchewan Archives Board, Regina)

was pulling out of the Santa Fe depot, a local farmer held up three fingers, signifying three dollars a day, and one of the men was persuaded to leap from the moving train. He took a nasty spill, but worse, "several bottles of perfectly good beer fell to the brick pavement and were totally destroyed. With the stringent Mahan [bone-dry] Law in effect, such an occurrence was no less a tragedy, especially to a Missourian who brought this sustenance to tide him through the hot harvest."[80] Neither was it regarded as surprising one night in 1938 in Devil's Lake, North Dakota, when after a spell of rain that brought

the men in off the farms, forty-seven were jailed for public drunkenness.[81]

Lodging was another important concern of the hands, and here again they had realistic expectations corresponding to the stage of civilization of the area in which they were working: Pioneer times wrought pioneer conditions for all. A thresherman reported from Kingfisher, Oklahoma, in 1912, "The straw pile is everybody's bed here. Sometimes we don't get near a house all week."[82] As their own circumstances permitted, farmers did better for harvesting and threshing crews. Lescohier found that in 1921 about two-thirds of

The burlap-covered, crockery water jug was the recourse of these threshers near Rockyford, Alta., 1929. (Glenbow Archives)

farmers lodged men in their own houses. The majority of the rest provided sleeping places in barns or granaries, and a few erected bunkhouses or tents. Except when there was severe exposure to cold on the northern plains, hands seldom griped about their quarters; but they complained severely if denied bathing facilities. Many farmers provided use of their own bathrooms, but hands were fairly satisfied if the farmer just cleaned up a watering trough for them. At mealtime they wanted sufficient basins of water, soap, and towels for washing up, and they appreciated combs and mirrors so that they could be presentable when they came to the table.[83]

Employers were wise to feed and lodge their help well, for they expected unrelenting toil from them. The hours seemed long to hands who did not come from farms themselves; but farmers did not regard ten to twelve hours a day as excessive because they and their families did chores before and after the fieldwork. Asked if any farmers of his experience were tough to work for, Milo Mathews replied, "They all were in those days. They had to be tough to survive, and they intended everyone who worked for them to do a hard day's work." The religious commitments of certain farmers and threshermen might provide reprieve from the toil on Sundays (or Saturdays), but the Lord's Day Act could not do so in the prairie provinces of Canada. The attorney general of Canada received frequent inquiries about

The Independence Day holiday in 1913 brought no break in the work except for lunch on the Ernest Anschutz farm, central Kansas. (Halbe Collection, Kansas State Historical Society, Topeka)

whether it was permissible to thresh on Sundays; he refused to rule on the question, leaving it to individual farmers and threshermen.[84]

The question of safety in the field seldom came up, for the risks of transient harvest hands were greater on the road than in the field. In 1914 a physician in Joplin, Missouri, gathered information about thirty-four deaths or serious injuries of transient harvesters in the adjacent winter-wheat belt. Of these, eleven died or were hurt in railroad accidents; four were victims of violent incidents, including one who was shot by a railroad brakeman; and two somehow drowned. Only seven of the deaths or serious injuries were definitely attributable to work in the fields: Three suffered the effects of heat, and five suffered simple exhaustion from

work. The remaining six deaths or serious injuries were victims of lightning, which may have taken place in the field or elsewhere.[85]

In the main, when laborers were at work alongside farmers in the field, troubles and disputes were few; however, when authorities attempted to manage and manipulate large numbers of laborers, even if their intentions were honorable, the problems were massive and scandalous. Some of the outrages that took place on the Canadian harvest excursions were such that it was ridiculous for American authorities to praise Canadian practice as they sometimes did in print. Every year there were fist fights and petty crime and vandalism on the trains, stimulated by supplies of liquor taken aboard; but in some years the situation degener-

The hands, bedrolls, and tent of the Jake Zook crew, Pawnee County, Kans., ca. 1918. (Santa Fe Trail Center, Larned, Kans.)

ated into outright riot as harvesters left trains at stops to ransack stores and to brawl with railroad trackmen. The most infamous episode was the harvest excursion of 1908. That year a particularly disreputable collection of excursionists got the upper hand on the trains and utterly ransacked them, terrorized residents and businesspeople in every town through which they passed, carried on a running battle with immigrant trackmen, committed multiple rapes and assaults, and generally were completely out of the control of Canadian Pacific Railroad detectives or law enforcement authorities.[86]

A more basic problem with the excursion system lay not in its execution but rather in its design. Authorities responsible for estimating needs for laborers as well as for recruiting them operated on unreliable intelligence and were subject to political pressures, including issues not directly related to the harvest, such as assimilation of immigrants and promotion of settlement. The outstanding example of miscalculation was the importation of British harvesters in 1928. Fearing shortages of labor that year, the Department of Immigration of Canada gave in to pressure and allowed the hasty setup of a recruitment program in Britain. The recruitment aspect of the program was effective, and the harvesters were transported to the west; but organizers had failed utterly to provide for the orderly dispersal of these harvesters to points of need. Canadian officials had hoped that the British importation of 1928 would be a spur to immigration, but the movement was such a fiasco, and criticism by both the press and the participants was so bitter, that the whole affair turned out to be a source of international enmity.[87]

A disturbance that Canadian authorities did prevent was the organization and agitation of the Industrial Workers of the World (IWW), or Wobblies. The authorities kept careful watch for them. In 1923 a writer for the *Regina Morning Leader* felt compelled to inform his readers that they need not fear an influx of Wobbly organizers among American harvesters entering Saskatchewan through North Portal. The Royal Canadian Mounted Police was questioning them at the border and making sure no Wobblies were coming in, he reported: "There is no doubt that many carry the tell-tale 'red card' while traveling on freights in the U.S. as this is the recognized passport for freight travel by members of the fraternity. . . . They, however, leave the card for owners of poolrooms and restaurants on the Dakota side of the line who, for a consideration, keep them until called for on the harvester's return."[88]

The Wobblies were indeed the source of great speculation and concern on the American side of the border. They were, however, but one element in a set of circumstances during the years 1914 through the early 1920s whereby bindlestiffs of the wheat belt were exploited by organizers intent not on helping the harvest hands, or even on offering them unbiased brokerage

(as that envisioned by such progressives as Lescohier), but rather on their own partisan agendas.

Organizers of the Industrial Workers of the World became interested in harvest labor because they perceived the bindlestiffs as ideal instruments of "revolutionary unionism," as a writer in *Solidarity* made clear. The bindlestiffs were men who traveled freely, without families, and so were "admirably fitted to serve as scouts and advance guard of the labor army." This Wobbly writer foresaw the day when former harvest hands would constitute "the guerilla of the revolution."[89] Consequently, in the fall of 1914 the IWW called for representatives of its locals in cities adjacent to the wheat belt to assemble in Kansas City the following spring and plan an effort to organize among the migrant harvest workers. Thus in 1915 the representatives formed a new Wobbly organization—the Agricultural Workers Organization, or, more commonly, "No. 400." The AWO planned to organize bindlestiffs mainly through traveling delegates rather than by stationary locals.[90]

For the next few years IWW organizers in the wheat belt sought to overthrow capitalism by using transient laborers as their instruments. The IWW frequently appeared to function as a legitimate union representing the wage and other interests of harvest hands, and many hands joined it for that reason; but the key indication of the intent of the organization was that its representatives called for the stiffs to strike against any proffered wage, whatever it was. As one Wobbly proclaimed to a group of workers in Colby, Kansas, in 1921, "We don't want an honest day's work for an honest day's pay, we want the abolition of the wage system."[91] Traveling delegates, backed but only loosely supervised by a headquarters in Minneapolis, used a variety of tactics, the most important being to infiltrate harvesting and threshing crews in the field. Organizers frequently concealed their red cards and their sentiments in order to be hired by farmers; once upon the job, they encouraged the men to strike unless given better wages. Wobbly policy specifically sanctioned sabotage and violence where necessary; this was particularly addressed at petty capitalist threshermen. Violence against fellow workers, too, was justified in Wobbly doctrine. Wobblies took control of transient camps in many communities and expelled nonmembers from them. More important to traveling harvesters was the Wobbly practice of boarding freight trains and kicking off riders who refused to take out membership. Their tactics were evidently fairly effective, at least in the recruitment of members, for by the fall of 1916 the AWO claimed twenty thousand members. The infusion of their dues reinvigorated the entire Wobbly organization.[92]

By unhappy coincidence, at about this time other parties of diametrically opposite philosophy from the Wobblies took action to implement their own designs on harvest laborers. Early in 1914, with the backing of a private organization known as the National Farm Labor Exchange, the Division of Information of the United States Bureau of Labor undertook a massive campaign to attract transient laborers to the wheat belt for the harvest. Throughout the country it distributed press releases and handbills extolling the opportunities available for laborers, not only saying with some truth that wages were up to three dollars a day but also proclaiming that the term of labor was from three to six months, which was patently false. The reckless irresponsibility of employment officials was matched by that of newspaper editors who, boosting their own localities, greatly exaggerated their needs for labor. As a result, stated one reporter, "men came from every direction."[93] The requirements for labor had been grossly overestimated. Overall, the labor bureau had called for more than one hundred thousand men; but this gross figure was composed of innumerable wild, seat-of-the-pants figures quoted by local authorities. In a published report, Barton County, Kansas, alone demanded that four thousand men be sent. Combined with the lack of secondary direction to assist men to particular needy localities, the scene was set for a fiasco.[94]

Already in late May the *Topeka Daily Capital* headlined, "Men Flood Kansas Wheat Belt Seeking Employment." Farmers along railroad lines found themselves besieged by hands who had been attracted by the publicity and were arriving far too early for the harvest and begging for sustenance. As the harvest got under way, moods turned ugly. Bindlestiffs overpowered freight train crews in Columbus and Cherryvale, no longer seeking passage surreptitiously but rather demanding it belligerently. In Hutchinson, a great gathering point for harvesters every year, the men piled up and "General" William Baumgardner, a laborer out of the oil fields, led hundreds in a march on the city police station. "We have had nothing to eat today and we want the city to feed us," Baumgardner announced, and the city responded. The mayor gave the stiffs tickets for free meals in cafés, and within the next two days they had fanned out to other points in the wheat belt. Smaller centers of the harvest were forced to the same recourse, issuing tickets for meals or, in the case of Hoisington, opening a municipal kitchen to feed the harvesters.[95]

The labor bureau continued its irresponsible recruiting through the early 1920s while at the same time the IWW labored energetically to convert the often disillusioned bindlestiffs to its cause. Chaos did not result—the harvest was not crippled or capitalism shaken; but numerous individuals suffered. Beginning in 1914 and accelerating through 1916, as IWW strength grew and its notoriety increased, local law enforcement authorities throughout the plains reacted more and more violently and often illegally. County sheriffs and deputies, often aided by local vigilantes, raided hobo jungles and searched boxcars, running out of town anyone suspected of being a member of the IWW or of just not

being needed in town at that particular time. The wildest rumors circulated and gained exposure in the public press so that it was impossible to sort genuine disturbance from malicious gossip. In early July 1916 a reported twelve hundred Wobblies gathered near WaKeeney, Kansas, and threatened to raid the town. The story was that the town sent for aid from Governor Arthur Capper, who replied that he could send none because the National Guard had been sent to patrol the Mexican border. Citizens of the town armed themselves, and farmers, fearing for safety in the country, came to stay in town; such scenes had not been enacted in Kansas since Dull Knife's Cheyennes raided the state in 1878. Eastward, in Salina, Sheriff August Anderson swore in fifty deputies to go through the hobo camps and run six hundred to eight hundred men out of town, arresting twelve Wobblies. Meanwhile, two hundred Wobblies took over a train in Oakley and forced the crew to take them to Colby. The state fire marshal was said to be discovering fire bombs in wheat stacks throughout the western part of the state. In Lincoln, Nebraska, the local sheriff, whose father had been hit on the head with a skillet brandished by a Wobbly, cached firearms and swore in deputies to defend the jail against a reported Wobbly force of up to six thousand men. What was mostly smoke in Kansas and Nebraska turned out to be fire by the time the harvest had proceeded to the spring wheat region. Two farmers in North Dakota were shot by

Wobblies in separate incidents during the harvest of 1916.[96]

The crisis deepened as the United States entered the war in 1917, bringing both a quickening of the wheat economy and a stirring of pseudo-patriotic antiradicalism. An odd interlude first occurred in North Dakota when the agrarian socialist Nonpartisan League, attempting to ensure a peaceful harvest for its farmer members, negotiated an agreement whereby the IWW would be recognized as the bargaining agent for harvest hands in the state. The membership across the spring wheat belt refused to approve this unlikely arrangement, however, and the agreement died except for a feeble attempt by Thorstein Veblen, the political economist, to persuade federal authorities to sanction it as a wartime measure. Meanwhile, local authorities throughout the plains, gaining inspiration from the national mood condemning radicalism during wartime, acted with unprecedented vigor to disperse Wobblies wherever they might gather. Their vigor was such that during the harvest of 1917 Governor Lynn J. Frazier of North Dakota felt compelled to issue a proclamation to peace officers charging them to cease illegal persecution of Wobblies. In Nebraska fifty-one Wobblies were charged by the United States Department of Justice with conspiracy to violate the Selective Service Act and the Espionage Act, but they were never brought to trial. Over the next few wartime and postwar years, the Wobblies disintegrated as an organization to the point

that they could only muster brief flurries of resistance in isolated localities. For instance, during the harvest of 1921 they staged a week-long stoppage of work at Colby, Kansas, but the men who gathered in town were ultimately dispersed by gun-wielding railroad detectives. The last significant event concerning Wobblies in the wheat belt involved the arrest of an organizer named Harold Fiske in 1923 in Geneseo, Kansas. Fiske was convicted of violating the Kansas Criminal Syndicalism Act; his appeal to the United States Supreme Court resulted in a landmark victory for free speech under the First and Fourteenth amendments to the United States Constitution.[97]

The Nonpartisan League's position notwithstanding, farmers' attitudes toward the IWW were tolerant at best and more commonly bitter. "If you heard of the IWWs they were troublemakers," recalled George Hitz. "What they tried to accomplish I don't know." Fellow North Dakotan William Lies said that farmers wryly joked that the initials IWW stood for "I won't work," "I want women," or "I want wine." Farmers cited with approval examples such as a neighbor of Lies who "had some trouble with a group, and he pulled out a revolver, 'I'll give you SOBs five minutes to get off the place.'"

For their part, bindlestiffs were greatly disillusioned by the way they had been manipulated by employment authorities, and they ceased believing what was announced to them in the press. A song propagated by the Wobblies and sung to the tune of "Beulah Land," entitled in this case "Harvest Land," played upon this disillusionment. In successive stanzas of the song, farmers and public authorities were depicted as promising harvesters feather beds, pleading with them to come to their fields, and then treating them shabbily. All in all, as Lescohier observed, it was "unfortunate that the first organized effort of the migratory laborers to better their condition should have fallen into the control of an organization that is more interested in socialism than in the welfare of the migratory laborer." It was equally unfortunate that laborers were not dealt with responsibly by public authorities.[98]

Furthermore, the lifestyle of harvest hands was not portrayed accurately to the reading public of North America. The story of harvest labor was so broad and so complicated that the tendency of journalists was to reduce it to stereotypes, a cast of simple characters. In these narratives, students figured out of all proportion to their documented numbers in the harvest. It was good style to throw in a bit of variation—for example, one journalist's student character stated an aspiration to write an epic novel about wheat and democracy, another's group of students alighted at the station chanting "Rah, rah, Harvard," and still another writer's traveling students were in the charge of a benevolent Professor Poindexter. However, the stereotype always took shape: The students were terribly naive but willing workers who proved to be good. When they had no Professor

Poindexter to shepherd them, the students depicted in the press commonly fell under the influence of some savvy hobo who showed them the ropes. Factory workers, too, acquitted themselves well in such accounts, especially when compared with soft-handed white-collar types who came out of the cities or with simple bums who dodged work wherever it appeared. All, of course, rejected the overtures of the misguided Wobblies.[99]

Although not many of their reflections reached print, farm families generally achieved a better understanding than did others of the bindlestiffs who came among them at the harvest. Ernest Claassen recalled that one day he was binding his wheat and one of his shockers commenced grumbling that the bundles were not tied properly. "He walked up and began examining the knotter. I thought that was a good one, what did you know about knotters?" The hand quickly saw, however, that the knife that cut the twine was dull and needed sharpening. The problem was corrected, and Claassen came away with a different view of the man. It was not unlike the conclusion reached by Doris A. Copeland, a farm woman from Saskatchewan, who wrote a long poem called "The Harvest Trains," about the hands who worked on the family farm. The final stanza contained the lines "For they had earned / Our respect and our trust."[100]

Children had a particular fascination with the hands who came to the place each year. A woman who grew up in Saskatchewan, the daughter of a thresherman, recalled many of the characters who worked for her father. There was the stout fellow who gave such new meaning to the old phrase "eating like a harvest hand" that the entranced girl forgot to eat when she watched him. Or there was the notable occasion when her father brought home a black laborer from the Canadian Pacific Railroad station. The children at first looked at him with "round-eyed wonder" and then quickly took to following him around the place "like puppies."[101]

Down in western Kansas, a veteran threshing hand patiently taught young Guy Bretz a folk poem, making a gentle point about the hours he was working on the crew:

> The farmer stood on the wheat stack,
> The hobo sat on the ground.
> Says the hobo to the farmer,
> "Will you quit when the sun goes down?"
> "Hell, no," says the farmer.
> We will work as long as it is light."
> Says the hobo to the farmer,
> "Give me my time tonight.
> I'll roam this wide world over,
> I'll travel from town to town,
> Until I find some damned old farmer
> That will quit when the sun goes down."

The thoughts of harvest hands themselves found their way into print more frequently, but those published were not representative of bindlestiffs as a class. Those who wrote for publication were atypically educated and articulate. Taken as a body, their writings formed a branch of that literary genre common to the nineteenth century—the personal narrative of travel and adventure. As in *Robinson Crusoe, Three Years before the Mast,* or *The Oregon Trail,* the summer harvesters left civilization and traveled among the strange peoples and customs of the wheat belt. They returned home to relate what they had seen, and they concluded that they had been much improved by the experience. "Back on Chicago Street again, with the tang of frost in the air, I felt like a bull moose straight from the woods," concluded one.[102] Another harvester, Robert L. Yates, was sufficiently moved by his experience on a harvest excursion to the Canadian west to pen a book about it entitled *When I Was a Harvester.* This coming-of-age memoir, like other published personal narratives, emphasized the romance of travel and the flowering of manhood.[103]

Alongside these published accounts of the educated elite in the harvest stands the unpublished memoir of a relatively uneducated common laborer, Robert G. Trussler, who had been a Canadian harvest excursionist in 1925. Remarkably, without mouthing any such clichés as might have been learned from the press and without any evident stretching of the truth, Trussler penned a narrative that corresponded closely in theme to the writings of his more educated colleagues but was more effective because of his lack of self-consciousness and ostentation. He was a farm boy in Ontario who felt he just had to get away from home. He made the journey west, and what he saw fascinated him—the rich productivity of the wheatlands and the more barren reaches of the Canadian plains, the city lights of Winnipeg and the verdant valley of the South Saskatchewan River.[104]

The poet Vachel Lindsay worked among harvesters to the south, in Kansas, and wrote,

> We feasted high in Kansas
> And had much milk and meat.
> The tables groaned to give us power
> Wherewith to save the wheat.
> And we felt free in Kansas
> From any sort of fear,
> For thirty thousand tramps like us
> There harvest every year.[105]

What did it mean when an uneducated laborer could scrawl an account that in its perceptive romance corresponded so closely to that of a popular American poet? Does this in any way explain why bindlestiffs of diverse social and economic background continually came to the plains when abundant testimony had it that they were unlikely to enrich themselves much by their extended travel and wearisome toil? How do these things relate to Carey McWilliams's mourning of the passing of transient labor in the wheat belt as an end to the opportunity for farmers from neighboring regions to earn extra money?

In some senses McWilliams obviously was off the mark. The wheat harvest could not have been a reliable source of supplementary income for many farmers from surrounding areas, for the pay was not good enough to make up for the time and risks involved. McWilliams also reckoned too little with the exploitation of laborers, who were manipulated by both employment officials and radical labor organizers. Still, McWilliams was absolutely right in perceiving that bindlestiff labor in the wheat belt was a story different from that of casual transient labor elsewhere in North American agriculture. There existed in the wheat belt no clear-cut situation of exploitation of laborers by an employer class. When the harvesting movement ended, something appealing in its own way died. If it was not an economic opportunity, it was a personal opportunity important to tens of thousands of individuals at a certain stage in their lives. The published adventures of the western harvest may not have revealed the whole story, but they were nevertheless true tales of the North American plains.

CHAPTER FIVE.
COMBINES

To Henry J. Allen—editor of the *Wichita Beacon,* former governor, and Kansas progressive—it was a godsend, a "wonder," a "marvel." For years farmers of the wheat belt "had been dependent wholly upon the peregrinetic harvest hands," had awaited each year the "picturesque lot" of "Wops," "slow Swedes," and "bohunks," with Wobblies "breathing discontent" among them and old hoboes corrupting young hands through drinking and gambling. But no more as of 1927, when Allen reported for *American Review of Reviews* on the advent of "the new harvest hand"—the combined harvester. "No mechanical advancement has ever wrought a revolution so nearly complete in any agricultural region as has the 'combine' in the western wheat fields," he asserted. As a result, the bindlestiffs had "gone to join the buffalo hunters, the hard-riding cowboys, the bartenders, the gamblers, the herds of wild horses, and the other elements which have helped this wide agricul-

tural country at various periods of its development from its raw state to its present circumstance." [1] Allen celebrated the combine as parcel to the mechanization of wheat farming on the plains, a process that he regarded as wholly good and liberating. Few plains folk would have disagreed with him then, although nostalgic ones would later. All would concur, however, that the change was important, more important even than Allen realized.

Over the previous generation, certain patterns of harvesting and threshing had evolved to suit the agriculture of the plains. Given the environment and the type of agriculture practiced there, both binders and headers had come into use, depending on local conditions; both cooperative and custom threshing had been employed, depending again on local conditions; and both resident and transient labor had come together to make the systems work. These systems were not in crisis or atrophy when combines arrived. They

Rumely Oil-Pull powering the McKinney threshing outfit in Texas, ca. 1920. (Courtesy of Ned Mc-Kinney)

were flourishing, despite frequent adversity for wheat farmers. These patterns did not fail but rather gave way to general mechanization, which in turn derived from both economic and technological developments. The process of giving way took place in stages, with various parts of the plains responding in different fashion, but with the same result everywhere: adoption of the combine and an end to previous systems of harvesting and threshing.

The gasoline (or kerosene) tractor was at the center of the mechanization that changed harvesting and threshing in the wheat belt. (This might have

been expected, for when John Froelich built the first successful gasoline tractor in Iowa in 1892, his first use for it was to hitch it to a separator.) Tractors became big news in wheat country after around 1909, when the Rumely Company introduced its popular Oil Pull and other old firms came up with comparable machines. These great early tractors borrowed much of their engineering from their steam traction predecessors. They were good for pulling big gang plows across wide open spaces or powering bull threshers next to wheat stacks. Some custom men and big farmers bought them, but most just

A fuel tank replaced the coal car on the Voth outfit, ca. 1910. (Courtesy of Moses Voth)

read in farm journals about their hero-
ics at the annual Winnipeg tractor
trials.[2]

It was at these Winnipeg trials, in
1913, that company designers
broached the idea of smaller tractors;
thereafter, manufacturers sought mass
sales of tractors that were lighter,
cheaper, and more versatile. Shortages
of horseflesh and human labor during
World War I spurred tractor development and sales. The small tractor definitely had arrived when Henry Ford
brought out his Fordson in 1917, after
which the automakers and farm machinery makers fought for the tractor
market. Farmers benefited from the

competition. The John Deere D tractor,
released in 1923, and the International
Harvester Farmall, released in 1924,
became great favorites.[5]

Statistics on tractor ownership recorded by the Kansas State Board of
Agriculture exemplified the process of
adoption in the winter wheat region
(see Figure 5.1). Prior to the Great War,
the number of tractors was insignificant except that certain custom men no
doubt gave their machines heavy use.
In 1915 the state boasted fewer than
2,500 tractors. Thereafter, through the
1920s, adoption of the tractor proceeded rapidly. By 1931 the state had
56,545 tractors. Distribution was not

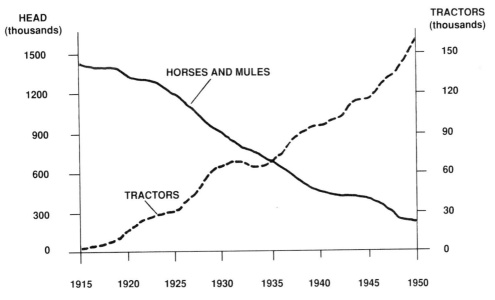

HEAD
(thousands)

TRACTORS
(thousands)

Figure 5.1 Horses, Mules, and Tractors on Kansas Farms, 1915–1950. *Source:* Data from the Kansas State Board of Agriculture document on mechanization of agriculture through replacement of horses by tractors, *Biennial Report, 1949–1950* (Topeka: State Printer, 1951). (Data from January 1 of each year.)

even across the state, however; tractors were concentrated in areas where winter wheat farming predominated. Reno led all counties with 1,752 tractors, followed by McPherson with 1,532. These, and all other leading counties that adopted the tractor, were in wheat country. Eastern counties, where farming was much more diversified, had few tractors; Johnson County had but 316, for instance, and Anderson County only 265. Generally, then, the winter wheat region converted to tractors during the 1920s; the 1930s brought a pause in mechanization; and once the depression had eased, adoption of the tractor proceeded throughout the state.[4]

Figures compiled on the number of tractors sold in the three prairie provinces of Canada indicated that a parallel process occurred a few years later in the spring wheat area (see Table 5.1). There tractor sales flurried during prosperous times just after World War I, stagnated during the early 1920s, and swelled during the late 1920s, before the depression dampened them again. Completion of the conversion to tractors would have to await the return of better times.[5]

The presence of large numbers of tractors affected both harvesting and threshing in the wheat belt. Big farmers of the northern plains first tinkered with devices whereby they could draw

Early gas tractors were just as massive as the steamers they replaced. The C. R. Voth crew sits next to tractor, ca. 1910. (Courtesy of Moses Voth)

Oiling valves on an Erie tractor in western Kansas, 1923. (Courtesy of Franz Goossen)

Table 5.1. Number of Tractors Sold in the
Prairie Provinces, 1919–1931

Year	Alberta	Saskatchewan	Manitoba	All
1919	1,703	3,514	3,627	8,844
1920	2,379	4,229	3,671	10,279
1921	716	1,665	1,057	3,428
1922	386	2,475	1,361	4,222
1923	731	2,524	911	4,166
1924	434	1,213	465	2,112
1925	869	2,176	1,008	4,053
1926	1,311	3,704	1,498	6,513
1927	2,885	5,727	1,414	10,026
1928	6,231	8,703	2,209	17,143
1929	5,228	6,906	2,423	14,557
1930	3,100	4,350	1,541	8,991
1931	334	267	186	787

Source: Adapted from R. Bruce Shepard, "Tractors and Combines in the Second Stage of Agricultural Mechanization on the Canadian Plains," *Prairie Forum* 11 (Fall 1986): 260.

three or more binders in tandem behind their large tractors. The hitching worked satisfactorily, but the whole idea was impractical: Such harvesting required not only a tractor driver but also a man on each binder, and if one had mechanical trouble, they all stopped. The advent of small tractors (particularly those with power take-off) was much more important in the mechanization of binding; but the change was in the source of power only, not in the system. The tractor replaced the team. Moreover, tractors were never used to a significant extent to power headers, except when they were combined with stack-barges.[6]

The effect of tractors on threshing was more profound. If farmers ac-

McCormick-Deering tractor hauling grain to the elevator in Saskatchewan, late 1920s. (Courtesy of Hal Lewis)

Binders hitched in tandem by G. L. Mumma near Dighton, Kans., ca. 1925. (Lane County Historical Museum, Dighton, Kans.)

Three binders and five men with an oil-pull tractor on the William Phillips farm, Belpre, Kans., ca. 1920. (Santa Fe Trail Center, Larned, Kans.)

quired their own engines, then they would be tempted to also get their own separators and do away with custom threshing altogether. Small separators (twenty- to thirty-inch cylinder), suitable for one or a few farmers to use, were available and seemed particularly attractive in developing areas where

steam rigs were slow in getting to all farms—such as in much of western Canada.

In 1914 the minister of agriculture of Saskatchewan sent an agent, W. G. Mawhinney, into the field to check out the work of small threshing machines.[7] He observed twenty-seven rigs in the

Small thresher in Saskatchewan, 1927. (Courtesy of Hal Lewis)

field and talked to the owners, who "were very enthusiastic about them, and thought that they were the only machine for farmers on small farms." Mawhinney found the machines "working along quite smoothly" and "doing just as good threshing as larger, and perhaps a little better, because they cannot be over-crowded." He thought that farmers would be little interested in small separators if they could get timely service from big rigs, but that was too often not the case. Mawhinney's report on farmers' satisfaction with small separators could not have been much of a surprise, for in 1911 his boss, W. R. Motherwell, had bought

a small separator and portable gas engine and had dispensed with the services of the Stueck brothers' steam rig on his farm, Lanark Place.[8]

Major implement manufacturers supplied small separators along with large ones while small entrepreneurial companies in both the United States and Canada challenged them for the small-thresher market with populist, regional appeals. Thus the Southwest Manufacturing Company of Oklahoma City called its product the Homestead Thresher. A Quebec firm owned by Stanley Jones named its small thresher the Call of the West and promoted it in poetry, or what passed for poetry:

And while the thresher sits and
  moans
He hears the hum of a STANLEY
  JONES
"If only I had one of THEM," he
  groans,
With watery eye
A year has flown; a new crop comes,
A "CALL OF THE WEST" in his field
  hums,
Good-bye repair bills and feed for
  bums,
Big rig—GOOD-BYE.[9]

With gas tractors, not just portable
engines, becoming available to power
the little rigs, custom men were dis-
turbed, and some were even incensed.
Already in 1911 steam thresherman
F. J. Main was denouncing "the *gasites*"
who, "hypnotized with their own elo-
quence," regarded themselves as "God's
chosen people" and the wheat country
as their promised land. He was conservative. "It seems highly presumptu-
ous to assume," said Main, "that the
steam engine which has been in the
process of development for over one
hundred fifty years and is the one absolutely dependable motive power in
the world today can be thrust aside so
easily by a motive power that is in the
incubator stage, and which, at best,
does not possess the inherent power of
steam." He cited results of the Winnipeg trials, where steam-powered engines had compared favorably with
gasoline-powered ones, except for fuel
economy. Shame on any steam man,
Main chided, who went "chasing after

this species of *ignis-fatuus*. . . . It's too
much like selling one's birthright for a
mess of pottage."[10]
   For a half-generation thereafter
steam and big-rig loyalists reiterated
Main's arguments (usually with less
spleen), although their ranks gradually
thinned. In 1926 a Lebanon, Kansas,
man declared himself still "in the class
with the 'Big Boys' " and proud of it.
He denounced the "Midgets," which he
said the manufacturers promoted only
because they broke down so often that
the dealers could sell plenty of parts.
"Stick to it, brethern, and history will
repeat itself bye and bye," he admon-
ished.[11] One of the "brethern" from
South Dakota vowed the same year, "I
own and operate a large machine and
expect to do so for the next 25 or 30
years." He said that he threshed the
past two years for a group of farmers
who had a small machine but had
found the cooperative arrangement
unworkable.[12] Another chimed in that
small threshers were uneconomical
both in their waste of grain through
poor threshing and in their excessive
capitalization and depreciation. Moreover, he said, farmer-operators fooled
themselves about their ability to "run
both ends" of the rig, that is, be both
tractor man and separator man: "It is
amusing and ridiculous to see the two-
job man trying to break the world's record for a 50-yard dash from the separator to the tractor when something
goes wrong."[13]
   Although the romance of the big rigs
was powerful, threshermen were inno-

vative, and most were prepared to adapt to changing technology. *Canadian Thresherman* observed already in 1911 that "to the man who has watched the threshing proposition carefully, there is evidence of a change. That change will not be toward larger outfits. . . . This change has been brought about by the advent of the gas tractor and the introduction of a system of power farming."[14] A few years later a Nebraska enthusiast proclaimed, "you fellows can take all the steam engines you like but for my part I will take gas as long as I can get it."[15]

Such pronouncements were premature but prescient. A survey performed by International Harvester Company confirmed that small separators, powered by gas tractors, were proliferating and changing the whole business of threshing. The small machines, although usually owned individually, had become "neighborhood machines." "The owner of this small machine has become a farmer-thresherman," commented a writer for *Power Farming,* "and he is the man who is replacing the custom or professional thresherman."[16]

Neither was this a phenomenon confined to small-farm areas. In Big Sky Montana, researchers reported in 1924 that "small threshing outfits with cylinders of 20 to 26 inches and which are operated by, say, a 15-30 tractor, are growing in popularity."[17] C. E. Lyons ran one of the small rigs in Montana. He reported that the proliferation of small outfits disrupted runs, made determination of rates difficult, some-

times caused neighborly disputes, and was not the answer in all localities; but he concluded that "every type of machine has its legitimate place."[18]

The reasons for the switch to gas and small rigs were more complex than admitted by the friends of steam and big rigs, who commonly confined discussion to narrowly defined points of horsepower and economics. In parts of the Canadian plains, for instance, the water limed up steam engines rapidly; there gas tractors were particularly welcome. In other places, coal was the problem. "The coal is also high priced here," wrote a North Dakotan who had bought a gas rig, "and, as it makes a lot of hauling, the fuel bill for a season's run amounts to large figures."[19] The cost of a small separator seemed reasonable if the buyer already had a tractor, and kerosene was cheap.

The most important point to a farmer who was thinking about buying a separator was timely threshing. Under the old system, asked a writer in *Canadian Thresherman,* "Does he get his threshing done when and how he would like it? I am afraid in the majority of cases we would get an answer in the negative."[20] In some respects the concern was concrete. Grain did deteriorate if rains came while it awaited threshing, especially if the grain was rusty. In their hearts, though, the buyers craved autonomy more than economy. "It is not a matter of economy. Far from it," remarked an author in *American Thresherman.* "It is a matter of every man having the privilege of

The Moore-Hascall combine in Michigan, early 1850s. (Agricultural History Center, University of California–Davis)

doing as he pleases with his own property."[21]

"Can steam come back?" asked a journalist in 1931. "I know it is hard for old-time threshermen to think of forsaking their old steam tractors, and I do not blame them for hanging on as long as possible [—but] there is no turning back."[22] The previous year George Hitz's thresherman-father had given in: "Through the course of those years smaller threshing machines started to take over so my dad and uncle traded the steam outfit in 1930 for a 28-in. cylinder separator and tractor, both John Deere." That was the same year a Montana thresherman announced, "The old large rigs with 12 to 15 teams and cook cars are almost a thing of the past, the 28-inch machine

with 15-30 tractor being the most popular rig."[23]

All this meant that when the combine arrived on the North American plains, it landed in the middle of a movement by farmers toward both mechanization and independence. Both before and during the time that power farming was recasting systems of harvesting and threshing on the plains, the machine that was to displace these systems utterly—the combined harvester-thresher, or combine—was passing through a series of modifications in other regions. The first working combine was the invention of Hiram Moore and John Hascall of Kalamazoo County, Michigan, who tested it in the late 1830s. Andrew and Abner Moore (no relation to Hiram Moore) operated combines built according to the inventors' design in Michigan at least until 1853. The early combines incorporated most of the features basic to later combines. A reciprocating sickle cut the stalks; a toothed reel pushed the grain onto the platform; and a canvas apron delivered it to a threshing cylinder. Screens and a fan cleaned the threshed grain. The header, twelve feet wide, extended to the right. Each combine required sixteen horses, for the moving parts were driven from a ground wheel.

Although competition from the relatively inexpensive reaper prevented general adoption of the combine in Michigan, an intriguing sequence of events established it in the expansive wheat ranches of California. In 1854 Andrew Moore and his partner, George Leland, shipped a combine around Cape Horn to the Santa Clara Valley, where Leland that year combined about six hundred acres for wheat ranchers on a custom basis. His clients failed to pay him for the work. Worse yet, in 1856 the combine was destroyed by fires in the field.[24]

From this apparent false start, the combine took root in the Golden State. Local mechanics and farmers constructed new combines along similar lines, and during the 1880s, commercial production began. Combines built by Daniel Best, Benjamin Holt, and other manufacturers replaced headers in California in the 1890s, and after 1900, equipped with leveling devices, they rolled into the hilly wheatlands of

Figure 5.2 Areas Where Wheat Was Cut with Combines in 1919. *Source:* Data from J. H. Arnold and R. R. Spafford, "Farm Practices in Growing Wheat: A Geographical Presentation," *Yearbook of the* [U.S.] *Department of Agriculture* (Washington, D.C.: GPO, 1919), pp. 123–50.

Washington's Palouse Valley. These combines of the Far West were cumbersome but effective. Their headers were as wide as twenty feet or more, and thirty-two or more horses pulled each machine.[25]

Only a few of these monsters roamed east of the Rocky Mountains prior to World War I (see Figure 5.2). As early as 1901, F. Neeland Thomas of Great Bend, Kansas, celebrated the Fourth of July with a demonstration of a sixteen-foot Best combine. This was a "field-to-mouth" demonstration, with wheat combined by Thomas rushed to a mill, the flour to a bakery, and bread put on sale the same evening. The Loewen brothers of Meade, Kansas, tried out a

Prairie combine with auxiliary engine in Lane County, Kans., 1928. (Lane County Historical Museum, Dighton, Kans.)

thirty-foot Holt in 1915, drawing curious crowds. Isolated introductions also took place in Montana and Saskatchewan. Two men named Shaw and Edwards used a combine near Spy Hill, Saskatchewan, in 1908. In 1910 Harry Edmonds and Colin Shand, farming near Welby, Saskatchewan, imported a twenty-foot Holt combine, which they used for three years. Reports on the Edmonds-Shand machine were mixed, although the two gave the Holt company a testimonial for advertising. All these attempts were premature: First, some economic jolt was required to force farmers to abandon the headers, binders, threshers, and bindlestiffs to which they were accustomed; next, the ungainly combine had to be adapted to the specific needs of farmers on the plains.[26]

World War I provided the economic stimulus. Rising prices for grain brought advancement of the wheat frontier at the same time that conscrip-

tion and defense work absorbed many of the seasonal laborers wheat farmers needed. In 1917 or 1918 farmers on the southern plains began to purchase combines. The machines they chose were known as prairie models, with headers nine to sixteen feet wide. These filled the need for swift harvesting with limited labor but were not so large and expensive that the cost was prohibitive. Prairie combines, pulled either by horses or tractors, bore auxiliary engines to drive the threshing parts.[27]

The prairie combine was a pivotal adaptation in the history of harvesting on the plains. A few combines of comparable size had been tried a decade earlier in Idaho and the Pacific Northwest but had not been popular there. Introduced east of the Rockies with the label "prairie," this same machine found a ready market. Conflicting accounts placed the first few prairie combines in Kansas in 1917 or 1918, and

Massey-Harris No. 7 combines, bought secondhand for five hundred dollars, in Thomas County, Kans., 1929. (Courtesy of Franz Goossen)

they arrived in other winter wheat states of the southern plains at about the same time; seven were reported in northwest Texas in 1919. The important facts were that both public authorities and farmers immediately recognized the potential of combines for their region and that farmers purchased them enthusiastically within but a few years. In 1920 a writer for the Kansas State Board of Agriculture termed the combine "the greatest advance in farm labor-saving machines." He also pointed out that its adoption was practical only because of the simultaneous advent of the tractor; the tractor, his report noted, "gives a steady movement over the ground—much more so than any team of horses can

ever do."[28] He might have added that to have hitched horses to a noisy prairie combine with a gas engine on it would have been a perilous prospect.

Kansas, with more winter wheat than any other state, also had more combines from the outset. Adoption proceeded rapidly during the 1920s (see Table 5.2), and by 1930, nearly one-third of the combines in the United States were in Kansas. By this time, beginning with International Harvester in 1926, farmers could also purchase one-man combines operated from the tractor platform and powered by the tractor power take-off.[29]

The combine won this acceptance despite a few objections and problems. "The first combines came into our part

Table 5.2. Number of Combines in Use in
Kansas, 1923–1936

Year	Number	Year	Number
1923[a]	2,796	1930	21,303
1924	3,116	1931	24,656
1925	3,828	1932	25,474
1926	5,412	1933	24,197
1927	7,562	1934	25,185
1928	11,203	1935	24,743
1929	16,631	1936	24,128

Source: Derived from statistical tables in biennial
reports of the Kansas State Board of Agriculture.

[a]First year data reported.

of the country in 1918," recalled Guy
Bretz. "Big, clumsy looking piece of
machinery. I well remember my father
saying that they would never be a success; that it was hard enough to save all
the wheat with a threshing machine
setting still, so how did they expect to
do a good clean job going down
through a rough field." His father was
an old-time thresherman, of course, as
was Perry Wiseman, of Hill City, Kansas. The combine, he said, was like the
"flying machine," which "gets you there
in real style, but railroads and steam-
ships will still be doing real service
after our grandchildren join us in a
better world." [30]

The more specific concern of farmers was that with the combine, they had
to let grain stand in the field until dead
ripe, thus exposing it to greater risk of
hail, lodging, or other loss. Fear of
such loss frequently caused new combine owners to cut wheat that was too
green or too wet, resulting in its being
graded down at the elevator. Small
farmers also questioned whether the
expense of a combine—more than two

thousand dollars—was justifiable, and
those with stock objected to leaving
good straw in the field instead of stacking it in the yard. [31]

Nevertheless, when a journalist
asked combine owner C. C. Slattery of
Dodge City, Kansas, what problems the
combine entailed, Slattery answered,
"There are absolutely no objections at
all." Farmer-grain dealer Claude M.
Cave of Sublette, Kansas, told the same
reporter, "Tell the folks back east that
nothing has ever happened that has so
completely benefited and revolution-
ized wheat raising as the combine." [32]
Numerous farmers gave general reports of reduced costs of threshing;
one, Fred Wagner of Clinton, Oklahoma, gave detailed accounts showing
that combine harvesting cost him only
sixteen cents per bushel, whereas
binder harvesting and stationary
threshing had cost him thirty-five
cents. [33] Labor was the biggest savings,
users of combines said again and again,
and that was a savings both of money
and of trouble. Henry Allen's piece for
American Review of Reviews documented
the economic side of such savings, but
his emphasis was on how the combine
made the farmer independent of labor
requirements. Said a farmer in Woods
County, Oklahoma, "With my tractor,
truck, and combine, I expect never to
hire another man." [34]

A particularly popular theme with
agricultural writers was the way that
the combine liberated farm women of
the southern plains from the toil of
cooking for harvesters and threshers.
A farm woman, Henry Allen said,

Allis-Chalmers combine connected to tractor power take-off on the Alvin Isern farm, Barton County, Kans., ca. 1940. (Courtesy of Bernice Isern)

Perry Counter (on tractor) and his Nichols and Shepard combine near Oberlin, Kans., ca. 1932. (Courtesy of Mr. and Mrs. Lowell Ayers)

could easily get in an automobile and take a good meal out to the few men needed to run a combine.[35] A woman from southwestern Kansas who, in ear-

lier years, had "learned to dread harvest as I had never dreaded anything in my life," found that with the acquisition of a combine, "for the first time in

"I Am Perfectly Satisfied With My Four John Deere Combines–"

H. S. Carpenter of Hugoton, Kans., in March 1930 testified for the John Deere Corporation that he was "perfectly satisfied" with his combines. (From American Thresherman*)*

the six years of my married life, a piece of machinery was placed on the farm which would lighten my work."[36] Other (generally male) writers gave similar reports, but no farmer ever stated that he had bought a combine to make life easier for his wife.[37]

In certain circumstances, the combine held particular advantage. Sophisticated farmers intent on prompt and proper tillage rejoiced that they could plow or disk immediately after harvest with a combine. Old custom men who

bought combines found opportunities to continue custom work with them, cutting for small-farmer neighbors who had not bought the new machines. Where hail or lodging struck the crop, much grain could be salvaged, it was found, with a combine. Richard Goering remembered that in 1925, the year his father bought his combine, he had two quarters of insured wheat hailed on—50 percent damage on one, 100 percent on the other, the adjuster ruled. "I'm going to pick it up, whatever I get," the elder Goering said, and he did—twenty bushels per acre from the first quarter, seven from the totaled quarter.[38]

The coming of the combine to the southern plains became of consuming interest to scientists from the state experiment stations and the United States Department of Agriculture. Agricultural engineer H. P. Smith brought in a report on the combine in northwest Texas, finding the innovation a success in all respects. J. O. Ellsworth and R. W. Baird, agricultural engineers for the Oklahoma station, concurred with only slight qualification, saying in 1927 that the combine was "past the experimental stage and is at present the most economical method of harvesting when conditions are favorable for its use."[39] L. C. Aicher at the Fort Hays, Kansas, station, after wet harvest seasons in 1928 and 1929, defended the combine against critics who blamed the machine for wet and weedy wheat brought to elevators. The weather was bad for all methods, he said; wheat threshed from stacks came in wet and damaged, too. He insisted that "it isn't the fault of the combine so much as the fact that we are inexperienced in the handling of the combine."[40]

A covey of agricultural economists from the United States Department of Agriculture, headed by L. A. Reynoldson, weighed in with the most comprehensive combine study in 1928—*The Combined Harvester-Thresher in the Great Plains*.[41] This bulletin, exhaustive and scholarly, ranks among the most historically portentous documents in the

chronicles of the North American plains. Its interest, however, is largely historical, for it merely reported on the adoption of the combine; it did not shape the process. American agricultural scientists in general did not experiment with the combine. Rather, they asked farmers what they had done, and by the time the researchers published the results, they were history. As of 1928, when the Reynoldson bulletin appeared, that history had progressed to the point where the advantages of the combine on the southern plains were obvious and the "general satisfaction" of farmers was documented. On the northern plains, however, except in the Judith Basin of Montana, the history of the combine was only beginning.

From Michigan to the Far West and finally to the southern plains, the combine had undergone adaptations. Introduction of the prairie model had facilitated adoption of the combine on the southern plains, for farmers there preferred the twelve- or sixteen-foot size to the mammoth machines used on the West Coast. The larger combines required too great a capital investment for a region where risk of crop failure was high. Farmers on the plains also chose the auxiliary engines of the prairie models over ground wheel drive because the engines made possible a constant threshing speed, even when ground speed varied. With the arrival of the tractor, conversion to combine harvesting in the winter wheat belt of the southern plains was a mere matter of transition.

Twenty-foot, horse-drawn, ground-wheel-driven Holt combine at Ensleigh, Alta., 1927. (Glenbow Archives)

Conditions on the northern plains were somewhat different, and the adoption of the combine was delayed in that region. From 1913 to 1919 Curtis Baldwin used a prairie combine at Aneroid, Saskatchewan, but this introduction did not attract significant attention. Only Montana provided the combine with a pathway of relatively early entry into the northern plains. In 1917 the Montana Farming Corporation, soon to become the famous Campbell Farming Corporation, near Hardin, bought four combines; but by the end of World War I, there probably were not fifty of them in Montana. Although a few farmers bought combines each year thereafter, still only one hundred forty-four were sold in 1925. Sales increased rapidly in the next few years as the combine entered every part of the state where wheat was grown. The combine succeeded in the winter wheat region of Montana for the same reasons that it had farther south: Farms were larger and workers were fewer than they had been before World War I.[42]

During the 1920s, while farmers in the winter wheat regions were embracing the combine, farmers in the Dakotas and in the prairie provinces of Canada were developing a catalog of stock arguments why the machine could not succeed in the spring wheat region, mainly because conditions there were different. Some of the arguments were valid. The first objection was that use of the combine postponed the beginning of harvest too long. Harvesting with the combine began seven to ten days later than harvesting with the binder. During this time, a hailstorm might level the crop, insect pests might attack it, lodging might occur, or the grain might bleach out. In addition, wheat that stood until dead ripe was more likely to shatter at the cutter bar.

Caterpillar tractor and Holt combine, Saskatchewan, ca. 1928. (Courtesy of Hal Lewis)

These objections weighed more heavily on spring wheat farmers (nearly all of whom used binders) than on winter wheat farmers (many of whom used headers) because the binder started harvesting a week or more earlier than the combine; the header, on the other hand, started only a few days earlier. Forced delay led to premature harvesting. Combine owners grew impatient when they saw their neighbors start up their binders, and they began cutting too soon. Wet wheat thus produced was unsafe to store in the bin, and elevators refused it. It was easy to blame the combine, forgetting that the machine had been improperly used.[43]

Another problem in the northern plains concerned weeds. Spring wheat was more subject to infestation with weeds than was winter wheat. When the weather was dry, Russian thistles outgrew the wheat; when it was wet, other species sprang up. Chunks of green stems and weed seeds passed into the threshed grain, and the green materials raised the moisture content and caused spoilage, even if the wheat itself was dead ripe. A related problem was uneven ripening of spring wheat, often exacerbated by low spots or mixed seed.[44]

The brevity of the combining day on the northern plains raised yet another objection to the combine. Dew was often heavy during harvest in the early fall, meaning that combining had to wait at least until late morning, whereas on the southern plains, combiners could start earlier and work later.[45]

The counsel of agricultural researchers and of implement manufacturers was hardly designed to ease the initial qualms of spring wheat farmers about the combine. Especially skeptical were such spokesmen in Canada. Agricultural scientists there were firmly convinced that the combine was unfit for Canadian conditions. Judging by their writings, they were little versed in technical literature on the combine in the United States. Implement company spokesmen averred outright that because the combine was most effective in areas where the grain ripened evenly, the machine would not be successful on the Canadian plains. Canada's own Massey-Harris Company argued in 1922 that "the very fact that we have built these machines for many years and have never attempted to market them in Canada forms the best evidence that we do not believe there is a future for the machine in Canada."[46] The International Harvester Company argued a similar line the same year. "In order for . . . these machines to work satisfactorily, it is necessary for them to be used in a country where the climate will permit of the grain standing until it is ripe enough to thresh," the company's spokesman insisted. "The machines necessarily would not be satisfactory where the grain does not ripen evenly, and because of that fact we have

not undertaken to introduce them into the Dominion of Canada."[47]

Weighing and repeating these arguments, spring wheat farmers, Canadian and American, then considered the initial cost of the combine—about twenty-three hundred in United States dollars for a sixteen-foot prairie combine in the late 1920s.[48] This seemed high because they were used to buying a relatively inexpensive binder and hiring their threshing. These farmers decided, therefore, to keep their binders. Theirs was a comfortable stance: The arguments they repeated against the combine supported the maintenance of the system of harvesting to which they were accustomed.

Manufacturers' failure to recognize the Canadian plains as a market for the combine did not stop experimentation with the machine in the area. In 1922 both International Harvester and Massey-Harris had their machines tested at federal experimental farms in Saskatchewan, the former at Cabri and the latter at Swift Current. Initial tests at Swift Current showed the manufacturers to be wrong and were so successful that the federal government purchased the machine the same year.[49]

The Swift Current tests were the beginning of a seven-year experiment that culminated in the publication of a booklet by the Canadian federal government. This publication revealed the advantages of the combine for the Canadian plains. Although tests showed some problems due to the uneven ripening of grain, overall savings to the farmer were considerable—in the order of 50 percent. There was also less crop loss using a combine. The 1928 tests showed a 1.16 percent loss when straight combining, compared with a 3.58 percent loss with the traditional binder and separator.[50]

Unlike the scientists at Canadian experimental farms, those at American experiment stations on the northern plains, as had those on the southern plains, relied entirely on reports from farmer-users to compile their bulletins on the combine. Personnel at the Montana station, enthusiasts for mechanization of all types, in 1930 forthrightly declared the combine "a part of the new era in wheat production in Montana," part of the "revolution" attendant to introduction of the tractor. Researchers in both Dakotas were more restrained; the predominance of spring wheat in their areas worked against quick adoption of the combine.[51]

In addition to these official tests and reports, individual farmers, including Canadians, began experimenting with the machines. In 1924 the J. I. Case Threshing Machine Company sold three machines in the Rosetown district of Saskatchewan. In 1925 manufacturers sold fourteen of the machines to Canadian plains farmers—thirteen in Saskatchewan and one in Alberta. Manitoba lagged behind its plains neighbors in trying the combine—the first units did not appear in that province until 1926, when two were sold.[52]

Among the farmers to experiment with the combine in the 1920s was the prominent Albertan C. S. Noble. Noble was an American who had migrated from North Dakota in 1902 to what would become the province of Alberta. He was initially successful in farming and real estate. High wheat prices during World War I led Noble to purchase the Cameron Ranch, twenty thousand acres of rangeland that he broke with ten steam traction engines.[53]

Noble's willingness to experiment and his large-scale operation led him to purchase a J. I. Case combine in 1926. His initial experience must have been positive because the following year he bought two Holt combines. By 1929 Noble had seven machines operating in his fields—six twenty-foot Holts and a mammoth California-type Harris combine. This latter machine was the largest combine produced at the time. It cut a thirty-four-foot swath through standing grain and could thresh one acre of grain every seven and a half minutes.[54]

The success of experimenters such as C. S. Noble and the Campbell Farming Corporation was followed by other northern plains farmers through the agricultural press. Evan Hardy of the University of Saskatchewan was watching the adoption of the combine from a somewhat different perspective. Hardy had been born and raised in Sioux City, Iowa, the son of a farmer and blacksmith. He attended Iowa State University, majoring in agricultural engineering, and later took his master's degree in that field from the same school. Upon graduation Hardy eagerly accepted a position as lecturer in agricultural engineering at the University of Saskatchewan in Saskatoon and rapidly became one of the leading authorities on agricultural mechanization on the Canadian plains. His unassuming manner and practical knowledge were welcomed by farmers. He was in constant demand as a speaker by farm, industry, and government groups. Hardy also maintained an extensive correspondence with farmers, answering an estimated four thousand to five thousand letters a year on various agricultural engineering questions.[55]

During the late 1920s many of these inquiries concerned the combine. Hardy was well placed to answer, having published an article on the new machine in 1927, which suggested even earlier research. In the paper Hardy outlined how the high cost of grain production had caused an analysis of harvesting and had led to the spread of the combine into the Canadian plains from the United States. He then briefly outlined earlier experiences with the machine in Saskatchewan and the distribution of the new machines in the province.[56]

Hardy carefully examined the results from the Swift Current tests, noting in particular that the cost of harvesting was reduced with the combine. He also noted the impact of the machine on the harvest labor problem. Hardy then turned his attention to questions such as the quality of the grain when harvested with a combine, the risk of loss due to shattering, the risk of freezing, the growth of weeds, and the problem

of irregular ripening. He also discussed the problems of pests such as wireworm and the wheat-stem sawfly. Hardy concluded by arguing that "the use of the Combine is not a cure-all for farm ills. The use of it may assist, however, in solving some of the problems of the harvest. The successful Combine users are those who farm throughout the year with the use of the Combine as a goal."[57]

Hardy's cautious endorsement of the combine gave way to moderate enthusiasm in 1928. In that year he addressed an agricultural society meeting and noted that "the use of the combine has increased more than the most ardent enthusiast could have expected during the 1927 harvest."[58] He went on to say that heavy frost and rust in most areas had worked against the use of combines and that many farmers were disappointed as a result. In addition, Hardy observed that a large amount of tough grain was being harvested because farmers were not waiting for the crop to dry in the morning before beginning to combine. Still, when properly used, the combine had its advantages, and Hardy concluded by citing the case of a farmer from Ponteix, Saskatchewan, who claimed that he would have had to give up farming had his combine not helped him get his badly frozen crop off.[59]

In his speech Hardy referred to areas where combines were in use. The areas of greatest combine use on the Canadian plains in the 1920s were within a line running from the United States border to Estevan, up the Soo

Line to Moose Jaw, back toward a point northeast of Regina, and up the eastern side of Last Mountain Lake to an apex at Saskatoon. From the peak in Saskatoon the line ran to the southwest toward Calgary and the United States border, including the Rosetown-Kindersley district of Saskatchewan and the farming areas east and south of Calgary.[60]

The area in which combines were initially popular is generally a broad, open plain and tends toward larger fields and larger farms. With the cost of a combine being between twelve hundred dollars and three thousand dollars at the time, it was not surprising that larger farmers were the first to consider them. In addition, a survey taken in 1929 discovered that "the combine will be most profitable on large acreages and can be run most efficiently on large fields where few turns are necessary. It was also brought out that where the combine and its auxiliaries were to be used the fields should not be rough and should be free of stones, stumps and deep dead-furrows."[61]

The dramatic increase in sales of combines in 1928 and 1929 were likely factors in Evan Hardy's eventual complete endorsement of the machine. It was an important conversion because of Hardy's position as an authority on agricultural mechanization. The restraint in his 1927 and 1928 comments gave way to a promotional tone in a 1929 publication distributed by the University of Saskatchewan. In this brochure Hardy and his colleagues in Saskatoon advised farmers that "the advantages of harvesting with the combine are well recognized by the farmers of Western Canada. The use of the straight combine where the grain is ripened standing in the field and is cut, threshed, and delivered to the wagon or truck in one operation is most desirable."[62]

The conversion of Evan Hardy on the combine question was not so radical a turnabout as it seemed. There were extenuating circumstances. Hardy was in touch with working farmers, paid attention to what they said and did, and knew that during the 1920s the more innovative spring wheat farmers had overcome the perceived disadvantages of the combine. They had adapted the most technologically sophisticated machine in wheat farming, the combine, to their needs by advances of folk technology.

Because it had evolved in winter wheat areas where grain ripened evenly, the combine had been limited to what was known as "straight combining," that is, cutting and threshing the standing grain in one operation. The problem with combining unevenly ripened grain was that it was tough or damp. Tough grain commanded lower prices and posed storage problems. Not that the combine was entirely to blame. Echoing L. C. Aicher of Kansas, a University of Alberta specialist recognized that "new combine owners may, very naturally, become over-anxious. They see their neighbours out with binders or they fear the approach of an early snowstorm. What is more natural

A transition image: Caterpillar-drawn combine dumping in horse-drawn grain wagon, Saskatchewan, ca. 1928. (Courtesy of Hal Lewis)

than they should commence cutting a little too soon."[63]

Most spring wheat farmers were willing to embrace the combine only in conjunction with some other device that suited it to their environmental needs. One answer, certain Canadians found, was to take a folk invention—the header stack-barge—and use it to cut their unevenly ripened grain. The header stack-barge proved as handy to use with a combine as it had been with headers and separators. As a farmer from Ponteix, Saskatchewan, observed,

> Almost from the beginning I realized the necessity of constructing a twin implement to the combine, an implement to work in conjunction with it, therefore, in order to give the combine a deserving, permanent place on the farm. I constructed a homemade barge or stacker with which to dump the stacks automatically on the land. It was a success from the start, as it permitted me to select the grain fields which did appear to be unwilling to ripen evenly, or grain fields which proved badly infested by sawflies and cut them invariably on the green side.[64]

In a feature article on the adoption of the combine in 1929, the *Western Producer* concurred:

> The header-barge showed up very well in the past season. Fields where

ripening was particularly uneven and fields infested by green weeds were successfully harvested by the header-barge. The stacks dried out perfectly and the grain when threshed was of good color and the grades obtained compare favorably with those obtained for binder-cut grain or windrowed grain.[65]

Although use of the header stack-barge with the combine was to prove of some importance during the 1930s as an emergency device to handle short crops, it was not a sufficiently convenient or efficient device during ordinary times to have accomplished the general adoption of the combine in the spring wheat area. The adaptation, the "twin implement," that spread the combine across the northern plains was the windrow harvester. In 1926 managers of the Campbell Farming Corporation in Montana improvised windrowers by hitching binders in staggered formation with the tying mechanisms removed and with extension canvases delivering the cut grain to a single windrow. They threshed the windrows using Holt combines with the headers removed and with hay loaders lifting the grain into the cylinders.[66]

Although highly publicized, this experiment hardly marked the invention of windrow harvesting. In 1907 August Hovland, a South Dakota farmer, had patented a "central delivery reaper," or swather. With his brother and three other backers, he then organized a joint stock company to manufacture his invention. One was built in 1910, but

the idea was ahead of its time and little came of it. The concept was revived by Helmer and Ellert Hanson, who had known the Hovlands in South Dakota. The Hansons had moved to Lajord, Saskatchewan, southeast of Regina. In 1926 the Hanson brothers developed two twenty-foot swathers and rigged a combine to pick up the windrows. The Hansons earlier had decided not to patent their machines for fear of losing all that they owned in a patent fight. They therefore welcomed engineers from implement companies to their farms. Officials of the International Harvester Company were among the observers, which probably was why that company was the first to market swathers in 1927.[67]

Other companies followed suit that year and the next. Some of the early windrowers discharged the cut grain at the end of the platform, others at the middle. Most were powered by a bull wheel, although after a few years, models connected to the tractor power take-off were more common. The first pickup attachments were merely hay loaders that emptied into the combine cylinder, but manufacturers soon sold pickups that bolted onto the combine header, and later they developed complete combine headers designed exclusively for picking up swathed grain.

The windrower cut standing grain and let it slide gently from a pan onto the six to eight inches of stubble left standing. It was important that the grain not fall to the ground but remain suspended on top of the stubble, with air circulating underneath to facilitate

McCormick-Deering swather at work on the E. C. Nelson farm near Saskatoon, Sask., 1928. (Courtesy of Hal Lewis)

drying. The heads of the grain would be on top of the windrow and pointing toward the rear. After a few days, the combine picked up the windrow in the same direction as it had been laid down.[68]

Although farmers generally recognized the advantages of swathing, they did not all rush to buy the new machines. Many just converted their old binders into swathers by removing the knotters. Others had lingering doubts about whether the swather could solve the problems with combines. They questioned the additional expense of the extra trip through the field with a swather and cited the danger of sprouting if the swaths were left out for too long in warm, wet weather. Yet most thought that the advantages of swathing were too obvious and argued

that the new machine would be used where the grain did not ripen uniformly, thereby extending the area where combines could be used successfully.[69]

The debates doubtless continued around cook stoves during the winters of the late 1920s. By 1929 the argument was on its way toward being settled, and the Department of Agriculture at the University of Saskatchewan could report that

the windrow method of harvesting small grains with a combine spread last year by leaps and bounds. In many sections where the combine had been used in the past to cut and thresh standing grain, crops were windrowed for the first time this past season and picked up later

Header, with the elevator removed, being used as a swather in Thomas County, Kans., 1929. (Courtesy of Franz Goossen)

from the windrow with the combine. In other parts of the country, the windrow method has made combining possible, where before it was considered impractical.[70]

Windrow harvesting resolved most of the objections to the combine voiced by spring wheat farmers. The windrower could begin the harvest about the same time as could the binder. It eliminated the problem of farmers starting to combine too early, for it kept them busy swathing. Green weeds swathed with the grain dried out in the windrow. Swath harvesting had certain disadvantages, too: The windrower was one more piece of machinery to buy; the necessity of going over the field twice instead of just once cost additional labor and fuel; and grain in the windrow was not quite so safe as grain in the shock because it was subject to winds rolling the windrows or rains driving them to the ground. Nevertheless, the advantages were sufficient to enable farmers of the northern plains to embrace the labor-saving combine already utilized by their southern brothers.[71]

Farmers who compared costs soon recognized the economic advantage of combining. Repeated trials showed that the cost of operating a prairie combine was less than US $1.50 an acre. Including costs for swathing, the expense of harvesting and threshing with the combine still totaled less than US $2.00 an

Professors from the University of Saskatchewan observing a new combine pickup at work, ca. 1929. (*Courtesy of Hal Lewis*)

acre. The cost of harvesting and threshing the same crop with a binder and a stationary separator consistently totaled more than US $3.00 an acre. In addition, losses of grain were less with the combine. Most early owners of combines on the northern plains bought fifteen- or sixteen-foot machines with which they harvested seven hundred or more acres in a season. Within a few years, the second most popular size of machine was a ten-footer, connected to the tractor power take-off and capable of handling at least five hundred acres in a season.[72] "The combine," testified a typical owner from Williams County, North Dakota, "is the greatest money-saving implement I have on my farm."[73]

Somewhat later than on the southern plains, then, the combine, abetted by the windrower, found its place in the spring wheat region. Use of the combine intensified in Montana, where both straight-cutting and windrowing were practiced. Within Montana the combine was most prevalent in the west-central wheat regions, especially the Judith Basin. There farmers raised both winter wheat and spring wheat, giving them a staggered harvest and an extended period of use for the combine. The combine had already been taking root there in the mid-1920s, but

Table 5.3. Number of Combines in Use in Three States of the Northern Plains, 1925–1928

Year	Montana	North Dakota	South Dakota	All
1925	291	3	25	319
1926	575	27	—	—
1927	1,500	249	180	1,929
1928	3,185	1,172	648	5,005

Source: Derived from A. E. Starch and R. M. Merrill, *The Combined Harvester-Thresher in Montana,* Montana Agricultural Experiment Station Bulletin 230 (1930); Alva H. Benton et al., *The Combined Harvester-Thresher in North Dakota,* North Dakota Agricultural Experiment Station Bulletin 225 (1929); Gabriel Lundy, K. H. Klages, and J. F. Goss, *Progress Report on the Use of the Combine in South Dakota,* South Dakota Agricultural Experiment Station Bulletin 244 (1929).

Table 5.4. Number of Combines Sold in the Prairie Provinces, 1926–1931

Year	Alberta	Saskatchewan	Manitoba	All
1926	26	148	2	176
1927	195	382	21	598
1928	1,095	2,356	206	3,657
1929	858	2,484	158	3,500
1930	541	939	134	1,614
1931	54	92	33	179

Source: Derived from R. Bruce Shepard, "Tractors and Combines in the Second Stage of Agricultural Mechanization on the Canadian Plains," *Prairie Forum* 11 (Fall 1986): 262.

the advent of the windrow harvester accelerated the trend. The number of combines in use multiplied quickly in 1927 and 1928 (see Table 5.3).[74]

The impact of the windrower on North and South Dakota was even more pronounced. There, prior to the distribution of the swather, the number of combines had remained insignificant. With first use of the manufactured windrower in 1927, the number of combines increased, and in 1928, the number expanded remarkably. In the Dakotas the combine displaced the binder more quickly in the central and western parts than in the eastern parts. The binder remained entrenched in the eastern prairies but could not withstand the combine on the plains.[75] In the prairie provinces of Canada, too, the advent of the windrower was pivotal in farmer acceptance of the combine. Sales of combines (see Table 5.4) ballooned in 1928–29 with the appearance of the windrower and were damp-

ened only by the onset of economic depression.[76]

By 1930 observers had to admit that the combine, abetted by the windrower, was a success on the northern plains, but economic depression set in so deeply that general adoption of the machine was tabled. Labor was cheap, capital was dear, and farmers kept their binders. Sales of combines in the spring wheat areas of both the United States and Canada dropped to little more than replacement levels. In 1938 a survey of eight counties across North Dakota disclosed that only about one-fourth of the small grains were harvested by combine, either windrowed or straight-cut. Farmers in the eastern and northern portions of the state used the combine the least, and when they did, they generally used the swather. Farmers in the western and southern parts of the state were more favorable to the combine and practiced straight-cutting; but even there, many clung to the binder.[77]

The drought that accompanied the depression during the 1930s forced

Header stack-barge built by a farmer near Conquest, Sask., to harvest short crops, ca. 1935. Ray Frey of the University of Saskatchewan is standing next to it. (Courtesy of Hal Lewis)

Pickup adapter fitted onto sickle platform of a combine in Saskatchewan, ca. 1930. (Courtesy of Hal Lewis)

many farmers to adapt what combines they had to harvesting short, thin crops. This they did by using them in conjunction with header stack-barges, a technique at least as old as 1929. A farmer using this method cut his grain with a header or, more commonly, a binder or swather modified to deliver the loose heads to the high-sided barge traveling alongside. The barge dumped the grain in stacks. The farmer then pulled his combine from stack to stack, using it as a stationary separator. The advantage of this method was that the header barge concentrated a thin crop in a few stacks, saving the combine from covering the whole field. With the sparse yields of the 1930s, this advantage was important.[78]

It remained for World War II to compel conversion to the combine throughout the northern plains. In 1939, 42.4 percent of the farmers in a study area of central and western Saskatchewan still used stationary separators; the rest used combines, either straight-cutting or swathing. In 1943 only 12.3 percent still used stationary separators. Obviously, World War II had rekindled interest in combines, mainly because it produced a labor shortage but also because it restored farmers' purchasing power. Rationing of steel limited the supply of combines on the market, but farmers snatched them up whenever they were available. Within the United States, a black market flourished, with southern dealers

R. L. Lewis picking up grain with a self-propelled combine near Gray, Sask., 1939. (Courtesy of Hal Lewis)

shipping combines to the Dakotas. Within the three Canadian prairie provinces, combine sales reached 1,756 in 1940, but availability remained a limiting factor: In 1945 Saskatchewan alone, according to one study, needed 18,688 combines, far more than would be manufactured. Particularly in demand were the new Massey-Harris self-propelled machines. The shortage of combines was a spur for itinerant custom combiners.[79]

At war's end, farmers quickly invested their wartime profits in combines. Once resumed, then, the conversion to combines was rapid. In most of

the northern plains it was substantially complete by 1950, when a study in central Saskatchewan found only 8 percent of farmers—a large proportion of whom were probably part-time or near retirement—using stationary threshers for wheat. By 1950, even in North Dakota, 70 percent of the small grains were combined from the windrow, with additional acres being straight-cut. Thereafter, attrition eliminated the last few advocates of the binder.[80]

The adoption of the combine on the plains caused or suggested a number of related changes in the region, changes easier to catalog than to measure, for the combine was intertwined with other technological adoptions and economic forces. Farmers and agricultural scientists quickly recognized that the combine entailed a general revision in agricultural practices to accommodate it. Combine owners had to be more meticulous in removing rocks and stumps from fields and had to work their fields smooth, for combines threshed poorly traveling over bumpy ground. Farmers on the southern plains ceased using listers and other furrowing implements. In the same area, farmers realized that because the combine cleared the field immediately with the harvest, they could begin tillage sooner, thus conserving moisture. Employment of the combine made it more difficult to save straw from the field for livestock, but if left in the field, it resulted in the return of more organic matter to the soil. Spring wheat farmers liked the way that straw and stubble left in the fields caught snow in winter, but they disliked the way it balled up their implements; so they often lost the organic benefit by burning it. If they wished to straight combine they needed to use good seed in properly calibrated drills and perhaps cross-seed low spots to ensure even ripening. They also had to minimize weeds through careful tillage, choose varieties of grain (preferably Marquis) not likely to lodge or shatter, and cooperate with neighbors to reduce sawflies, which also caused lodging. Overall, as Evan Hardy put it, farmers began "farming for the combine."[81]

The combine precipitated or exacerbated problems of storage and transfer of grain. In conjunction with trucks, combines gave farmers the capacity, in some cases the necessity, to deliver grain much more rapidly than before. Threshing with stationary separators had gone on for months, but combines shortened the time to two or three weeks. Absorbing the entire small-grain harvest into storage or market in such a short time demanded additional elevator space and more boxcars. On-farm storage and (in Canada) marketing quotas moderated this problem.[82]

The most profound consequence of the combine was its contribution toward mechanization. The increase in numbers of tractors and combines was not only simultaneous but also symbiotic: Purchase of one encouraged purchase of the other, both directly (because tractors pulled combines) and indirectly (because combines required farmers to do better tillage). Together, tractors, trucks, and combines permitted farmers to farm larger acreages and to eliminate horsepower. "Combines made it possible," said Canadian agricultural engineer Hal Lewis, a protégé of Evan Hardy, "to farm completely without horses by use of the combine, tractor, and truck." Relieved, then, of the bottleneck of harvesting, successful farmers were able to expand their acreage and purchase still more machinery. With operating costs lowered, wheat farmers were encouraged to extend operations farther into marginal lands on the plains.[83]

After the advent of the combine, the harvest required not only fewer horses

The tractor, combine, and truck accomplished the full mechanization of grain farming. Shown is a six-speed International truck in Saskatchewan, 1928. (Courtesy of Hal Lewis)

but also fewer men. Combines, which Hal Lewis called "the greatest labor saving device introduced into western Canada," eliminated most of the need for transient harvest labor.[84] The comment by a writer to the *Western Producer* that the combine was "a great boon to the farmer and his wife" echoed similar earlier language from the southern plains on the departure of crews of hungry, rude bindlestiffs.[85] A wheat farmer from Montana was also enthusiastic; he reported that after his first season of combining, "my wife did not know we harvested this year."[86] However, as a later scholar pointed out, the combine also destroyed the cooperative threshing ring, thereby eroding neighborliness.[87] The custom thresherman departed, too, of course, but he was not without heirs. During the next generation, itinerant custom combiners would provide farmers with machinery, labor, and expertise in a fashion similar to the old-time thresherman, except on a more far-flung itinerary—Texas to Saskatchewan for some of them—which would have astounded their predecessors.[88]

The effects of adopting the combine were similar in both the northern plains and the southern plains, as were the economic motives that persuaded farmers to utilize the machine. The differences between the two regions lay in the time period and manner in which they converted to the combine. Farmers on the southern plains, stimulated at first by the circumstances of the Great War, turned to the combine as soon as the prairie model was offered. During the 1920s, a period of intense mechanization, they accomplished for the most part the transition to the combine, a transition that provided them with a system of harvesting that was most suitable to their environment. Entry of the combine into the northern plains came later. Farmers there embraced the combine only after it had undergone additional mechanical adaptations (most notably the introduction of the windrower), after they had weathered the Great Depression, and after the economic incentive to adopt the combine had been renewed.

The combine, then, once the proper circumstances came together to permit its adoption, was the key to the completion of mechanization all over the North American plains. It became the towering, rumbling symbol of modern, capital-intensive agriculture in the region. On the Saskatchewan plains, when Regina's Western Canada Farm Progress Show presents its celebration of modern technology, similar to other expositions in other plains cities, what event fills the central arena and is featured on the program to attract the public? The Battle of the Combines, of course.

Yet something is missing. No one gathers hands, neighbors, family, dogs, vehicles, tools, and shacks around for a picture. If a photographer came to the harvest fields of Saskatchewan or Kansas today, took his exposures, and printed them with the same chemicals as had his itinerant brethren of the turn of the century, would his prints be fixed with the same golden hue?

CHAPTER SIX.
THE PLAINS

I was born a little too late to pitch bundles onto the feeder, or even to buck straw around for the engineer. I can barely remember the last pull-type, tractor-drawn combine on our farm in Barton County, Kansas; every one since has been self-propelled. Today I would not dare to climb into the cab of a combine, with all those lights and beepers and digital gizmos monitoring more shafts and circuits than I want to know about. The closest thing that I can remember to an old-time hindlestiff on our farm is Lowell. I cannot remember his last name, and I cannot remember the town in Missouri he came from. I guess I am about as vague as those journalists who wrote about the harvest hands of the early twentieth century; but I do know that Lowell showed up every year for harvest, drove one of the combines (and was loath to do any other kind of work), and then moved on to drive a combine for someone farther north. Today I have plenty of

friends who custom combine all over the plains, but that is not the same.

It is a legitimate question whether I have the authority to say anything about those radically different ways of harvesting and threshing that prevailed on the plains before the era of the combine and me. I am a historian, though, and I am supposed to sort through the documents and make some sense of them, to do my best to recreate their times. Documents there are aplenty, true accounts from the thousands of folks who experienced the things I am writing about; but every one of them experienced only certain things in certain places at certain times, and none can lay out the whole story for me.

I decided right away that I could not derive an overall interpretation from such a literary light as Herbert Krause.[1] His powerful novel, *The Thresher*, is sound on the technical details of harvesting and threshing and on the technological stages of development. But the book is not about threshing; rather it is about human obsession, about evil. J. Sanford Rikoon's book, *Threshing in the Midwest, 1820–1940,* confirms my contradictory impression that threshing was one of the more attractive elements in the culture of farm life on the middle border, not one of its perversions. These books deal with harvesting and threshing in the American Midwest, which is east of the region I am concerned with here, the North American plains. In reconstructing the story on the plains, I have before me the works of many fine scholars, whose names appear in my footnotes; but each has taken up only a part of the story, and besides, I trust them only when I can confirm their interpretations by a mass of first-person authorities.

If Krause's depiction of threshing was typical, then those who performed this craft on the plains either lacked perception of its nature or participated in a conspiracy of silence and deceit, for they found threshing a much more benign obsession than did Krause. Consider again the albumen prints with which I began my research and this book, how forthright the pride of labor and accomplishment staring out of the golden tones. Even if we relegate these photographic artifacts to the realm of symbolism, not evidence, and proceed inductively to the most conservative of primary historical sources, the documents we find soon echo the impressions of the photographs to the point of redundancy. Wrote T. E. Randall of Independence, Kansas, in 1917, "I am still a thresherman and although it is a hard, dirty job, I like the work and after twenty years of following the business I am far from being ready to quit."[2] And this from Earl G. Rex of Rocky Ford, Colorado:

> There is lots of work, lots of dirt and a good many knocks in the threshing business but nevertheless it is fascinating. That little chuffle-chuffle of the engine and the hum of the cylinder is music to many an old thresherman. It is hard to quit. He hears a whistle toot, gets a whiff or two of new straw or grain and he can't stop himself, he feels that he must go. I have not yet reached middle age but I began threshing when very young. . . . I have my engine painted a shiny black all over and paint it every year. I paint the head end about every week when I am working it hard. I wipe it all over every day, keep the brass bright and it shines in the sunlight like any other well groomed locomotive.[3]

Were such testimonials extraordinary, they would be insignificant; but placed amid a veritable prairie of documents similar in tone if not so explicit in sentiment, they become credible.

Looking for what is behind these documents, I prowl the threshing bees that take place today throughout the midsection of the continent. There are at least fourteen annual threshing and

Steam engine buffs on an engine at the Pawnee Threshing Bee, Pawnee, Okla., 1977. (By the author)

engine shows in my home state of Kansas alone. A company in Pennsylvania puts out a directory of such events every year; the same company publishes the magazines *Iron Men Album* and *Gas Engine*.[4] The meaning of these modern threshing bees—and I have attended them from Oklahoma to Manitoba—is obscured by all manner of peripheral hoopla. People set up booths and sell genuine Pennsylvania Dutch funnel cakes on paper plates, or embroidered chickens that hold rolls of toilet paper. Tourists and recreational vehicle people throng around, seeking shade. None of these things count. In the middle of the event are a bunch of dedicated hobbyists who restore and operate their threshing equipment. They are competent fellows who not only become learned in their own technical areas but also perform a public service by exhibiting the massive artifacts that they have preserved. Amid the tourist-trap trappings, they do thresh, putting on some of the best living history to be found. They do not thresh for long, though—not long enough for the pitchers to develop blisters, let alone callouses.

In those few minutes while the belt is taut comes the chance to look through

Pitching bundles onto feeder at the McLouth Threshing Bee, McLouth, Kans., 1980. (By the author)

the peripheral foolishness, even past the preoccupied preservationists, and find history on the hoof—or, more likely, on top of the separator. Almost anyone can throw some bundles on if he takes it easy on the feeder, and lots of younger fellows have read up and apprenticed and learned to operate engines; but up on top, the separator man is usually an old hand, getting older every year. He is the only one on the scene who knows exactly what is supposed to be happening in the guts of the bull thresher, how it is supposed to sound. As I watch him up there listening, I know that he is the only fellow here who may speak as one having authority. Soon there will be only us

scribes. At all those threshing bees, I have never met a historian.

It was in 1979, when the chic environmental movement of the 1960s and 1970s had crested, that Donald E. Worster's *Dust Bowl: The Southern Plains in the 1930s* was published. The book won the Bancroft Prize for History. Its analysis of the greatest environmental holocaust in the human history of the North American plains was sophisticated and full of insights, but it was also in at least one sense offensive to the people of the plains. Focusing on Sublette, Haskell County, Kansas—an area that happened to have been the

Binding wheat to be threshed at Goessel Museum Threshing Days, Goessel, Kans., 1984. (By the au-thor)

subject of two major community stud-ies by scholars working for the federal government—Worster depicted the southern plains as a place with no cul-ture of its own. Sublette was, he said, "a study in national clichés, . . . a blank page upon which men and women had not yet begun to write about what was really there." The commercial, cash-grain agriculture that supported the region was no different from the American mass culture of "the radio, the automobile, and the can of Burma Shave"; consequently, "there was no opportunity for an indigenous culture to take firm root here or for man and nature to find a stable equilibrium." In-stead the people would be obsessed by consumerism and at the mercy of "ur-ban hucksters."[5]

To describe the plains as without in-digenous culture is to confuse the fa-çade of Main Street with the face of the land, to dismiss the possibility that people in the region acted rationally according to their lights, and to ignore the centrality of work in the lives of people on the land. Certainly the civili-zation of the plains has suffered col-lapse more than once in the relatively brief history of European-American-Canadian occupation, but there existed in times and in places remarkable net-works of ways and things that consti-

Shocking wheat for the Goessel Threshing Days, Goessel, Kans., 1984. (By the author)

tuted complex regional cultures. The ways and things of harvesting and threshing were an example of this, as people of the region selected and crafted the features of their culture that enabled them to survive and, at times, prosper. They could survive and prosper only by work, however, and because the gathering of their crops was the hardest work of all, the ways and things of harvesting and threshing became the classic statement of their regional culture. This integral aspect of

their lives was subject to continual evaluation, experimentation, and adaptation and therefore was never static. It is no contradiction to say that the agriculture of the plains forged a tradition of change.

Tradition and change are points at which this book diverges from Rikoon's *Threshing in the Midwest*. Rikoon's work was in progress during the same years as was mine, and although we are acquainted with each other, similarities between our books did not derive from

A separator man and a crew that bears watching at Pawnee Threshing Bee, Pawnee, Okla., 1977. (By the author)

consultation. We emphasize the commonplaces of life—the everyday ways of doing things and talking about them—and approach them through a variety of grass-roots primary sources. We both recognize a public fascination with past threshing that must represent something more than nostalgia. We both show respect for farm folk as actors working out their own ways, not just dummies pummeled by circumstance. On tradition and change, however, we differ. Rikoon speaks of the midwestern farmers' "confrontation with change" as producing a "constant and perhaps irreconcilable tension"; I,

on the other hand, find plains farmers, particularly farmer-threshermen, comfortable with technology, adopting, adapting, and contributing to it.[6] Even when steam men railed against gasoline tractors, it was hardly a case of hidebound cultural conservatism but rather a rivalry between two different modern technologies. Although this may be a regional difference between the Midwest and the Great Plains, more likely it is a difference in our authorial perspectives.

The other great difference between this study and Rikoon's has to do with place. It is good to study one place in depth, then another in depth, whether or not the two are eventually pulled together in comparison or synthesis. Rikoon, as a social scientist, says, "Interregional variations demonstrate that similar threshing technologies adopted into contrasting farming systems result in different occupational styles depending on variances in settlement patterns, eco-zones, agricultural cycles, regional concepts of reciprocal labor, and existing systems of neighborhood cooperation."[7] The historian is more likely to say, "The Great Plains is a different place from the Midwest, and people there do things differently." "Place," too, is a more potent term for a historian than it is for any social scientist— more potent even than "space" is for a geographer. In Rikoon's study, place is a location or, at most, a setting. In this historical work, place is prerequisite and parcel to the action.

Where a culture of the plains place flourished, we must look to other scholarly contributions to interpret it. American scholars of the plains customarily begin with the work of Walter Prescott Webb, *The Great Plains,* first published in 1931.[8] Webb's history set forth an environmental interpretation of regional history with broad applicability. The plains he characterized as a region of physiographic integrity—flat, treeless, semiarid—that defeated North American pioneers and compelled them to adapt their ways before settlement could succeed. Such adaptations as barbed wire, windmills, and dry farming were so obvious as to defy refutation. But in at least one respect

Webb's work was limited: It concentrated on pioneering and settlement, a transitory process. It fell to such followers as James C. Malin and Carl Frederick Kraenzel to extend Webb's concept of adaptation to environment into the twentieth century and even, hazardously, into prescriptions for the future.[9]

In certain respects the environmental regionalism inspired by Webb is basic to understanding the harvesting and threshing of the plains. The plains from Texas to Saskatchewan shared certain commonalities of agricultural practice, chiefly emphasis on small grains and recourse to extensive farming as opposed to diversified farming on small acreage. The region, too, was sparsely populated throughout. All these things were related to environmental constraints on agriculture and on the capacity of the land to support people. In attempting to carry on small-grain farming under such conditions (which seemed to most residents to be the logical land use), farmers up and down the plains discovered that the local labor supply was inadequate for such peak periods of activity as harvesting and threshing. Everywhere they sought a means, cooperative or commercial, of redressing the shortage of labor, and everywhere they were enthusiastic about mechanizing any aspect of the process that was susceptible to it. These are constants in the history of harvesting and threshing on the plains.

The environmental approach wants refining if it is to be of use in explaining much more of this history, however. In the first place it must be refined to recognize that overlaid on the commonalities of the region are variations of subregion and locality. The most obvious division within the region is that between the winter wheat area of the southern plains and the spring wheat area of the northern plains. This great division shaped preferences for harvesting implements, consequent variation in threshing practices, and, finally, differing attitudes toward adopting the combine. Another important overlay across the map of the plains as an agricultural region is the differences between the eastern and western reaches in any particular latitude. Western Kansas is not eastern Kansas, nor is Alberta Manitoba. To complicate the scheme of things further, every locality has its own environmental nuances. Steam engines bog down in the sand hills of Nebraska and lime up on the Regina plains of Saskatchewan.

The emphasis on environment as an influence on harvesting and threshing, even if refined to the local level, neglects the key elements of human initiative and personal choice that also affected practices. This is related to what contemporary geographers have come to call "geographic possibilism," the idea that people in any particular place might get along by any one or combination of strategies, within certain environmental constraints.[10] Evidence from the history of harvesting and threshing on the plains shows elements of initiative and choice even finer than the broad strokes of geographic possi-

bilism. Of three farmer-neighbors, for instance, one might choose to harvest with the binder, another with the header, and a third with a push binder that combined the features of both, and all three might prosper or fail together. Within a locality a group of farmers might organize a threshing ring to handle their grain while others in the same locality choose to bring in a custom man, and the preference for one method or the other might not go according to what a farm economist would expect. A farmer and his family might take a shine to a particular harvest hand and invite him back year after year, and a harvest hand might settle into a routine or perhaps decide to sever ties and see another part of the country. Thus the broad patterns that can be mapped on the plains are composed of myriad individual decisions among alternatives. Individuals might even forge their own new alternatives, as repeated instances of folk invention and homespun technology show. These range from the local and picturesque (such as mounting a beer barrel on a binder to give it traction) to the regional and consequential (such as the invention of the windrower).

In the end, however thoroughly considered, environmental considerations will not explain everything that happened in the history of the plains or all of its aspects. Many interpreters of the plains do not even consider the Webb tradition the best approach. This was amply documented by the lack of enthusiasm, even the muted hostility, of Canadian scholars toward the works of two Americans, Paul F. Sharp and John W. Bennett, who applied Webb-style environmental interpretations to the Canadian plains. This seemed logical to Sharp and Bennett, and although they produced splendid works on aspects of the Canadian plains, they cut no swath in Canadian scholarship.[11]

Canadian scholars were cool toward American environmentalism because they came from a wholly different scholarly tradition, the genealogy of which ran back to political economist Harold A. Innis. Innis and his followers were concerned mainly with explaining Canadian nationhood, and in their writings, the Canadian plains were the means by which the nation's destiny would be fulfilled. The plains (or "prairies," as they would say) were of importance to Canada because they provided a staple (grain) important to Canadian self-sufficiency and nationhood. Scholars such as Vernon C. Fowke turned such interpretation around from a celebration of nationhood into a protest against oppression of the west for the sake of a national agenda, but they did not change the basic staples theory framework of analysis.[12]

Staples theorists illuminate the history of harvesting and threshing through the realization that not all decisions about what happened on the plains were made on the plains. Many developments—and staples theorists would say the most important of them—came from agendas set elsewhere or from movements generated outside the region. The economic situation—including the relative prosperity of the early twentieth century, the crisis-laden expansionism of World War I, the tense transition (economic and technological) of the 1920s, and the advent of the Great Depression—shaped harvesting and threshing on the plains as much as environment did. Authorities located outside the plains also played key roles in how farmers within the region adapted to environmental and economic conditions. Both implement manufacturers and experiment station scientists sought to influence farmers in the technologies they employed. Both railroad companies and government officials sought to organize the flow of harvest labor.

Still another approach to the history of the plains comes from those who emphasize continuity rather than change. They believe that ethnicity and cultural heritage were the important determinants of cultural ways on the plains. For example, the dean of Manitoba historians, W. L. Morton, insisted that whatever was culturally distinctive about the Manitoba prairies derived from the mixing of ethnic cultures there.[13] At the other end of the plains, geographer Terry G. Jordan has traced the cultural vestiges of German immigrants and southern Anglo-Americans in Texas and devised sophisticated theories on how those influences were expressed.[14] This point of view contributes little to the history of harvesting and threshing on the plains, however. In antiquity, and through early North American history, cultural antecedents were important determinants in harvesting and threshing. Cultural features such as the Doukhobors' use of sickles for harvesting and treading for threshing came to the plains with immigrants, but they did not last long under environmental and economic influences. Only variations in minor detail and in terminology (such as "shocks" and "stooks") survived as ethnic vestiges.

Thus the cultural heritage introduced to the plains by settlers and immigrants was the starting point for the history of the region; but in relation to harvesting and threshing, it was merely the starting point. The gathering of crops was the crucial climax to a year's work. Knowing this, plains folk did not hesitate to reform their ways in this area, initially and repeatedly. Their first and obvious adaptations were to the environment of the plains. They took up methods of farming, particu-

larly of harvesting and threshing, that worked, and they were ever willing to discard those ways if they found new ones that seemed to work better. This process of adaptation did not take place with the farmer facing the land alone and in isolation, however. Forces from outside his class and region continually sought to influence his choice of adaptations and generally determined whether the product of his efforts would be profitable.

With so many conditions beyond the control of agriculturalists on the plains, and with every success dependent not only on hard work but also on good judgment and appropriate adaptation, it is no wonder that pride of accomplishment exudes from those faces in the old albumen prints. The wonder is that the civilization they represent reached such a state and then receded so swiftly.

NOTES

CHAPTER 1. ANTIQUITIES

1. Graeme R. Quick and Wesley F. Buchele, *The Grain Harvesters* (St. Joseph, Mich.: American Society of Agricultural Engineers, 1978), p. 2.

2. Ibid., p. 3; Merritt Finley Miller, *The Evolution of Reaping Machines,* U.S. Department of Agriculture, Office of Experiment Stations Bulletin 103 (Washington, D.C.: GPO, 1902), p. 7.

3. Miller, *Evolution of Reaping Machines,* pp. 7–9; Quick and Buchele, *Grain Harvesters,* pp. 6–7; Eliot Cecil Curwen, "Implements and Their Wooden Handles," *Antiquity* 21 (1947): 155–58; V. Gordon Childe, "The Balanced Sickle," in W. F. Grimes, ed., *Aspects of Archeology in Britain and Beyond* (London: H. W. Edwards, 1951), pp. 39–48.

4. Pliny, *Natural History,* Book 18, vol. 5, Loeb Classical Library Edition (Cambridge, Mass.: Harvard University Press, 1961), p. 375; Lucius Junius Moderatus Columella, *On Agriculture,* Book 1, Loeb Classical Library Edition (Cambridge, Mass.: Harvard University Press, 1960), p. 287; Marcus Terentius Varro, *On Agriculture,* Loeb Classical Library Edition (Cambridge, Mass.: Harvard University Press, 1960), pp. 282–85;

Miller, *Evolution of Reaping Machines,* p. 9; Quick and Buchele, *Grain Harvesters,* pp. 7–8.

5. Miller, *Evolution of Reaping Machines,* p. 10; Quick and Buchele, *Grain Harvesters,* p. 8. For techniques of cradling among the Pennsylvania Dutch, see Beauveau Borie IV, *Farming and Folk Society: Threshing among the Pennsylvania Germans* (Ann Arbor, Mich.: UMI Press, 1986), pp. 37–42.

6. R. Douglas Hurt, *American Farm Tools: From Hand Power to Steam Power* (Manhattan, Kans.: Sunflower University Press, 1982), pp. 40–41; Leo Rogin, *The Introduction of Farm Machinery in Its Relation to the Productivity of Labor in the Agriculture of the United States during the Nineteenth Century* (Berkeley: University of California Press, 1931), pp. 69–72; Quick and Buchele, *Grain Harvesters,* p. 10; Miller, *Evolution of Reaping Machines,* pp. 10–11. Rogin provides an authoritative source on the advent of discrete technologies in American agriculture and on their respective time and labor requirements.

7. Norman Lee, *Harvests and Harvesting through the Ages* (Cambridge, Eng.: Cambridge University Press, 1960), pp. 81–82; John F. Steward, *The Reaper: A History of the Efforts of Those Who Justly May Be Said to*

Have Made Bread Cheap (New York: Greenberg, 1931), pp. 16–17; Pliny, *Natural History,* Book 18, p. 375; Barton Lodge, ed., *Palladius on Husbandrie* (London: Early English Text Society, 1873; Millwood, N.Y.: Kraus Reprint Company, 1973), p. 159; K. D. White, *Greek and Roman Technology* (Ithaca, N.Y.: Cornell University Press, 1984), pp. 60–62; K. D. White, *Roman Farming* (Ithaca, N.Y.: Cornell University Press, 1970), pp. 182–83; Quick and Buchele, *Grain Harvesters,* pp. 13–16.

8. Steward, *The Reaper,* pp. 18–19; Miller, *Evolution of Reaping Machines,* p. 12.

9. Miller, *Evolution of Reaping Machines,* pp. 12–13; Quick and Buchele, *Grain Harvesters,* pp. 20, 26.

10. Steward, *The Reaper,* pp. 19–20; Miller, *Evolution of Reaping Machines,* pp. 13–14; Quick and Buchele, *Grain Harvesters,* p. 18.

11. Steward, *The Reaper,* pp. 24–25; Miller, *Evolution of Reaping Machines,* pp. 14–15.

12. Steward, *The Reaper,* pp. 22–24; Miller, *Evolution of Reaping Machines,* pp. 14–15; Quick and Buchele, *Grain Harvesters,* pp. 20–21.

13. Steward, *The Reaper,* p. 30; Quick and Buchele, *Grain Harvesters,* pp. 22–23.

14. Quick and Buchele, *Grain Harvesters,* pp. 22–23; Steward, *The Reaper,* pp. 28–31; Miller, *Evolution of Reaping Machines,* pp. 15–16.

15. Steward, *The Reaper,* pp. 28–30.

16. Ibid., pp. 31–43; Quick and Buchele, *Grain Harvesters,* pp. 23–26; Miller, *Evolution of Reaping Machines,* pp. 16–17.

17. Steward, *The Reaper,* p. 48. The "favorable environment for invention" was more evident in the United States than in Canada; no early, notable technological innovations came from Canada. "Throughout the [nineteenth] century the industry in Canada relied almost entirely on the American industry to point the direction of technological advance" (W. G. Phillips, *The Agricultural Implement Industry in Canada: A Study of Competition* [Toronto: University of Toronto Press, 1956], p. 37).

18. Hurt, *American Farm Tools,* pp. 41–42; Steward, *The Reaper,* pp. 49–51; William T. Hutchinson, *Cyrus Hall McCormick: Seed-Time, 1809–1856* (New York: Century Company, 1930), pp. 64–68.

19. Hurt, *American Farm Tools,* p. 42; Steward, *The Reaper,* pp. 82–95; Hutchinson, *Seed-Time,* pp. 74–98; Miller, *Evolution of Reaping Machines,* pp. 24–25; Rogin, *Farm Machinery,* pp. 72–77, 87–91.

20. Hurt, *American Farm Tools,* pp. 42–44; Steward, *The Reaper,* pp. 56–81; Hutchinson, *Seed-Time,* pp. 150–65; Miller, *Evolution of Reaping Machines,* pp. 25–26; Rogin, *Farm Machinery,* pp. 72–77, 85–87; Paul Wallace Gates, *The Farmer's Age: Agriculture, 1815–1860* (New York: Holt, Rinehart and Winston, 1960), p. 286.

21. Steward, *The Reaper,* pp. 149–85; Hurt, *American Farm Tools,* p. 44; Hutchinson, *Seed-Time,* pp. 165–202, 377–408, 409–52.

22. Hurt, *American Farm Tools,* p. 44; Gates, *Farmer's Age,* p. 286; Hutchinson, *Seed-Time,* pp. 203–75.

23. Percy Wells Bidwell and John I. Falconer, *History of Agriculture in the Northern United States, 1620–1860* (New York: Peter Smith, 1941; reprinted as Carnegie Institution of Washington Pub. No. 358), p. 290; Clarence H. Danhof, *Change in Agriculture: The Northern United States, 1820–1870* (Cambridge, Mass.: Harvard University Press, 1969), pp. 243–49; Paul W. Gates, *Agriculture and the Civil War* (New York: Alfred A. Knopf, 1965), p. 232; Hurt, *American Farm Tools,* pp. 44–45; Rogin, *Farm Machinery,* pp. 78–84.

24. Hutchinson, *Seed-Time,* pp. 422–23; William T. Hutchinson, *Cyrus Hall McCormick: Harvest, 1856–1884* (New York: D. Appleton–Century Company, 1935), pp. 394–95; Hurt, *American Farm Tools,* p. 46; Miller, *Evolution of Reaping Machines,* p. 29; Rogin, *Farm Machinery,* p. 97.

25. Miller, *Evolution of Reaping Machines,*

p. 31; Rogin, *Farm Machinery*, pp. 96–97; Hurt, *American Farm Tools*, pp. 46–47; Steward, *The Reaper*, pp. 221–24.

26. Miller, *Evolution of Reaping Machines*, pp. 31–33; Rogin, *Farm Machinery*, pp. 100–103; Hurt, *American Farm Tools*, p. 47; Steward, *The Reaper*, pp. 221–26.

27. Hurt, *American Farm Tools*, pp. 47–49; Rogin, *Farm Machinery*, pp. 102–3.

28. Hurt, *American Farm Tools*, p. 52; Steward, *The Reaper*, pp. 237–56; Hutchinson, *Harvest*, pp. 525–29; Miller, *Evolution of Reaping Machines*, p. 35; Rogin, *Farm Machinery*, pp. 107–10; Merrill Denison, *Harvest Triumphant: The Story of Massey-Harris* (New York: Dodd, Mead & Company, 1949), pp. 78–79.

29. Rogin, *Farm Machinery*, pp. 110–15; Hurt, *American Farm Tools*, pp. 52–54; Hutchinson, *Harvest*, pp. 537–41.

30. Miller, *Evolution of Reaping Machines*, pp. 36–37; Rogin, *Farm Machinery*, pp. 115–19; Hurt, *American Farm Tools*, pp. 54–55; Steward, *The Reaper*, pp. 268–343; Hutchinson, *Harvest*, pp. 551–62; F. B. Swingle, "The Invention of the Twine Binder," *Indiana Magazine of History* 10 (September 1926): 35–41.

31. Miller, *Evolution of Reaping Machines*, p. 37; Hurt, *American Farm Tools*, pp. 55–56.

32. Hurt, *American Farm Tools*, pp. 49–52; Miller, *Evolution of Reaping Machines*, pp. 37–39; Rogin, *Farm Machinery*, pp. 103–6.

33. Lillian Church, *Partial History of the Development of Grain Threshing Implements and Machines*, U.S. Department of Agriculture, Bureau of Agricultural Engineering, Information Series 73 (Washington, D.C.: GPO, 1939), pp. 1–3; Quick and Buchele, *Grain Harvesters*, pp. 3, 11.

34. Varro, *On Agriculture*, p. 287; White, *Greek and Roman Technology*, p. 62; Quick and Buchele, *Grain Harvesters*, p. 39.

35. Pliny, *Natural History*, Book 18, p. 337; White, *Roman Farming*, p. 185; Lee, *Harvests and Harvesting*, p. 83; Quick and Buchele, *Grain Harvesters*, p. 11; Church, *Threshing Implements and Machines*, p. 3.

Borie, *Farming and Folk Society*, pp. 55–64, gives an elaborate typology for flails, mainly ones from Pennsylvania.

36. Donald P. Greene, "Prairie Agricultural Technology, 1860–1900" (Ph.D. dissertation, Indiana University, 1957), p. 290; Quick and Buchele, *Grain Harvesters*, pp. 43–53; Church, *Threshing Implements and Machines*, pp. 5–8.

37. Quick and Buchele, *Grain Harvesters*, pp. 53–57.

38. Columella, *On Agriculture*, Book 1, p. 287; Greene, "Prairie Agricultural Technology," pp. 290–91; Quick and Buchele, *Grain Harvesters*, pp. 47–50.

39. Quick and Buchele, *Grain Harvesters*, pp. 55–56; E. J. Hobsbawm, "The Machine Breakers," *Past and Present* (February 1952): 57–70. The standard work on the troubles of 1830 is E. J. Hobsbawm and George Rude, *Captain Swing* (Woking, Eng.: Lawrence & Wichart, 1969). This book includes an appendix, "The Problem of the Threshing Machine," pp. 359–65.

40. Quick and Buchele, *Grain Harvesters*, pp. 51–52; Hurt, *American Farm Tools*, pp. 67–68; Danhof, *Change in Agriculture*, p. 221; Rogin, *Farm Machinery*, pp. 157–60; J. Sanford Rikoon, *Threshing in the Midwest, 1820–1940* (Bloomington: Indiana University Press, 1988), pp. 1–19; Borie, *Farming and Folk Society*, pp. 15–36, 55–76.

41. Greene, "Prairie Agricultural Technology," p. 290; Hurt, *American Farm Tools*, p. 69; Church, *Threshing Implements and Machines*, p. 12; Quick and Buchele, *Grain Harvesters*, pp. 57–58.

42. Greene, "Prairie Agricultural Technology," pp. 291–93; Hurt, *American Farm Tools*, pp. 69–70; Quick and Buchele, *Grain Harvesters*, pp. 58–59; Church, *Threshing Implements and Machines*, pp. 12–15; Edward Carpenter, "The Groundhog Thresher: An Enigma," *Wisconsin Magazine of History* 37 (1954): 217–18; Rikoon, *Threshing in the Midwest*, pp. 22–23.

43. Greene, "Prairie Agricultural Technology," pp. 291–92; Quick and Buchele,

Grain Harvesters, p. 60; Hurt, *American Farm Tools,* pp. 70–73; Gates, *Farmer's Age,* p. 288; Danhof, *Change in Agriculture,* p. 223; Church, *Threshing Implements and Machines,* pp. 15–16.

44. Greene, "Prairie Agricultural Technology," pp. 291–92; Quick and Buchele, *Grain Harvesters,* p. 60; Danhof, *Change in Agriculture,* p. 223; Church, *Threshing Implements and Machines,* p. 16.

45. Greene, "Prairie Agricultural Technology," p. 292; Quick and Buchele, *Grain Harvesters,* pp. 61–62.

46. Greene, "Prairie Agricultural Technology," pp. 293–94; Quick and Buchele, *Grain Harvesters,* p. 62; Hurt, *American Farm Tools,* pp. 73–74; Church, *Threshing Implements and Machines,* pp. 19–20.

47. Rikoon, *Threshing in the Midwest,* pp. 32–38; Greene, "Prairie Agricultural Technology," pp. 294–97; Hurt, *American Farm Tools,* p. 70; Gates, *Farmer's Age,* p. 288; Danhof, *Change in Agriculture,* pp. 224–27.

48. Rikoon, *Threshing in the Midwest,* pp. 27–32; Greene, "Prairie Agricultural Technology," pp. 302–5; Hurt, *American Farm Tools,* p. 70; Rogin, *Farm Machinery,* p. 173.

49. Greene, "Prairie Agricultural Technology," pp. 303–6; Church, *Threshing Implements and Machines,* pp. 32–34; Rogin, *Farm Machinery,* pp. 173–75.

50. Church, *Threshing Implements and Machines,* pp. 34–35; Greene, "Prairie Agricultural Technology," pp. 306–7.

51. Quick and Buchele, *Grain Harvesters,* p. 57; Hurt, *American Farm Tools,* p. 101; Church, *Threshing Implements and Machines,* pp. 34–35.

52. Standard general histories of plains settlement include Gilbert C. Fite, *The Farmer's Frontier, 1865–1900* (New York: Holt, Rinehart and Winston, 1966); Fred A. Shannon, *The Farmer's Last Frontier: Agriculture, 1860–1897* (New York: Farrar & Rinehart, 1945); and Gerald Friesen, *The Canadian Prairies: A History* (Toronto: University of Toronto Press, 1984). Vernon C. Fowke, *The National Policy and the Wheat Economy* (Toronto: University of Toronto Press,

1957), and James C. Malin, *Winter Wheat in the Golden Belt of Kansas: A Study in Adaptation to Subhumid Geographical Environment* (Lawrence: University of Kansas Press, 1944), are required reading for a basic understanding of the wheat culture of, respectively, the Canadian plains and the American plains. Solid studies on the agricultural settlement of the plains include David C. Jones, *Empire of Dust: Settling and Abandoning the Prairie Dry Belt* (Edmonton: University of Alberta Press, 1987); Paul Voisey, *Vulcan: The Making of a Prairie Community* (Toronto: University of Toronto Press, 1988); Craig Miner, *West of Wichita: Settling the High Plains of Kansas, 1865–1890* (Lawrence: University Press of Kansas, 1986); Paula M. Nelson, *After the West Was Won: Homesteaders and Town-Builders in Western South Dakota, 1900–1917* (Iowa City: University of Iowa Press, 1986); and Jan Blodgett, *Land of Bright Promise: Advertising the Texas Panhandle and South Plains, 1870–1917* (Austin: University of Texas Press, 1988).

53. Robert C. Williams, *Fordson, Farmall, and Poppin' Johnny: A History of the Farm Tractor and Its Impact on America* (Urbana: University of Illinois Press, 1987), p. 3; R. Bruce Shepard, "Tractors and Combines in the Second Stage of Agricultural Mechanization on the Canadian Plains," *Prairie Forum* 11 (Fall 1986): 254.

54. In this paragraph I acknowledge the thesis of Earl Hayter, *The Troubled Farmer: Rural Adjustment to Industrialism, 1850–1900* (DeKalb: Northern Illinois University Press, 1968), while remaining more in tune with the views of Williams (*Fordson, Farmall, and Poppin' Johnny*) and Danhof (*Change in Agriculture*).

CHAPTER 2.   HARVESTING

1. J. H. Arnold and R. R. Spafford, "Farm Practices in Growing Wheat: A Geographical Presentation," *Yearbook of the* [U.S.] *Department of Agriculture* (Washington, D.C.:

GPO, 1919), pp. 123–50.

2. Ibid., p. 148.

3. Allen R. Turner, "Pioneer Farming Experiences," *Saskatchewan History* 8 (Fall 1955): 47.

4. Questionnaires from Michael Ewanchuk, Winnipeg, Man.; F. M. Redpath, "Cradle to Combine," undated typescript, Kansas State Historical Society Library, Topeka; Seventieth Anniversary Edition, *Washington* [Kansas] *Weekly Republican,* 1938; Robert H. Porter, "Texan Recites Harvesting's Evolution," *The Farmer-Stockman* 60 (October 1947): 37; Vera Meredith, "Memoirs of Mr. J. S. McLain," interview, 26 June 1936, Panhandle Plains Historical Museum, Canyon, Tex.; Mandie Meredith, "Memoirs of Rev. R. E. L. Muncy," interview, 25 June 1936, Panhandle Plains Historical Museum; Sadie Summers, "Memoirs of John Bell Porter," interview, 4 August 1936, Panhandle Plains Historical Museum.

5. James C. Malin, *Winter Wheat in the Golden Belt of Kansas: A Study in Adaptation to Subhumid Geographical Environment* (Lawrence: University of Kansas Press, 1944), p. 247.

6. Ibid., pp. 61–62; Diary of Arthur C. Smith, Manuscript Collections, Santa Fe Trail Center, Larned, Kans.

7. Malin, *Winter Wheat,* p. 63.

8. Arnold and Spafford, "Farm Practices," pp. 137–38, 143–45 (quote on p. 145).

9. *Wheat in Kansas,* Quarterly Report of the Kansas State Board of Agriculture (Topeka: State Printer, September 1920), p. 88; Leslie A. Fitz, *Handling Wheat from Field to Mill,* U.S. Department of Agriculture, Bureau of Plant Industry Circular 68 (Washington, D.C.: GPO, 1910), pp. 3–4; N. C. Donaldson, *Grains for the Montana Dry Lands,* U.S. Department of Agriculture, Farmers' Bulletin 749 (Washington, D.C.: GPO, 1916), pp. 8–9.

10. Ewanchuk questionnaires; questionnaires from Alexander Boan, Briarcrest, Sask.

11. Questionnaires from George Hitz, New Rockford, N. Dak.; questionnaires from William J. Lies, New Rockford, N. Dak.

12. Interview with Ernest Claassen, Peabody, Kans., 3 September 1982; interview with Milo Mathews, Linwood, Ore. (conducted in Emporia, Kans.), 17 November 1980; questionnaires from Guy Bretz, Buffalo, Missouri.

13. Interview with Richard Goering, Cassoday, Kans., 21 September 1981.

14. Sheaf loader advertisements recur in *Canadian Thresherman* (hereafter cited as *CanTh*) for the period under discussion; see also W. R. Porter, *New Labor Saving Machinery for Harvesting Grain,* North Dakota Agricultural Experiment Station Bulletin 128 (1919), pp. 3–5.

15. Porter, *Labor Saving Machinery,* pp. 5–6.

16. Ibid., pp. 6–8.

17. For an overview of the history of the header stack-barge, see Thomas D. Isern, "The Header Stack-Barge: Folk Technology on the North American Plains," *Social Science Journal* 24 (Autumn 1987): 361–73.

18. My material on the Jacobs machine comes from *Wheat in Kansas,* pp. 281–83, and from M. L. Wilson and H. E. Murdock, *Reducing Wheat Harvesting Costs on Montana Dry Lands,* Montana Extension Service Bulletin 71 (Bozeman: Montana State Extension Service, 1924), pp. 30–31.

19. Porter, *Labor Saving Machinery,* pp. 8–13.

20. Wilson and Murdock, *Reducing Harvesting Costs,* pp. 23–30.

21. Gabriel Lundy, *The Header Stack-Barge for Harvesting,* South Dakota State College, Special Extension Circular 7 (1930), pp. 1–16.

22. "Farmers Okay Header Barge," *Western Producer* (Saskatoon), 29 June 1929, clipping in private manuscript collection of Hartford A. Lewis, Gray, Sask.; "Header Barge," undated typescript, Lewis collection; J. K. MacKenzie, "The Barge Method of Combine Harvesting," *Agricultural Engineering* 14 (April 1933): 95; J. MacGregor Smith and Donald Cameron, *The Header*

Barge Method of Harvesting, University of Alberta, Extension Circular 14 (1933), p. 24.

23. This quote and other Murphy material are from A. P. Murphy, "A Bundle Rack That Satisfies," *American Thresherman* (hereafter cited as *AmTh*) 31 (October 1928): 9.

24. Redpath, "Cradle to Combine," p. 11.

25. Arnold P. Yerkes and L. M. Church, *Cost of Harvesting Wheat by Different Methods,* U.S. Department of Agriculture Bulletin 627 (Washington, D.C.: GPO, 1918), p. 17.

26. Wilson and Murdock, *Reducing Harvesting Costs,* p. 15.

27. Ibid., p. 10; Yerkes and Church, *Cost of Harvesting,* pp. 3–6; Turner, "Pioneer Farming Experiences," p. 47; Redpath, "Cradle to Combine," p. 4; *Wheat in Kansas,* pp. 90–91, 134–35.

28. These generalities about the vernacular of harvesting are based on usage in articles, bulletins, and (especially) interviews cited throughout the harvesting sections of this book.

29. Wilson and Murdock, *Reducing Harvesting Costs,* p. 10.

30. E. B. McCormick and L. L. Beebe, *Care and Repair of Farm Implements,* U.S. Department of Agriculture, Farmers' Bulletin 947 (Washington, D.C.: GPO, 1918), p. 9.

31. Ibid., pp. 3–15; W. R. Humphries, *Care and Repair of Mowers and Binders,* U.S. Department of Agriculture, Farmers' Bulletin 1757 (Washington, D.C.: GPO, 1936), pp. 1–20; R. Milne and W. J. Gilmore, "The Grain Binder," *CanTh* 18 (August 1913): 60, 62, 92–93.

32. Questionnaires from Wornall, Ewanchuk, McKinney, and Lies; Goering interview.

33. Redpath, "Cradle to Combine," p. 3.

34. Ibid., p. 4; Boan questionnaires; Goering interview.

35. Donald P. Greene, "Prairie Agricultural Technology, 1860–1900" (Ph.D. dissertation, Indiana University, 1957), pp. 257–58; Claassen interview; Lies and McKinney questionnaires.

36. "Good Binders Help the Threshers," *AmTh* 25 (June 1922).

37. Ibid.; Yerkes and Church, *Cost of Harvesting,* p. 4; Claassen and Goering interviews; Lies and Ewanchuk questionnaires.

38. "Good Binders Help the Threshers"; Worrall, McKinney, Hitz, and Ewanchuk questionnaires; Claassen and Goering interviews.

39. "Good Binders Help the Threshers."

40. Ibid.; C. M. Hennis and Rex E. Willard, *Farm Practices in Grain Farming in North Dakota,* U.S. Department of Agriculture, Farmers' Bulletin 757 (Washington, D.C.: GPO, 1919), p. 11; quote is from Hitz questionnaires; Claassen interview; *Topeka Daily Capital,* 16 May 1914, "Binder Twine Short" (unidentified clipping dated 1914), and *Kansas City Times,* 11 June 1914, all in clippings collection, Kansas State Historical Society Library, Topeka.

41. Redpath, "Cradle to Combine," p. 5; author's notes of conversations with groups at the Life Enrichment Program, Bethel College, North Newton, Kans., 1981; "An Early Binder Engine Experience," *AmTh* 16 (February 1914): 70–71; quote from advertisement in *CanTh* 17 (June 1912): 23; Goering interview.

42. *Wheat in Kansas,* p. 92; Yerkes and Church, *Cost of Harvesting,* p. 11.

43. Yerkes and Church, *Cost of Harvesting,* p. 11; Wilson and Murdock, *Reducing Harvesting Costs,* p. 11.

44. *Wheat in Kansas,* pp. 93–94; Mathews interview.

45. Life Enrichment notes; Mathews, Claassen, and Goering interviews.

46. *Wheat in Kansas,* pp. 92–95.

47. Questionnaires from J. A. Boan, Briarcrest, Sask.; Ewanchuk and Lies questionnaires; Claassen interview.

48. Mathews and Claassen interviews; Lies and Ewanchuk questionnaires.

49. Timothy Parson, "Building Good Wheat Stacks," *AmTh* 28 (June 1925): 4; *Wheat in Kansas,* p. 96; Hennis and Willard, *Farm Practices,* p. 13; M. R. Cooper and R. S. Washburn, *Cost of Producing Wheat on 481 Farms in the States of North and South Dakota, Minnesota, Kansas, Nebraska, and Mis-*

souri, for the Crop Year 1919, U.S. Department of Agriculture Bulletin 943 (Washington, D.C.: GPO, 1921), p. 5.

50. Yerkes and Church, *Cost of Harvesting,* p. 13.

51. *Wheat in Kansas,* pp. 97, 153.

52. Ibid., pp. 97–98, 159–61.

53. Ibid., pp. 98–99.

54. Ibid., pp. 99–100.

55. Ibid., pp. 153–57.

56. Ibid., pp. 157–58.

57. Bretz questionnaires; Yerkes and Church, *Cost of Harvesting,* pp. 15–16; Wilson and Murdock, *Reducing Harvesting Costs,* p. 12; *Wheat in Kansas,* pp. 90–91; also interviews as cited above.

58. *Wheat in Kansas,* pp. 91–92.

59. Ibid., pp. 100–101.

60. Wilson and Murdock, *Reducing Harvesting Costs,* pp. 12–13.

61. Ibid., p. 13.

62. Ibid., pp. 13–14.

63. Bretz questionnaires; Goering and Mathews interviews.

64. Bretz questionnaires; Goering interview.

65. Ibid.; Mathews interview.

66. Goering interview.

67. Bretz questionnaires; Mathews and Goering interviews; *Wheat in Kansas,* pp. 101–2.

68. Wilson and Murdock, *Reducing Harvesting Costs,* pp. 14–16.

69. Fitz, *Handling Wheat,* p. 6.

70. Ibid., pp. 7–10.

71. *Wheat in Kansas,* pp. 103–5.

72. Ibid., p. 103.

73. Modern grain scientists do not identify any specific chemical process associated with moisture and heat in the stack that would vindicate the more elaborate beliefs about the sweat. One authority points out that the sweat as simply a drying process was discernible, with droplets forming on the bundles. Modern studies do confirm, however, that wheat cut at the binder stage is at approximately the optimum point for grain quality. Grain cut drier is inferior in test weight and protein content. Therefore,

grain cut early with a binder and put through the sweat in the stack probably was superior grain, not necessarily because of the sweat but because it was cut early (telephone interviews with Bob Bequette, Kansas State University, August 1989; letter from E. G. Heyne, Professor Emeritus, Kansas State University,14 August 1989; Gene E. Scott, E. G. Heyne, and K. F. Finney, "Development of the Hard Red Winter Wheat Kernel in relation to Yield, Test Weight, Kernel Weight, Moisture Content and Milling and Baking Quality," *Agronomy Journal* 49 [1957]: 509–13).

CHAPTER 3.   THRESHING

1. Allen R. Turner, "Pioneer Farming Experiences," *Saskatchewan History* 8 (Fall 1955): 47; Elizabeth Hampsten, "A German-Russian Family in North Dakota," *Heritage of the Great Plains* 20 (Winter 1987): 4–5; letter from Richard H. Schmidt, Newton, Kans., 18 February 1981; George D. Harper, "Eighty Years of Recollections," interview by Works Progress Administration, no date, Panhandle Plains Historical Museum, Canyon, Tex.; Sadie Summers, "Memoirs of John Bell Porter," interview, 4 August 1936, Panhandle Plains Historical Museum.

2. James C. Malin, *Winter Wheat in the Golden Belt of Kansas: A Study in Adaptation to Subhumid Geographical Environment* (Lawrence: University of Kansas Press, 1944), p. 65; "Threshing Machines in 1878," clippings file, Saskatchewan Archives, Regina; Robert H. Porter, "Texan Recites Harvesting's Evolution," *The Farmer-Stockman* 60 (October 1947): 37; "Memoirs of L. A. Pierce," interview, 3 August 1936, Panhandle Plains Historical Museum, Canyon, Tex.; T. Eugene Barrows, "Threshing in Montana at the Turn of the Century," *Montana* 38 (Autumn 1988): 63.

3. Clarence L. Petrowsky, "Kansas Agriculture before 1900" (Ph.D. dissertation, University of Oklahoma, 1968), p. 108; au-

thor's notes of conversations with groups at the Life Enrichment Program, Bethel College, North Newton, Kans., 1981; Graeme R. Quick and Wesley F. Buchele, *The Grain Harvesters* (St. Joseph, Mich.: American Society of Agricultural Engineers, 1978), pp. 103–12; R. Douglas Hurt, *American Farm Tools: From Hand Power to Steam Power* (Manhattan, Kans.: Sunflower University Press, 1982), pp. 103–5; *Regina Leader,* 13 March 1884, 27 November 1884, 13 November 1888, and 4 December 1888; Ernest B. Ingles, "The Custom Thresherman in Western Canada," in *Building beyond the Homestead: Rural History on the Prairies,* ed. by David C. Jones and Ian MacPherson (Calgary: University of Calgary Press, 1985), p. 136. A standard reference on steam engines is Jack Norbeck, *Encyclopedia of American Steam Traction Engines,* 3d rev. ed. (Sarasota, Fla.: Crestline Publishers, 1976).

4. Questionnaires from J. A. Boan, Briarcrest, Sask. (quote); diary of an unidentified thesherman, copy provided by Spike Jensen, Columbus, Mont.

5. Interview with Milo Mathews, Linwood, Ore. (conducted in Emporia, Kans.), 17 November 1980; "Farmers' Cooperative Threshing Outfits," *National Stockman and Farmer* 40 (July 1916): 4–5; Wilbert E. Sommer, "A Successful Threshing Club," *American Co-operative Journal* 11 (August 1916): 1204; Volney O. Applegate, "A Successful Threshing Ring," *National Stockman and Farmer* 41 (November 1917): 764–65; "Threshing Rings Displace Custom Work: Teamwork by Farmers Gives Benefits," U.S. Department of Agriculture *Weekly News Letter* 6 (June 1919): 5; "By-Laws of a Cooperative Threshing Outfit," *Wallace's Farmer* 43 (September 1918): 1309; "Organizing a Threshing Ring," *Wallace's Farmer* 45 (April 1920): 1177; "Threshing Rings," *Nor'West Farmer* 43 (5 May 1924): 466; Halley K. Dickey, "Community Threshing Outfits," *Biennial Report of the Kansas State Board of Agriculture, 1919–1920* (Topeka: Kansas State Board of Agriculture, 1921), pp. 124–

26; W. C. Smith, "Community Owned Threshing Outfits," *American Thresherman* (hereafter cited as *AmTh*) 26 (April 1924): 32; Donald Joe Wright, "The Squaw Creek Threshing Company," *Junior Historian* (Texas State Historical Association) 42 (November 1956): 13–14, 32; J. C. Rundles, "The Thrashing Ring in the Cornbelt," *Yearbook of the [U.S.] Department of Agriculture* (Washington, D.C.: GPO, 1918), pp. 247–68; James Sanford Rikoon, "The White Plains, Indiana, Threshing Ring, 1920–1943," *Indiana Magazine of History* 80 (September 1984): 227–63; J. Sanford Rikoon, *Threshing in the Midwest, 1820–1940* (Bloomington: Indiana University Press, 1988), pp. 58–134.

6. Lescohier discussed threshing practices in *Conditions Affecting the Demand for Harvest Labor in the Wheat Belt,* U.S. Department of Agriculture Bulletin 1230 (Washington, D.C.: GPO, 1924), pp. 24–30.

7. E. L. Currier, *The Cost of Growing Wheat on Typical Non-Irrigated Areas in Montana,* Montana Agricultural Experiment Station Bulletin 122 (1918), p. 159; C. M. Hennis and Rex E. Willard, *Farm Practices in Grain Farming in North Dakota,* U.S. Department of Agriculture Bulletin 757 (Washington, D.C.: GPO, 1919), pp. 12–13.

8. M. R. Cooper and R. S. Washburn, *Cost of Producing Wheat on 481 Farms in the States of North and South Dakota, Minnesota, Kansas, Nebraska, and Missouri, for the Crop Year 1919,* U.S. Department of Agriculture Bulletin 943 (Washington, D.C.: GPO, 1921), pp. 40–41; *Wheat in Kansas,* Quarterly Report of the Kansas State Board of Agriculture, September 1920, pp. 106–7.

9. *Annual Report of the Department of Agriculture of the Northwest Territories,* 1901, pp. 33–34; *Regina Leader,* 7 November 1901; *Final Report on Grain Crops of the Province of Saskatchewan for 1907,* Saskatchewan Department of Agriculture, Bureau of Information and Statistics Bulletin 6, pp. 29–32; *Annual Report,* 1915, Saskatchewan Department of Agriculture, p. 11; representative

file (others destroyed), "Movement of Threshing Machines," 1609, Saskatchewan Department of Agriculture, 1915, Saskatchewan Archives, Regina.

10. Interview with Floyd Bever, Sedan, Kans., 3 April 1976.

11. Questionnaires returned by A. O. Krueger.

12. Questionnaires from Ned McKinney, Alexander Boan, J. A. Boan, William Lies, and George Hitz; interview with Alexander Boan.

13. Interviews with Richard Goering, Cassoday, Kans., 21 September 1981, and Ernest Claassen, Peabody, Kans., 3 September 1982; unidentified clipping, Fred Barde Collection, Indian Archives, Oklahoma Historical Society, Oklahoma City; Ray Coates, "To the Golden West, 1904–08: Part II," *Saskatchewan History* 8 (Winter 1955): 17.

14. Citations for threshermen letters quoted, in order: *Canadian Thresherman* (herafter cited as *CanTh*) 16 (June 1911): 41; *AmTh* 2 (May 1908): 39; *AmTh* 12 (April 1910): 49, 52; *AmTh* 14 (September 1911): 68; *CanTh* 16 (May 1911): 38; *AmTh* 16 (May 1913): 45; *AmTh* 16 (August 1913): 84–85.

15. *CanTh* 16 (July 1911): 62–63.

16. See Chapter 4 for the history of harvesting and threshing labor.

17. *AmTh* 2 (August 1908): 46.

18. *AmTh* 18 (May 1915): 38.

19. Letter from Dyck, *AmTh* 2 (July 1908): 36; letter from Vaughn, *AmTh* 2 (July 1908): 36.

20. Letter from Turry Anderson, *AmTh* 20 (July 1917): 36.

21. McKinney questionnaires; see also letter from George Young, Brencepeth, Sask., *CanTh* 16 (April 1911): 52–53.

22. *American Thresherman* and *Canadian Thresherman* carried frequent notices of opportunities for engine education and many articles by Evan A. Hardy and other academics. The Connor work is *Science of Threshing: Treating the Operation, Management and Care of Threshing Machinery* (St. Joseph,

Mich.: Thresherman's Review Company, 1906), quotes on pp. 155–56. For another profile of the engineer, see Ingles, "Custom Thresherman," pp. 138–39.

23. Letter from John Grigwire, *AmTh* 12 (June 1909): 38.

24. Letter from Sander L. Rude, *AmTh* 12 (May 1909): 42.

25. *AmTh* 12 (March 1909): 39–40.

26. Life Enrichment notes; questionnaires from Guy Bretz, Worrall, and Hitz.

27. *AmTh* 20 (May 1917): 11, 15, 19; H. R. Tolley, *The Efficient Operation of Threshing Machines*, U.S. Department of Agriculture, Farmers' Bulletin 991 (Washington, D.C.: GPO, 1918); U.S. Department of Agriculture, *Weekly News Letter* 6 (23 April 1919): 9, (25 June 1919): 4, (4 June 1919): 12; "Mobilizing Threshermen to Save Grain," *Co-operative Manager and Farmer* (June 1918): 45.

28. J. E. Hill, "Adjusting and Running the Thresher," *Dakota Farmer* 41 (August 1921): 706.

29. The literature on these and other concerns about the separator is abundant—see Tolley, *Efficient Operation of Threshing Machines*; Hill, "Adjusting and Running the Thresher"; Elmer Johnson, *Care and Repair of Farm Implements*, U.S. Department of Agriculture, Farmers' Bulletin 1036 (Washington, D.C.: GPO, 1919); Connor, *Science of Threshing*, pp. 7–9; John Scott, *The Complete Text-book of Farm Engineering* (London: Crosby Lockwood and Company, no date); P. S. Rose, "Practical Talks to Threshermen, Talk No. XLIX," *CanTh* 16 (September 1911): 34, 76; P. S. Rose, "Practical Talks to Threshermen, Talk No. LIII," *CanTh* 17 (January 1912): 36; James Beamish, "The Lubrication of Threshing Machinery," *CanTh* 17 (August 1912): 66–68; R. Milne, "The Grain Separator," *CanTh* 18 (September 1913): 18, 20, 50–51; F. N. G. Kranich, "The Care and Handling of Separators," *AmTh* 13 (August 1910): 74–76, 78; F. N. G. Kranich, "The Waste of Threshing," *AmTh* 13 (December 1910): 52–53; P. S. Rose,

"Threshers' School of Modern Methods, Lesson LX," *AmTh* 14 (June 1911): 16; Evan A. Hardy, "Overhaul Your Separator Early," *AmTh* 27 (May 1924): 5; Timothy Parson, "Before Storing Your Separator," *AmTh* 27 (November 1924): 5–6; James R. Stone, "Save More Grain in Threshing," *Power Farming* 27 (June 1918): 18, 20; M. H. Crosbie, "How to Get Good Work from the Thresher," *Power Farming* 29 (July 1920): 11–13. On separator men, see also Ingles, "Custom Thresherman," p. 139.

30. Bretz, Lies, McKinney, Hitz, and Alexander Boan questionnaires; Alexander Boan interview; Ingles, "Custom Thresherman," pp. 139–40.

31. Interview with Hartford A. Lewis, Gray, Sask., 13 June 1985.

32. Lies, Hitz, and McKinney questionnaires.

33. J. A. Boan questionnaires.

34. Hitz questionnaires.

35. J. A. Boan questionnaires.

36. J. H. Hohaus, "Always Feed Bundles Head First," *Dakota Farmer* 45 (July 1925): 643.

37. McKinney questionnaires.

38. Rose, "Practical Talks to Threshermen," *CanTh* 17 (January 1912): 36.

39. Ibid.; P. S. Rose, "Threshers' School of Modern Methods, Lesson LX," *AmTh* 14 (June 1911): 16; quote from W. H. Belford, "The Threshing of the Grain," *Canadian Magazine of Politics, Science and Literature* 21 (October 1903): 499; quote from letter from L. J. Fargo, Stratford, S. Dak., *AmTh* 13 (May 1910): 45.

40. M. L. Wilson and H. E. Murdock, *Reducing Wheat Harvesting Costs on Montana Dry Lands,* Montana Extension Service Bulletin 71 (Bozeman: Montana State Extension Service, 1924), pp. 33–35.

41. Letter from Carl Nutsch, Morrowville, Kans., *AmTh* 29 (January 1927): 12.

42. Edna Sutherland, "The Threshers Are Coming," no date, clippings, Prairie Room, Regina Public Library.

43. F. M. Redpath, "Cradle to Combine,"

undated typescript, Kansas State Historical Society Library, Topeka.

44. Mary W. McFarlane, "Harvest Time in the Kitchen," *Biennial Report of the Kansas State Board of Agriculture, 1917–1918* (Topeka: Kansas State Board of Agriculture, 1919), pp. 90–91; see also Life Enrichment notes; Mathews interview; Aline Funk, "The Day of the Threshing Machine," *Kanhistique* 10 (June 1984): 11; Laverne Ritter, "Threshing in the Thirties," paper for Tallgrass Writers' Workshop, Emporia State University, 1987; "The Lore of the Wheatfield," paper for Great Plains Folklore seminar, Emporia State University, 1987; Henry T. Murray and John A. Murray, "Neighbors Helping Neighbors: Threshing in the Judith Basin," *Montana* 37 (Winter 1987): 56–59; "Threshing Gangs Put Farm Women on Test," clippings, Prairie Room, Regina Public Library; Mrs. F. M. Cantlon, "The Threshing Crews," *Alberta Historical Review* 16 (Autumn 1968): 17–18.

45. Anna May Handley, "Cook Car Apprentice Has Hard Existence," clippings, Prairie Room, Regina Public Library.

46. Bretz and Hitz questionnaires; see also Lies and McKinney questionnaires; Mathews interview.

47. Mrs. E. R. Ghan, "Memories of Harvesting at Hoffer, Sask.," clippings file, Saskatchewan Archives, Regina.

48. Lorena Hickok, unfinished autobiography, chapter 2, pp. 15–16, Lorena Hickok Papers, Franklin D. Roosevelt Library, Hyde Park, N.Y. For one more, fictionalized view of life in the cook car, see C. M. Harger, "The Mistress of the Cook Shack," *Outlook* 88 (September 1907): 209–13.

49. Bretz, Lies, and McKinney questionnaires; Goering and Mathews interviews.

50. Letter from E. J. Powers, Almeria, Nebr., *AmTh* 18 (July 1915): 52; letter from Frank L. Dodge, Morse Bluff, Nebr., *AmTh* 16 (December 1913): 48; letter from Ed Eike, Woodward, Okla., *AmTh* 17 (December 1914): 47–48; letter from F. G. Cour-

bot, Cimarron, Kans., *AmTh* 17 (August 1914): 79; clippings from *Fort Benton River Press,* provided by River Press Publishing Company.

51. P. S. Rose, "Thresher's School of Modern Methods," *AmTh* 2 (May 1908): 32; *AmTh* 2 (June 1908): 36; F. N. G. Kranich, "Belting," *AmTh* 14 (December 1911): 66–68; letter from Blaine Mills, Arborville, Nebr., *AmTh* 19 (September 1916): 48; C. C. Hermann, "Caring for the Tractor's Belt," *AmTh* 30 (August 1927): 8, 29; Evan Hardy, "Lagging Pulleys and Lacing Belts," *AmTh* 31 (May 1928): 5; A. J. Schwantes, "Lacing Belts with Leather," *AmTh* 33 (September 1930): 4; J. A. Boan, Worrall, McKinney, and Lies questionnaires.

52. McKinney questionnaires.

53. Bretz questionnaires.

54. Lies questionnaires.

55. Worrall questionnaires.

56. Letter from Emil Sobota, *AmTh* 13 (January 1911): 44; letter from Clarence Weldon, *AmTh* 25 (August 1922): 32–33; see also letter from John H. Nelson, Junction City, Kans., *AmTh* 12 (April 1910): 52; letter from J. B. Hermann, Chasely, N. Dak., *AmTh* 16 (January 1914): 18–19; "Fireman Killed Instantly," *AmTh* 25 (January 1923): 7; *Vinita* (Oklahoma) *Indian Chieftain,* 31 August 1893.

57. David J. Price and E. B. McCormick, *Dust Explosions and Fires in Grain Separators in the Pacific Northwest,* U.S. Department of Agriculture Bulletin 379 (Washington, D.C.: GPO, 1916); U.S. Department of Agriculture *Weekly News Letter* 3 (1916): 1; *Power Farming* 25 (July 1916): 30, 38; letter from N. M. Tipps, Zybach, Tex., *AmTh* 20 (November 1917): 19.

58. Letter from C. H. Everhart, *AmTh* 18 (February 1916): 38; photo feature in *AmTh* 12 (December 1909): 69; see also letter from George Schutt, Redfield, S. Dak., *AmTh* 2 (May 1908): 38; letter from Louis Nagengast, Howells, Nebr., *AmTh* 13 (May 1910): 48; "Crashed through Wooden Bridge," *AmTh* 29 (November 1926): 6; In-

gles, "Custom Thresherman," pp. 144–45.

59. Hennis and Willard, *Farm Practices,* p. 13.

60. Cooper and Washburn, *Cost of Producing Wheat, 1919,* p. 16.

61. Quote from letter from Merritt Harmon, Esmond, N. Dak., *AmTh* 14 (November 1911): 51. Statements about rates in succeeding paragraphs are based on hundreds of similar reports in *American Thresherman* and *Canadian Thresherman.*

62. M. T. Austin, "Threshing in Southwestern South Dakota," *AmTh* 13 (July 1910): 14.

63. Letter from Dobson, *CanTh* 16 (June 1911): 40; letter from Dibble, *CanTh* 16 (November 1911): 34; W. H. Belford, "Winning Out in the Threshing Game," *CanTh* 19 (June 1914): 18, 58–60; see also letter from John L. Kuhn, Minneapolis, Minn., *AmTh* 25 (June 1922); letter from J. L. Hickman, Tulia, Tex., *AmTh* 25 (September 1922).

64. This series of articles by Rose, part of his "Threshers' School of Modern Methods," ran from January through May 1909 in *American Thresherman.*

65. W. C. Smith, "Balancing the Thresherman's Books," *AmTh* 17 (April 1915): 34–35; W. C. Smith, "Collecting the Threshing Account," *AmTh* 18 (June 1915): 36–37; W. C. Smith, "The Thresherman's Expense Bill," *AmTh* 20 (June 1917); G. F. Connor, "Threshing Viewed as a Business Proposition," *Power Farming* 25 (March 1916): 12; "Custom Threshing as a Business," *AmTh* 23 (May 1920): 7, 70; A. P. Murphy, "Threshing Prices Produce Arguments," *AmTh* 26 (October 1923): 9, 14; A. P. Murphy, "Threshing Requires Business Ability," *AmTh* 26 (December 1923): 9; A. P. Murphy, "What It Costs to Thresh," *AmTh* 28 (July 1925): 5–6.

66. Letter to *AmTh* 17 (January 1915): 35.

67. Letter to *AmTh* 2 (August 1908): 45–46.

68. Letter from R. F. Anderson, Wilton,

N. Dak., *AmTh* 20 (March 1918): 37.

69. Letter from Lee Hinds, Cleburne, Tex., *AmTh* 16 (May 1913): 45; letter from A. E. Morris, McGregor, Tex., *AmTh* 16 (December 1913): 44–50; letter from Floyd L. Wilmoth, Crawford, Kans., *AmTh* 25 (June 1922): 28.

70. Claassen and Mathews interviews; Bretz questionnaires.

71. *AmTh* 12 (February 1910): 42; *AmTh* 18 (September 1915): 27; *AmTh* 2 (May 1908): 60; *AmTh* 2 (June 1908): 44–45; *AmTh* 2 (May 1908): 39; *AmTh* 2 (September 1908); *AmTh* 17 (September 1914): 39; *AmTh* 17 (May 1914): 76; *AmTh* 19 (December 1916): 54.

72. Letter from Frank Nyberg, Basalt, Colo., *AmTh* 19 (August 1916): 32; Bretz questionnaires; letter from H. G. Hewitt, Brighton, Colo., *AmTh* 12 (April 1910): 49, 52.

73. Bretz questionnaires; Mathews interview; letter from J. R. Huffman, Orman, S. Dak., *AmTh* 17 (September 1914): 39; letter from Hays, *AmTh* 20 (July 1917): 36; letter from Bignall, *AmTh* 2 (June 1908): 44–45; letter from Pasco, *AmTh* 2 (September 1908).

74. Letter from W. G. Stuard, Embden, N. Dak., *AmTh* 14 (August 1911): 80.

75. Letter from N. L. Walsted, Milton, N. Dak., *AmTh* 33 (May 1930): 23.

76. Letter from William Koester, Fairfax, S. Dak., *AmTh* 2 (January 1909): 34; in similar vein, see letter from J. R. Meile, Lincoln, Kans., *AmTh* 18 (May 1915): 38.

77. Letter from George Braschear, *AmTh* 20 (December 1917): 27.

78. Letter from Frank Fesler, Palco, Kans., *AmTh* 12 (September 1909): 41, 45.

79. Letter from J. W. Sibert, Bemis, S. Dak., *AmTh* 2 (May 1908): 60.

80. *AmTh* 19 (June 1916): 66–67; see also letter from John Grigwine, Clay Center, Kans., *AmTh* 12 (June 1909): 38; letter from Z. Thomas, Olivet, Kans., *AmTh* 14 (May 1911): 42; letter from F. J. Bignall, Sandorn, N. Dak., *AmTh* 18 (March 1916): 34.

81. Letter from Thomas Decker, *AmTh* 13 (August 1910): 85.

82. "Threshermen, Why Don't You Organize?" *AmTh* 2 (March 1909): 52–53; Ingles, "Custom Thresherman," p. 148.

83. *Stillwater Gazette*, 2 June 1898.

84. Ibid., 16 June 1898.

85. For other reports on local brotherhoods, see *Topeka Daily Capital*, 12 February 1903; letter from J. R. Morris, Sedgwick, Kans., *AmTh* 2 (May 1908): 42; letter from D. A. Skeiner, Bern, Kans., *AmTh* 2 (May 1908): 61–62; letter from Jerry Dunkelberger, Newton, Kans., *AmTh* 2 (August 1908): 41; letter from Lewis E. Doty, Hastings, Nebr., *AmTh* 13 (July 1910): 72; letter from Berrington, Nebr., *AmTh* 13 (August 1910): 93; letter from Clark Wilcox, Saratoga, Wyo., *AmTh* 16 (July 1913): 76; letter from the Sobota brothers, Schuyler, Nebr., *AmTh* 14 (May 1911): 48; letter from Roy Betts, Harlan, Kans., *AmTh* 16 (October 1913): 59; letter from Fritz Nelson, Regent, N. Dak., *AmTh* 17 (June 1914): 62; letter from Theodore Holmes, Bergen, N. Dak., *AmTh* 19 (April 1917): 18; letter from Grand Forks, N. Dak., *AmTh* 27 (September 1924): 32; see also Ingles, "Custom Thresherman," pp. 148–50.

86. Reports of brotherhood meetings in *AmTh* 12 (May 1909): 8; 13 (March 1911): 12; 13 (April 1911): 8; 14 (June 1911): 42–44; 14 (April 1912): 12–13, 80; 16 (April 1914): 36; 10 (April 1917): 8; 13 (April 1911): 10; 20 (March 1918): 29; 14 (May 1911): 8–9.

87. Reports of brotherhood meetings in *AmTh* 13 (June 1910): 8; 13 (April 1911): 10; 14 (March 1912): 43; 20 (March 1918): 28, 29; 25 (April 1923): 5; 27 (May 1924): 39; 31 (March 1929): 9; 2 (August 1908): 14; 27 (April 1925): 9, 12; 30 (May 1927): 6; 31 (May 1928): 3, 5; 31 (April 1929): 7–8; 32 (April 1930): 7–8; 34 (May 1931): 18–19; 14 (July 1911): 79; 27 (July 1924): 14; *CanTh* 19 (March 1914): 40–41; *AmTh* 34 (December 1931): 12.

88. *AmTh* 27 (July 1924): 14.

89. *Revised Statutes of Kansas, 1923* (To-

peka: State Printing Plant, 1923), 58-203–6; *General Statutes of Kansas, 1936* (Topeka: State Printing Plant, 1936). For cases interpreting the thresher's lien law, see (in *Kansas Reports*) *Rupp v. Dinkel*, vol. 112, pp. 534–35; *Kansas Wheat Growers Association v. Leslie*, vol. 126, pp. 694–99; *Taylor v. White*, vol. 131, pp. 791–94; *Miller v. Fike*, vol. 133, pp. 108–11; *Reeves and Michener v. Kansas Cooperative Wheat Marketing Association*, vol. 136, pp. 306–10; *Schmitz v. Stockman*, vol. 151, pp. 891–97.

90. "A Story of Threshing Liens," *AmTh* 25 (July 1922).

91. Diary of unidentified thresherman provided by Spike Jensen.

92. "Provincial Lien Laws," *CanTh* 19 (April 1914): 38–39; "Threshermen of Saskatchewan to Organize," *CanTh* 19 (March 1914): 40–41; A. W. Smith, "The Canadian Thresherman," *Farm Power* (October 1914): 57.

93. *Revised Statutes of Kansas, 1923*, 68-1129; notes on organizations in *AmTh* 2 (November 1908): 31; 13 (October 1910): 70; 13 (January 1911): 16; 14 (May 1911): 9; 14 (June 1911): 42; 25 (April 1923): 5; 27 (December 1924): 17.

94. *Regina Leader*, 15 October 1903; Smith, "Canadian Thresherman," p. 57; Ingles, "Custom Thresherman," pp. 138, 142–43; *AmTh* 18 (May 1915): 82.

95. Camrose Historical Society (collector), threshers' papers and beef ring record, 1892–1893 and 1908–1928 (includes ledgers of Haselwood and Son, rig registration, and noxious-weeds notice), Glenbow-Alberta Institute Archives, Calgary, Alberta.

96. Robson, notebook of farm, roadwork, and threshing records, 1931–1939, Glenbow-Alberta Institute Archives, Calgary, Alberta.

97. Records of the Spruce Home Threshing Syndicate, Saskatchewan Archives, Regina.

98. Threshing journal of Lowell Ayers, copy courtesy of Mr. and Mrs. Lowell Ayers, Oberlin, Kans.; letter to author from Lowell Ayers, 1981.

99. The discussion of the threshing operations of C. R. Voth is based on two sources: his thresherman's account books, which cover (although a few appear to be missing) the years 1903–1930 and which were lent to me by his son, Moses H. Voth, of North Newton, Kans.; and an interview with Moses H. Voth, North Newton, Kans., 2 April 1983.

CHAPTER 4.   HANDS

1. Carey McWilliams, *Ill Fares the Land: Migrants and Migratory Labor in the United States* (New York: Barnes and Noble, 1967), pp. 91–108 (Chapter 5), 95 (quote).

2. John Herd Thompson, "Bringing in the Sheaves: The Harvest Excursionists, 1890–1929," *Canadian Historical Review* 59 (1978): 469–70; G. C. Holtzman, "Harvest Excursions to Western Canada," student research paper, no date, Saskatchewan Archives, Regina; George V. Haythorne, "Harvest Labor in Western Canada: An Episode in Economic Planning," *Quarterly Journal of Economics* 47 (May 1933): 533.

3. Thompson, "Bringing in the Sheaves," pp. 470–71; Haythorne, "Harvest Labor," p. 539; Holtzman, "Harvest Excursions"; "Report on the Western Farm Excursion 1947," in File 14, R-262, Saskatchewan Department of Agriculture, Farm Labor Division, Saskatchewan Archives, Regina.

4. Holtzman, "Harvest Excursions"; Thompson, "Bringing in the Sheaves," p. 477; Department of Agriculture of the Northwest Territories, *Annual Report*, 1901, p. 33; Saskatchewan Department of Agriculture, *Annual Report*, 1905, pp. 20–21, 1906, pp. 13–14, 1907, pp. 108–10, 1908, pp. 92–93, 1909, pp. 82–83, 1911, pp. 14, 195–97, 1915, pp. 178–80, 1918, pp. 29–31; *Regina Morning Leader*, 12 October 1909, 25 July 1923, 15 August 1923, 14 September 1927.

5. Haythorne, "Harvest Labor," pp. 535–36.

6. Holtzman, "Harvest Excursions";

Thompson, "Bringing in the Sheaves," p. 473; Haythorne, "Harvest Labor," pp. 539–41.

7. Thompson, "Bringing in the Sheaves," p. 469; Haythorne, "Harvest Labor," pp. 538–39.

8. Thompson, "Bringing in the Sheaves," pp. 471–73.

9. Letter to *New York Times*, quoted in Allen G. Applen, "Migratory Harvest Labor in the Midwestern Wheat Belt, 1870–1940" (Ph.D. dissertation, Kansas State University, Manhattan, 1974), p. 69.

10. *Kansas City Star*, quoted in Applen, "Migratory Harvest Labor," p. 69; A. B. MacDonald, "The Moving Army of Harvest Hands," *Country Gentlemen* 89 (August 1924): 15.

11. William R. Draper, "Solving the Harvest Labor Problem of the Wheat Belt," *American Monthly Review of Reviews* 26 (July 1902): 72.

12. E. L. Rhoades, "Harvest Labor," in *Twenty-second Biennial Report of the Kansas State Board of Agriculture*, 1919–20 (Topeka: Kansas State Board of Agriculture, 1921), pp. 208–9. Roughly the same categories and descriptions were reproduced in H. Umberger and E. L. Rhoades, *Kansas Handbook of Harvest Labor*, Kansas State Agricultural College Extension Circular 23 (1921).

13. Lescohier's publications are "Harvesters and Hoboes in the Wheat Fields," *The Survey* 50 (July 1923): 376–82, 409–12; "Hands and Tools of the Wheat Harvest," *The Survey* 50 (August 1923): 482–87, 503–4; *Harvest Labor Problems in the Wheat Belt*, U.S. Department of Agriculture Bulletin 1020 (Washington, D.C.: GPO, 1922); *Conditions Affecting the Demand for Harvest Labor in the Wheat Belt*, U.S. Department of Agriculture Bulletin 1230 (Washington, D.C.: GPO, 1924); and *Sources of Supply and Conditions of Employment of Harvest Labor in the Wheat Belt*, U.S. Department of Agriculture Bulletin 1211 (Washington, D.C.: GPO, 1924). A summary of his work appeared as "Conditions of Harvest Labor in the Wheat Belt, 1920 and 1921," *Monthly Labor Review* 16 (February 1923): 44–50.

14. Lescohier, *Demand for Harvest Labor*, p. 7.

15. Ibid., pp. 8–9, 18–19.

16. Lescohier, *Harvest Labor Problems*, p. 14.

17. Lescohier, "Hands and Tools," pp. 379–80.

18. Lescohier, *Harvest Labor Problems*, p. 1, and *Sources of Supply*, p. 1.

19. Lescohier, "Hands and Tools," p. 380.

20. Lescohier, *Sources of Supply*, p. 2.

21. Lescohier, *Harvest Labor Problems*, p. 16.

22. Lescohier, "Hands and Tools," p. 378.

23. Ibid., p. 382.

24. Ibid.; Lescohier, *Sources of Supply*, p. 3.

25. Lescohier, *Harvest Labor Problems*, p. 19; Lescohier, *Sources of Supply*, p. 7.

26. Lescohier, *Harvest Labor Problems*, p. 18; Lescohier, *Sources of Supply*, p. 7.

27. Lescohier, *Sources of Supply*, p. 11.

28. Lescohier, *Harvest Labor Problems*, pp. 14–16.

29. Lescohier, *Sources of Supply*, p. 4.

30. The pie graph appeared on page 412 of Lescohier's article "Hands and Tools."

31. Ibid., p. 382.

32. Ibid., p. 376.

33. Ibid., pp. 381–82; Lescohier, *Harvest Labor Problems*, pp. 19–20.

34. Lescohier, "Harvesters and Hoboes," p. 485.

35. Ibid., pp. 485–86; Lescohier, "Hands and Tools," p. 382.

36. Lescohier, "Hands and Tools," p. 381.

37. Lescohier, *Harvest Labor Problems*, p. 18.

38. Lescohier, "Hands and Tools," p. 379.

39. Ibid., p. 378.

40. Ibid., p. 380.

41. Lescohier, "Harvesters and Hoboes," p. 483.

42. Donald G. Hay, *Rural Population Migration in the Northern Great Plains* (Lincoln, Nebr.: U.S. Bureau of Agricultural Eco-

nomics, no date), pp. 15–17; Robert M. Cullum, Josiah C. Folsom, and Donald G. Hay, "Men and Machines in the North Dakota Harvest" (mimeograph, U.S. Bureau of Agricultural Economics, 1942), pp. 9, 39, 42–44; see also Cullum et al., "Men and Machines in the North Dakota Harvest (Statistical Supplement)" (mimeograph, U.S. Bureau of Agricultural Economics, 1942), a companion publication.

43. Cullum et al., "Men and Machines," p. 33.

44. Ibid.

45. Applen, "Migratory Harvest Labor," pp. 118–19; Draper, "Harvest Labor Problem," pp. 70–71.

46. Applen, "Migratory Harvest Labor," pp. 136–37; Draper, "Harvest Labor Problem," pp. 71–72.

47. Applen, "Migratory Harvest Labor," pp. 140–42; Draper, "Harvest Labor Problem," p. 71.

48. Draper, "Harvest Labor Problem," pp. 70–72.

49. Applen, "Migratory Harvest Labor," pp. 116–18.

50. Ibid., pp. 123–24.

51. Ibid., pp. 126–31; Topeka Daily Capital, 11 July 1907 and 13 July 1907, Clippings, Kansas State Historical Society Library, Topeka; Lescohier, Harvest Labor Problems, p. 29; Rhoades, "Harvest Labor," p. 207; Umberger and Rhoades, Kansas Handbook.

52. Applen, "Migratory Harvest Labor," pp. 131–42; Kansas Department of Labor and Industry, Twenty-ninth Annual Report, 1913, pp. 219–22, Thirtieth Annual Report, 1914, pp. 240–44, and Combined Thirty-first and Thirty-second Annual Reports, 1915–16, pp. 200–215.

53. Applen, "Migratory Harvest Labor," pp. 142–44.

54. Lescohier, Harvest Labor Problems, p. 1.

55. Quote from Lescohier, Demand for Harvest Labor, p. 30.

56. Ibid., p. 1.

57. Quote from Umberger and Rhoades,

Kansas Handbook; Lescohier, Harvest Labor Problems, pp. 24–28; Lescohier, Demand for Harvest Labor, pp. 30–31; Rhoades, "Harvest Labor," p. 211; MacDonald, "Moving Army of Hands," pp. 15, 38.

58. Lee H. Gould, "Furnishing 'Help' to the Farmer," Nineteenth Biennial Report of the Kansas State Board of Agriculture, 1913–14, pp. 295–97; Edward C. Johnson, Handling the 1918 Wheat Harvest in Kansas, U.S. Department of Agriculture Circular 121 (old series) (Washington, D.C.: GPO, 1918); Umberger and Rhoades, Kansas Handbook.

59. Ibid.

60. Rhoades, "Harvest Labor," pp. 205–6; Lescohier, Harvest Labor Problems, pp. 22–23; Lescohier, Demand for Harvest Labor, pp. 2–3.

61. Lescohier, Harvest Labor Problems, p. 22.

62. Rhoades, "Harvest Labor," pp. 210–11; Umberger and Rhoades, Kansas Handbook.

63. Thompson, "Bringing in the Sheaves," pp. 482–85.

64. Ibid., pp. 484–85; Statutes of the Province of Saskatchewan, 1908–1909, Chapter 11; Office Consolidation of the Public Statutes of the Province of Alberta, 1906–1915, Chapter 17.

65. P. S. Rose, "Threshers' School of Modern Methods," American Thresherman (hereafter cited as AmTh) 2 (February 1909): 10.

66. Rhoades, "Harvest Labor," pp. 213–14; Umberger and Rhoades, Kansas Handbook.

67. Lescohier, Harvest Labor Problems, pp. 30–32; Lescohier, Employment of Harvest Labor, pp. 16–19; Lescohier, Demand for Harvest Labor, pp. 32–37.

68. Lescohier, Employment of Harvest Labor, pp. 17, 25–26.

69. Cullum et al., "Men and Machines," pp. 24–25.

70. Data compiled from letters to AmTh and Canadian Thresherman, for various years from 1909 to 1916.

71. Letter from Arthur Hanger, Sarles, N. Dak., *AmTh* 28 (August 1925): 18; letter from Saskatchewan "Old Timer," Aylesbury, *CanTh* 20 (July 1915): 26; letter from Wildeman brothers, Phillipsburg, Kans., *AmTh* 19 (December 1916): 54.

72. Holtzman, "Harvest Excursions," p. 19.

73. Lescohier, *Harvest Labor Problems*, p. 29; Lescohier, *Employment of Harvest Labor*, p. 11; Umberger and Rhoades, *Kansas Handbook*.

74. Lescohier, *Employment of Harvest Labor*, p. 12.

75. Ibid., pp. 12–13; interview with Milo Mathews, Linwood, Ore. (conducted in Emporia, Kans.), 17 November 1980.

76. Lescohier, *Employment of Harvest Labor*, p. 12; Mathews interview; John J. Hader, "Honk Honk Hobo," *The Survey* 60 (August 1928): 453–55; Cullum et al., "Men and Machines," pp. 28–29.

77. Lescohier, *Employment of Harvest Labor*, p. 14; questionnaires from Michael Ewanchuk, Winnipeg, Man., and Alexander Boan, Briarcrest, Sask.; Mathews interview and interview with Richard Goering, Cassoday, Kans., 21 September 1981.

78. Roy Winchester, "Caring for the Threshers," *AmTh* (September 1914): 24.

79. Ibid., pp. 24–25; letter from A. C. Rude, Mona, N. Dak., *AmTh* 28 (May 1925): 28; interview with Ernest Claassen, Peabody, Kans., 3 September 1982; Ewanchuk questionnaires; James M. Minifie, *The Homesteader* (Toronto: Macmillan of Canada, 1972), p. 79; Cullum et al., "Men and Machines," p. 26.

80. *Ellinwood Leader*, 26 June 1913.

81. Cullum et al., "Men and Machines," p. 32.

82. Letter from H. C. Kuntz, *AmTh* 14 (April 1912): 60.

83. Lescohier, *Demand for Harvest Labor*, p. 37; Ewanchuk questionnaires; Winchester, "Caring for Threshers," pp. 24–25.

84. Mathews interview; Cullum et al., "Men and Machines," p. 26; representative file, "Movement of Threshing Machines,"

1609, Saskatchewan Department of Agriculture, 1915, Saskatchewan Archives, Regina.

85. *Topeka Daily Capital*, 20 July 1914, Clippings, Kansas State Historical Society Library, Topeka.

86. Thompson, "Bringing in the Sheaves," pp. 473–74; W. J. C. Cherwinski, "The Incredible Harvest Excursion of 1908," *Labor: Journal of Canadian Labor Studies* 5 (Spring 1980): 57–79.

87. W. J. C. Cherwinski, "'Misfits,' 'Malingerers,' and 'Malcontents': The British Harvester Movement of 1928," in *The Developing West: Essays on Canadian History in Honor of Lewis H. Thomas*, ed. by John E. Foster (Edmonton: University of Alberta Press, 1983), pp. 272–302.

88. *Regina Morning Leader*, 11 August 1923.

89. *Solidarity*, 21 November 1914, quoted in Applen, "Migratory Harvest Labor," pp. 152–53.

90. Applen, "Migratory Harvest Labor," pp. 152–56; Philip Taft, "The I.W.W. in the Grain Belt," *Labor History* 1 (Fall 1960): 58–59; Charles James Haug, "The Industrial Workers of the World in North Dakota, 1913–1917," *North Dakota Quarterly* 39 (Winter 1971): 93–95; David G. Wagaman, "The Industrial Workers of the World in Nebraska, 1914–1920," *Nebraska History* 56 (Fall 1975): 296–97.

91. Don D. Lescohier, "With the I.W.W. in the Wheat Lands," *Harper's Magazine* 147 (August 1923): 376.

92. Applen, "Migratory Harvest Labor," pp. 155–62; Taft, "I.W.W. in Grain Belt," pp. 59–62; Haug, "Industrial Workers of the World in North Dakota," pp. 95–97; Lescohier, "With the I.W.W.," pp. 371–74; Wagaman, "Industrial Workers of the World in Nebraska," pp. 297–307.

93. George Creel, "Harvesting the Harvest Hands," *Harper's Weekly* 59 (September 1914): 292.

94. Ibid., pp. 292–93; *Topeka Daily Capital*, 19 May 1914, Clippings, Kansas State Historical Society Library, Topeka.

95. *Topeka Daily Capital,* 29 May 1914; *Kansas City Star,* 10 June 1914; *Coffeyville Daily Journal,* 12 June 1914; *Topeka Daily Capital,* no date; and *Kansas City Journal,* 12 June 1914—all in Clippings, Kansas State Historical Society Library, Topeka.

96. Creel, "Harvesting the Harvest Hands," pp. 292–94; *Topeka Daily Capital,* 9 July 1916, and *Kansas City Journal,* 13 July 1916, Clippings, Kansas State Historical Society Library, Topeka; Wagaman, "Industrial Workers of the World in Nebraska," pp. 298–307; Haug, "Industrial Workers of the World in North Dakota," pp. 98–99.

97. Charles James Haug, "The Industrial Workers of the World in North Dakota, 1918–1925," *North Dakota Quarterly* 41 (Summer 1973): 5–19; Joseph Dorfman, ed., "An Unpublished Paper on the I.W.W. by Thorstein Veblen," *Journal of Political Economy* 40 (December 1932): 796–807; Lescohier, "With the I.W.W.," pp. 378–79; Wagaman, "Industrial Workers of the World in Nebraska," pp. 308–25; Richard C. Cortner, "The Wobblies and *Fiske v. Kansas:* Victory amid Disintegration," *Kansas History* 4 (Spring 1981): 30–38.

98. Richard E. Lingenfelter, Richard A. Dwyer, and David Cohen, *Songs of the American West* (Berkeley: University of California Press, 1968), pp. 491–92; Lescohier, "Harvesters and Hoboes," p. 504.

99. Richard Washburn Child, "The Kansas Invaders," *Independent* 55 (September 1903): 2281–83; Charles Moreau Harger, "Journeying with Harvesters," *Scribner's Magazine* 36 (July 1904): 1–14; Altha Lea Bass, "The Harvest Vanguard," *The Survey* 52 (September 1924): 623; W. G. Clugston, "Harvest Days in Kansas," *Nation* 122 (June 1926): 720–21; MacDonald, "Moving Army of Hands," pp. 15, 38.

100. Unidentified clipping, Prairie Room, Regina Public Library, Sask.

101. Mrs. E. R. Ghan, "Memories of Harvesting at Hoffer, Sask.," Saskatchewan Archives, Regina.

102. Robert Donald, "Steam Thresher," *Kansas Quarterly* 12 (Spring 1980): 41–42.

103. Robert L. Yates, *When I Was a Harvester* (New York: Macmillan Company, 1930); other narratives include Edward R. Bushnell, "College Men as Kansas Harvesters," *Physical Culture* (August 1905): 122–26; Leslie Hartwell, "A Summer of Adventure in the West," *Pennsylvania State Farmer* 20 (March 1927): 8, 20–21; Cedric Worth, "The Brotherhood of Man," *North American Review* 227 (April 1929): 487–92; and P. W. Luce, "Memoirs of a Harvest Excursionist," *Family Herald,* 25 August 1960, pp. 21–22.

104. Robert G. Trussler, "Account of Trip West in 1925 and Harvesting Experience around New Norway, Alberta," Glenbow Museum Library, Calgary, Alberta.

105. Vachel Lindsay, *Collected Poems* (New York: Macmillan, 1952), pp. 150–52 (selected stanzas are from "Kansas").

CHAPTER 5.   COMBINES

1. Henry J. Allen, "The New Harvest Hand," *American Review of Reviews* 76 (September 1927): 279–80.

2. Robert C. Williams, *Fordson, Farmall, and Poppin' Johnny: A History of the Farm Tractor and Its Impact on America* (Urbana: University of Illinois Press, 1987), pp. 14–23.

3. Ibid., pp. 48–56, 66, 85–89.

4. Kansas State Board of Agriculture, *Twentieth Biennial Report* (Topeka: State Printer, 1915–16), p. 676, and *Twenty-eighth Biennial Report,* 1931–32, pp. 580–81.

5. R. Bruce Shepard, "Tractors and Combines in the Second Stage of Agricultural Mechanization on the Canadian Plains," *Prairie Forum* 11 (Fall 1986): 259–60.

6. C. V. Hull, "A Canadian Harvesting Scene," *American Thresherman* (hereafter cited as *AmTh*) 17 (September 1914): 50–51; Arthur L. Dahl, "Tractor Power Used for Harvesting," *AmTh* 29 (June 1926): 8–9.

7. Mawhinney's report, dated 3 October 1914, is in Records of the Saskatchewan Department of Agriculture, Statistics Branch, "Movement of Threshing Machines," Archives of Saskatchewan, Saskatoon; also

published in *Annual Report* of the Saskatchewan Department of Agriculture, 1914, pp. 316–19.

8. David Spector, *Agriculture on the Prairies, 1870–1940* (Ottawa: Parks Canada, 1983), pp. 238–39.

9. Mawhinney report; *Daily Oklahoman*, 26 August 1917; "The 'Call of the West,'" *Saskatchewan Times* (Western Development Museums), Summer 1988.

10. F. J. Main, "The Steam Tractor vs. the Gas Tractor," *AmTh* 14 (May 1911): 40–41.

11. Letter to *AmTh* 29 (October 1925).

12. Letter from Thomas Grocott, Humboldt, S. Dak., *AmTh* 28 (January 1926): 6.

13. R. E. Patterson, "Big Threshers Save More Grain," *AmTh* 29 (July 1926): 6.

14. "To the Threshermen of Canada," *Canadian Thresherman* (hereafter cited as *CanTh*) 16 (May 1911): 5.

15. Letter from Chris Wedeking, Jr., Ohiowa, Nebr., *AmTh* 17 (February 1915): 39.

16. A. C. Seyfarth, "Business of Threshing Undergoing a Change," *Power Farming* 32 (August 1923); also reprinted as "Threshing Operations Are Undergoing a Change," *Farmers Elevator Guide* 18 (May 1923): 15–16.

17. M. L. Wilson and H. E. Murdock, *Reducing Wheat Harvesting Costs on Montana Dry Lands*, Montana Extension Service Bulletin 71 (Bozeman: Montana State Extension Service, 1924), pp. 38–39.

18. C. E. Lyons, "Threshing with a Small Rig," *AmTh* 27 (May 1924): 8–9.

19. Interview with Hartford A. Lewis, Gray, Sask., 13 June 1985; quote from letter by Arthur C. Rude, Mona, N. Dak., *AmTh* 27 (September 1924): 16; Ernest B. Ingles, "The Custom Thresherman in Western Canada," in *Building beyond the Homestead: Rural History on the Prairies*, ed. by David C. Jones and Ian MacPherson (Calgary: University of Calgary Press, 1985), pp. 150–51; Spector, *Agriculture on the Prairies*, pp. 152–53.

20. W. C. Netterfield, "The Individual

Threshing Outfit," *CanTh* 7 (July 1911): 62–63.

21. R. J. Morrison, "Reducing Our Labor Costs," *AmTh* 29 (June 1926): 9.

22. E. W. Hamilton, "Can Steam Come Back?" *AmTh* 34 (October 1931): 4, 10.

23. Reuben Monson, "Harvest Conditions in Montana," *AmTh* 32 (February 1930): 17.

24. F. Hal Higgins, "The Moore-Hascall Harvester Centennial Approaches," *Michigan History Magazine* 14 (Summer 1930): 415–37; F. Hal Higgins, "John M. Horner and the Development of the Combined Harvester," *Agricultural History* 32 (January 1958): 14–17; "The Michigan-California Combine Link," undated typescript, F. Hal Higgins Library of Agricultural Technology, University of California–Davis.

25. Higgins, "John M. Horner," pp. 14–24; F. Hal Higgins, "The Cradle of the Combine," *Pacific Rural Press* 133 (February 1937): 284–85; C. C. Johnson, "Combine Long Known in Washington," *AmTh* 33 (May 1930): 26; Robert Terry, "The Combined Harvester-Thresher," *Implement and Tractor* 64 (August 1949): 45–46.

26. *Great Bend Tribune*, 26 July 1937, and *Larned Chronoscope*, 8 July 1927, Clippings, Kansas State Historical Society Library, Topeka; "Combine in 1915 Startled Kansans," *AmTh* 30 (February 1928): 6; A. E. Starch and R. M. Merrill, *The Combined Harvester-Thresher in Montana*, Montana Agricultural Experiment Station Bulletin 230 (Bozeman: Montana Agricultural Experiment Station, 1930), p. 6.

27. L. A. Reynoldson et al., *The Combined Harvester-Thresher in the Great Plains*, U.S. Department of Agriculture Technical Bulletin 70 (Washington, D.C.: GPO, 1928), pp. 2–3.

28. Reynoldson et al., *Combined Harvester-Thresher in Great Plains*, p. 3; Edwin A. Hunger, "Kansas Outstanding Leader in Use of Combine," Kansas State Board of Agriculture, *Twenty-seventh Biennial Report*, 1929–30, pp. 189–90; H. P. Smith and Robert F. Spilman, *Harvesting Grain with the*

Combined Harvester-Thresher in Northwest Texas, Texas Agricultural Experiment Station Bulletin 373 (1927), p. 5; quote from W. H. Sanders, "Some New Farm Machines," Kansas State Board of Agriculture, *Twenty-second Biennial Report,* 1919–20, p. 181.

29. H. B. Walker and E. L. Rhoades, "The Combine Harvester in Kansas," in *Wheat in Kansas,* Quarterly Report of the Kansas State Board of Agriculture (Topeka: State Printer, September 1920), p. 273; Hunger, "Kansas Leader in Use of Combine," p. 187; "Big Increase in Use of Combines Certain," *Power Farming* 36 (May 1927): 7.

30. Letter to *AmTh* 28 (February 1926): 18.

31. Clyde Walker, "Combine Owners Tell Their Story," *AmTh* 30 (August 1927): 5; E. G. Boerner, "Harvesting Wheat with a Combine," Kansas State Board of Agriculture, *Twenty-sixth Biennial Report,* 1927–28, pp. 210–11; letter from Mrs. Ellen Newman, Valley Falls, Kans., *AmTh* 31 (March 1929): 20.

32. E. R. Durgin, "Kansas Welcomes a Shorter Harvest," *AmTh* 29 (August 1926): 8.

33. *AmTh* 26 (March 1924): 27.

34. Earl W. Gage, "How the Combine Cuts Harvest Cost," *Power Farming* 31 (July 1922): 5; Allen, "New Harvest Hand," pp. 279–84; quote from J. O. Ellsworth, "Will Combine Solve My Labor Problems?" *Power Farming* 36 (December 1927): 7.

35. Allen, "New Harvest Hand," p. 280.

36. Fred A. Lyman, "The Second Romance of the Reaper," *Nation's Agriculture* 2 (June 1927): 3.

37. Mrs. Ellen Newman letter; Durgin, "Kansas Welcomes Shorter Harvest," p. 8; Hunger, "Kansas Leader in Use of Combine," pp. 191–92.

38. Sanders, "New Farm Machines," p. 183; Walker, "Combine Owners Tell Story," p. 5; C. W. Mullen, "Custom Combines," *Power Farming* 37 (April 1928): 8; interview with Richard Goering, Cassoday, Kans., 21 September 1981.

39. Smith and Spilman, *Harvesting Grain in Northwest Texas;* Ellsworth and Baird, *The Combine Harvester on Oklahoma Farms, 1926,* Oklahoma Agricultural Experiment Station Bulletin 162 (1927), p. 3.

40. L. C. Aicher, "Problems of the Combined Harvester," Kansas State Board of Agriculture, *Quarterly Report,* March 1930, pp. 101–5.

41. The bulletin by Reynoldson et al., besides being published by the department, was summarized in the department's *Yearbook of Agriculture,* 1927, pp. 692–95, and by C. D. Kinsman, "Results of the U.S.D.A. Investigation of Harvesting with the Combine," *Agricultural Engineering* 8 (April 1927): 85.

42. J. K. MacKenzie, *The Combined Reaper-Thresher in Western Canada,* Canada Department of Agriculture Pamphlet 83 (new series) (1927), p. 3; Hiram M. Drache, *Beyond the Furrow: Some Keys to Successful Farming in the Twentieth Century* (Danville, Ill.: Interstate Printers and Publishers, 1976), pp. 116–18; Starch and Merrill, *Combined Harvester-Thresher in Montana,* pp. 6–7.

43. Gabriel Lundy, K. H. Klages, and J. F. Goss, *Progress Report on the Use of the Combine in South Dakota,* South Dakota Agricultural Experiment Station Bulletin 244 (1929), pp. 5–6, 18–20; R. C. Miller and Alva H. Benton, *Combine Harvesting in North Dakota,* North Dakota Agricultural Experiment Station Bulletin 220 (1928), pp. 3, 7, 14–17; A. J. Schwantes, "The Combine in the Northwest," *AmTh* 34 (May 1931): 7; H. F. McColly, "The Combine in the Spring Wheat Area," *AmTh* 34 (May 1931): 8; R. C. Miller, "The Combine in North Dakota," *Agricultural Engineering* 8 (May 1927): 115–16.

44. Miller and Benton, *Combine Harvesting in North Dakota,* p. 17; "Weeds Reduce Combine's Efficiency," *AmTh* 31 (May 1928): 7; J. Fletcher Goss, "Field Problems in Combine Harvesting," *Agricultural Engineer-*

ing 10 (February 1929): 65; J. Fletcher Goss, "What Are Combine's Advantages?" *Dakota Farmer* 48 (January 1928): 35.

45. Lundy et al., *Combine in South Dakota,* pp. 20–24; Miller and Benton, *Combine Harvesting in North Dakota,* pp. 10–11; "Moisture May Spoil Combined Wheat," *AmTh* 31 (August 1928): 8.

46. *Nor-West Farmer* (Winnipeg), 5 May 1922.

47. Ibid.

48. Lundy et al., *Combine in South Dakota,* p. 45; Starch and Merrill, *Combined Harvester-Thresher in Montana,* p. 15.

49. Evan A. Hardy, "The Combine Harvester in Western Canada," *Scientific Agriculture* 12 (November 1931): 121–22; E. A. Hardy, "The 'Combine' in Saskatchewan," *Agricultural Engineering* 8 (August 1927): 206; Swift Current Dominion Experimental Farm, *Report of the Superintendent,* 1922.

50. J. G. Taggart and J. K. MacKenzie, *Seven Years' Experience with the Combined Reaper-Thresher,* Canada Department of Agriculture Bulletin 118 (new series) (1929), pp. 17–18; see also annual reports of Swift Current Dominion Experimental Farm for years under discussion, and J. K. MacKenzie, "The Combine in Saskatchewan," *Agricultural Engineering* 10 (February 1929): 57–58.

51. Starch and Merrill, *Combined Harvester-Thresher in Montana,* p. 5; Lundy et al., *Combine in South Dakota;* Miller and Benton, *Combine Harvesting in North Dakota;* Alva H. Benton et al., *The Combined Harvester-Thresher in North Dakota,* North Dakota Agricultural Experiment Station Bulletin 225 (1929).

52. Richard J. Friesen, *The Combine Harvester in Alberta: Its Development and Use, 1900–1950,* Background Paper 9 (Edmonton: Reynolds-Alberta Museum, 1983), p. 24.

53. S. F. Noble, "Dr. Charles S. Noble," *Lethbridge Herald,* 28 December 1967, quoted in Asael E. Palmer, *When the Winds Came* (Lethbridge, no date), p. 51; Grant MacEwan, *Charles Noble: Guardian of the Soil* (Saskatoon: Western Producer, 1983), pp. 143–49.

54. Friesen, *Combine Harvester in Alberta,* p. 27.

55. H. A. Lewis, "'And He *Was* Such a Man': The Story of Prof. Hardy," typescript, 1968, in private manuscript collection of Hartford A. Lewis, Gray, Sask.

56. Evan A. Hardy, *The "Combine" in Saskatchewan,* University of Saskatchewan Agricultural Bulletin 38 (1927).

57. Ibid.

58. *Western Producer* (Saskatoon), 26 January 1928.

59. Ibid.

60. Ibid.; Hardy, *"Combine" in Saskatchewan;* Friesen, *Combine Harvester in Alberta,* pp. 33, 35; E. G. Guest, "The Combine Harvester," *Scientific Agriculture* 15 (December 1934): 344. Two other articles on combines by Hardy not heretofore cited are "The Combine in the Prairie Provinces," *Agricultural Engineering* 10 (February 1929): 55–56, and "The Combine in Canada," *AmTh* 34 (May 1931): 9, 17.

61. W. W. Swanson and P. C. Armstrong, *Wheat* (Toronto, 1939), p. 58; *Western Producer* (Saskatoon), 13 June 1929.

62. *Farming for the Combine,* University of Saskatchewan, mimeograph, no. 120–29 (1929), Lewis collection.

63. *Western Producer* (Saskatoon), 5 April 1928.

64. Ibid., 20 June 1929.

65. Ibid., 13 June 1929.

66. Starch and Merrill, *Combined Harvester-Thresher in Montana,* pp. 34–35; "Windrow Combine Reduces Shattering," *AmTh* 30 (March 1928): 5; "Operating a 95,000-Acre Wheat Farm," *Mechanical Engineering* 50 (October 1928): 750–51; Drache, *Beyond the Furrow,* pp. 116–18.

67. Helmer H. Hanson, *History of Swathing and Swath Threshing* (Saskatoon, 1967), pp. 3, 5, 9–10, 12; see also Audrey Doerr,

"History of the Swather," in *Research and Development in the Farm Machinery Industry,* Study No. 7, Royal Commission on Farm Machinery (Ottawa: Queen's Printer, 1970), pp. 112–17.

68. "Windrow Combine Reduces Shattering," pp. 5, 11; I. D. Mayer, "Windrow and Pick-Up Attachments," *Agricultural Engineering* 10 (February 1929): 67–68; Ralph L. Patty, "Many New Improvements on the Combine," *Dakota Farmer* 489 (March 1928): 301; McColly, "Combine in Spring Wheat Area," p. 8; Starch and Merrill, *Combined Harvester-Thresher in Montana,* pp. 32–35; "Windrow Method of Combining Gaining in Favor," *Dun's International Review* 55 (March 1930): 57–58; T. J. Duffy, "Combines Invade Spring Wheat Belt," *Country Gentleman* 94 (March 1929): 9, 91, 176.

69. Friesen, *Combine Harvester in Alberta,* p. 33; *Western Producer* (Saskatoon), 1 March 1928 and 26 January 1928; C. R. Harrison, "Grain Windrowed with Binders," *AmTh* 32 (June 1929): 2.

70. *Right and Wrong Use of Windrowers,* University of Saskatchewan, mimeograph, F. P. Release No. 73, 20 November 1929, Lewis collection.

71. A. J. Schwantes, "Windrow Method of Combine Harvesting," *Agricultural Engineering* 10 (February 1929): 49–50; McColly, "Combine in Spring Wheat Area," p. 8; Starch and Merrill, *Combined Harvester-Thresher in Montana,* pp. 36–38; Lundy et al., *Combine in South Dakota,* p. 56; J. K. MacKenzie, "The Windrow Harvester," *AmTh* 34 (May 1931): 5, 18.

72. Lundy et al., *Combine in South Dakota,* pp. 43–54; Starch and Merrill, *Combined Harvester-Thresher in Montana,* pp. 10–20; Benton et al., *Combined Harvester-Thresher in North Dakota,* pp. 27–31, 40–47.

73. "Farmers Agree That Combines Are Practical," *Dakota Farmer* 47 (January 1927): 45.

74. Starch and Merrill, *Combined Harvester-Thresher in Montana,* pp. 6–9.

75. Miller and Benton, *Combine Harvesting in North Dakota,* pp. 3–6; Benton et al., *Combined Harvester-Thresher in North Dakota,* pp. 3–5; Lundy et al., *Combine in South Dakota,* pp. 4–5.

76. Data derived from Shepard, "Tractors and Combines," p. 262.

77. "Western Combine Sales for Past 18 Years" [1926–1943], typescript, Lewis collection; Robert M. Cullum, Josiah C. Folsom, and Donald G. Hay, "Men and Machines in the North Dakota Harvest" and "Statistical Supplement" (mimeographs, U.S. Bureau of Agricultural Economics, 1942).

78. Evan A. Hardy, *The Header and Header Barge for Grain Harvesting,* University of Saskatchewan Extension Bulletin 85 (1940); also numerous notes, manuscripts, mimeographs, photographs, and sketches of header barges in Lewis collection.

79. R. A. Stutt, "The Pattern of Mechanization and Wartime Changes on Farms in the Elrose-Rosetown-Conquest Area of Central and West Central Saskatchewan, 1944," Canada Department of Agriculture, Economics Division, Marketing Service, mimeograph, 1945, pp. 5–6; J. W. Clarke, "Farm Practices in Central Saskatchewan, Saskatchewan Department of Agriculture, Agricultural Representative Services, mimeograph, 1950, p. 16; "Farm Equipment Available in 1944," *Agricultural Situation* 27 (February 1944): 15–16; "Farm Machinery in Wartime," *Agricultural Situation* 29 (June 1945): 14–17; W. S. Johannson, "The Great Migration," *Implement and Tractor* (31 July 1943): 10–12, 23.

80. "Two-Thirds of Small Grains Combined," *Agricultural Situation* 31 (June 1947): 9–10; "More and More Combines Used by Farmers in Harvesting Grain," *Agricultural Situation* 36 (April 1952): 9–10.

81. *Western Producer* (Saskatoon), 5 April 1928, 27 June 1929, and 4 July 1929; George F. Boyd, *A Consolidation of Field Reports on the Combined Reaper-Thresher in Sas-*

katchewan, Saskatchewan Department of Agriculture Bulletin 78 (1926), p. 13; *Annual Report of the Swift Current Dominion Experimental Farm*, 1922, p. 13; MacKenzie, *Combined Reaper-Thresher in Western Canada*, p. 12; Taggart and MacKenzie, *Seven Years with Combined Reaper-Thresher*, pp. 24–27; Hardy, *Farming for the Combine*; Goss, "Combine's Advantages," p. 35; W. E. Grimes, "Effect of the Combined Harvester-Thresher on Farming in a Wheat Growing Region," *Scientific Agriculture* 9 (August 1929): 774, 777–78; John A. Martin, "The Influence of the Combine on Agronomic Practices and Research," *Journal of the American Society of Agronomy* 21 (July 1929): 768–72.

82. Reynoldson et al., *Combined Harvester-Thresher in Great Plains*, pp. 56–57; W. E. Grimes, "How Combines Affect Grain Storage," *AmTh* 33 (May 1930): 8; F. B. Nichols, "Combines Present Wheat Storage Problem," *Power Farming* 36 (September 1927): 76; *Western Producer* (Saskatoon), 6 September 1928.

83. Shepard, "Tractors and Combines"; quote from lecture notes, Lewis collection; Reynoldson et al., *Combined Harvester-Thresher in Great Plains*, p. 57; Grimes, "Effect of Combined Harvester-Thresher," pp. 773–82; Martin, "Influence of Combine," pp. 767–68; W. E. Grimes, *The Effect of the Combined Harvester Thresher on Farm Organization in Southwestern Kansas and Northwestern Oklahoma*, Kansas Agricultural Experiment Station Circular 142 (1928).

84. Lecture notes, Lewis collection.

85. *Western Producer* (Saskatoon), 27 June 1929 and 4 November 1928.

86. "Farmers Agree That Combines Are Practical," p. 45.

87. Jean Burnet, *Next-Year Country: A Study of Rural Social Organization in Alberta* (Toronto: University of Toronto Press, 1951).

88. See Thomas D. Isern, *Custom Combining on the Great Plains: A History* (Norman: University of Oklahoma Press, 1981; co-published by Western Producer, Saskatoon).

CHAPTER 6.   THE PLAINS

1. Herbert Krause, *The Thresher* (Sioux Falls, S. Dak.: Brevet Press, 1974).

2. *American Thresherman* (hereafter cited as *AmTh*) 20 (August 1917): 54–55.

3. *AmTh* 19 (September 1916): 50–51.

4. The company is the Stemgas Publishing Company, Lancaster, Pennsylvania.

5. Donald E. Worster, *Dust Bowl: The Southern Plains in the 1930s* (New York: Oxford University Press, 1979), pp. 167, 168, 169.

6. J. Sanford Rikoon, *Threshing in the Midwest, 1820–1940* (Bloomington: Indiana University Press, 1988), pp. iv, 154.

7. Ibid., p. 156.

8. Walter Prescott Webb, *The Great Plains* (Lincoln: University of Nebraska Press, 1981).

9. On Malin, see Robert S. LaForte, "James C. Malin, Optimist: The Basis of His Philosophy of History," *Kansas History* 6 (Summer 1983): 110–19, and especially Malin's book, *The Grassland of North America: Prolegomena to Its History* (Lawrence: By the author, 1948). Kraenzel's work is *The Great Plains in Transition* (Norman: University of Oklahoma Press, 1955).

10. A discussion of possibilism as applied to agricultural geography is in Howard F. Gregor, *Geography of Agriculture: Themes in Research* (Englewood Cliffs, N.J.: Prentice-Hall, 1970).

11. Sharp's works were *Agrarian Revolt in Western Canada: A Survey Showing American Parallels* (Minneapolis: University of Minnesota Press, 1948) and *Whoop-Up Country: The Canadian-American West, 1865–1885* (Norman: University of Oklahoma Press, 1973). Reaction to Sharp's works is documented in Thomas D. Isern and R. Bruce Shepard, "Paul F. Sharp and the Historiog-

raphy of the North American Plains," forthcoming in *The Historian*. The major work by Bennett is *Northern Plainsmen: Adaptive Strategy and Agrarian Life* (Arlington Heights, Ill.: Harlan Davidson, 1970).

12. A discussion of Innis's staples theory is in James N. McCrorie, "The Staple Theory in Canadian Social Thought," unpublished paper provided by McCrorie, executive director of the Canadian Plains Research Center, University of Regina. An analysis of Fowke is in T. D. Regehr, "Vernon C. Fowke and the Political Economy of the Canadian West," paper presented at the annual meeting of the Western Social Science Association, 1988. See also Fowke's major work, *The National Policy and the Wheat Economy* (Toronto: University of Toronto Press, 1957).

13. W. L. Morton, *Manitoba: A History* (Toronto: University of Toronto Press, 1957).

14. Terry G. Jordan, *German Seed in Texas Soil: Immigrant Farmers in Nineteenth-Century Texas* (Austin: University of Texas Press, 1966), and *Trails to Texas: Southern Roots of Western Cattle Ranching* (Lincoln: University of Nebraska Press, 1981).

INDEX

Combine (*continued*)
  invention and evolution of, 12–13, 184–85
  objections to, 192–94
  prairie, 186–87
Common, John, 5
Connor, G. F., 82, 84
Cook cars, on threshing outfits, 99
Cooking, for threshing crews, 96–100
Cooperative threshing. *See* Threshing rings
Copeland, Doris A., 171
Cox, John, 18
Cradle
  with scythe, 3–4
  use of, on plains, 25
Cumming, Donald, 5
Custom threshing, 73–80. *See also* Threshermen

Deering, William, 11
Dobson, E., 108
Dorsey, Owen, 9
Doukhobor immigrants, 69
Draper, William R., 148
Dropper, on reaper, 9–10
Drunkenness, among harvest hands, 162–63
Dust Bowl, The (Worster), 213–14
Dyck, Jacob F., 81

Edmond, Harry, 186
Ellsworth, J. O., 191
Employment services, for harvest hands, 150–52
Engebregtson, Olaf, 116
Engineers, of threshing crews, 68, 81–82, 84–85
Evers, William, 15
Ewanchuk, Michael, 29, 48
Explosions, of steam boilers, 103–4
Extension services, and harvest hands, 151–52

Fanning (of grain) and fanning mills, 15
Feeders, on threshing crews, 89–90
Fires, on threshing outfits, 104
Fisher (of Grand Forks, N.Dak.), 33
Fiske, Harold, 170
Fitz, Leslie A., 65
Flailing (of grain) and flails, 14, 16
Food, for harvest hands, 162
Fowke, Vernon C., 219
Frazier, Lynn J., 170

Garnett, W. G., 108
Gearhart, W. S., 115
Gerow, T. B., 147

Gladstone (inventor of reaper), 5
Goering, Richard, 30–31, 43, 45, 46, 57, 78, 190–91
Goodwin, Joe M., 56
Gordon, James, 10
Goucher, John, 15
Graham (of Carrington, N.Dak.), 34
Great Plains, historiography of, 217–20
Great Plains, The (Webb), 217
Groundhog threshers, 17–19

Haines, Jonathan, 11–12
Hall, Joseph, 18
Handley, Anna May, 98
Hanson, Helmer and Ellert, 199
Hardy, Evan, 195–97, 207
Harper, George D., 69
Hart, C. W., 34
Harvest excursions (to western Canada), 131–36, 165–67
Harvest hands, 130–73
  hired by threshermen, 80
  social characteristics of, 138–47
Harvesting
  definition of, 2
  methods of, on plains, 14–67
  technological history of, 2–13
Harvest labor. *See* Harvest hands
Hascall, John, 184
Haselwood and Son (threshing outfit), 116
Hauling grain, 94–96
Hays, Earl W., 111
Header
  harvesting with, on plains, 26–30, 57–62
  invention and evolution of, 11–12
Header barges
  construction of, 36–37
  driving of, 62
  See also Header stack-barges
Header stack-barges, 32–35
  used with combine in western Canada, 198–99, 205
Heberling, M. H., 54–56
Hellam (of Acadia Valley, Alta.), 34
Henry, T. C., 70
Hickok, Lorena, 99–100
Hitz, George, 29, 78, 98, 103, 170, 184
Hohaus, J. H., 89
Holt, Benjamin, 185
Holland brothers, 112
Horsepower sweeps, for threshing, 20–21, 70–71
Horses, use of, with binders, 38
Hovland, August, 199
Hradec brothers, 104
Hussey, Obed, 7–8